The Book
of
How It Works

This edition produced in **1995** for
Shooting Star Press Inc
Suite 1212
230 Fifth Avenue
New York, NY 10001

© Aladdin Books Ltd 1995

Designed and produced by
Aladdin Books Ltd
28 Percy Street
London W1P OLD

Printed in Czech Republic

ISBN 1-57335-145-8

Some of the material in this book was previouly
in the *How it Works* series.

CONTENTS

The Book of
How It Works

Written by
Ian Graham, Robin Kerrod
Kevin Gosnell, Lionel Bender

Illustrated by
Alex Pang, Ian Moores, Peter Harper,
Galiana Zolfaghari, Guy Smith, Aziz Khan,
and Ron Hayward Associates

SHOOTING STAR PRESS

INTRODUCTION

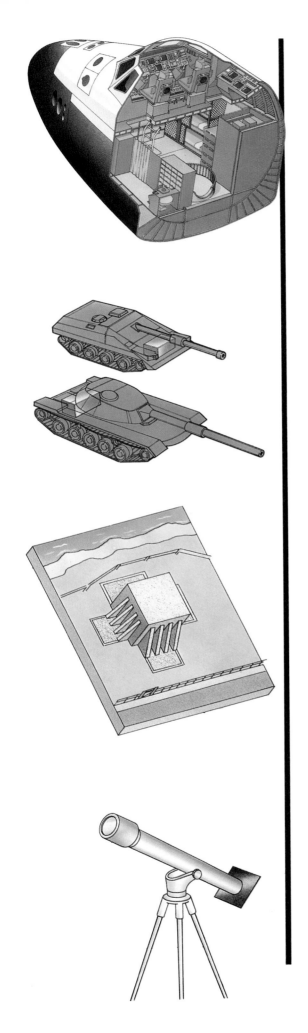

The massive technological advances of the twentieth century have completely transformed the way we live our lives. During the early 1900's cars slowly puttered around the countryside, primitive planes could only cover short distances and electricity in the home was virtually unheard of.

All types of vehicles have changed beyond recognition, to the point where today high performance racing cars scream around racetracks at hundreds of miles an hour. On the roads around our homes powerful trucks deliver loads to every corner of the country, while at the other end of the scale, two-wheeled motorcycles carry people quickly and efficiently during their work or play.

The advent of total world warfare has transformed the face of the modern battlefield. The first tanks that rolled across the muddy fields of Europe in the World War I have been superseded by fast, heavily armored battle machines that can deliver explosives miles from their target. At sea, silent missile launchers now prowl below the waves, avoiding the attention of complex radar and sonar detection systems, and small submarines dive into the depths of the sea to explore the strange worlds found there. In the skies above our heads, ultramodern jet fighters can now perform the most complex manoeuvres at the very edge of the atmosphere.

In more recent years, humans have been able to leave the boundries of our planet. This has culminated in landing on the moon, sending probes to explore the farthest planets in our solar system and beyond, and the creation of the reusable space shuttle which can launch satellites and telescopes that gaze far into the endless blackness of space.

Back in the home electricity is now commonplace , involved in almost every activity we choose to do. It powers the televisions and videos that entertain us, and the home computers that can help us with our work. As a result of this always increasing demand for electricity, power stations have been constructed. Some of these stations harness the energy unleashed by thetiny atom to create vast amounts of power. However, they have their drawbacks, such as nuclear waste from power stations is dangerous, and can remain so for hundreds of years.

The Book of How It Works takes the reader on an exciting journey through the world of technology that affect the way we live our lives, from the depths of the oceans to the highest mountain and beyond into space. With the help of bright, colorful artwork accompanying concise text, it sets out to explain the workings of the most complicated machines, from cameras that fit in the pocket to massive nuclear power stations.

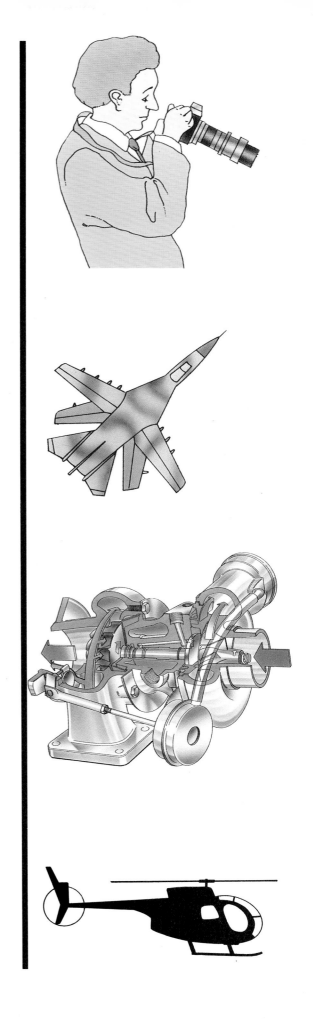

Chapter One

TELESCOPES

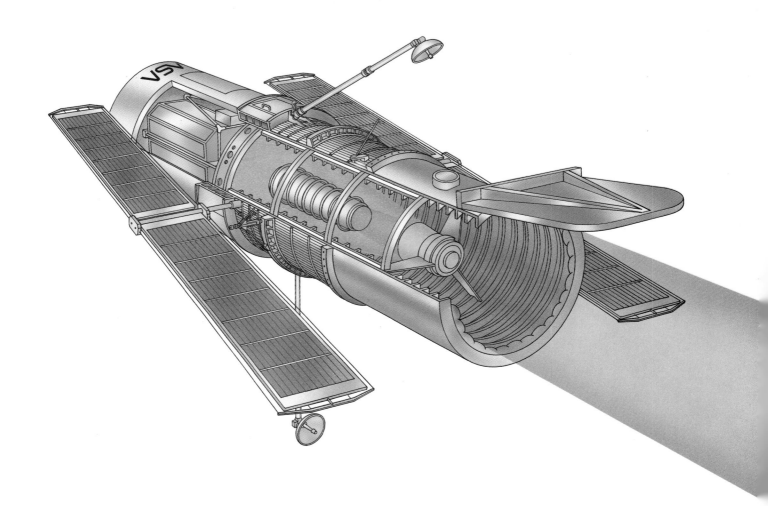

CONTENTS

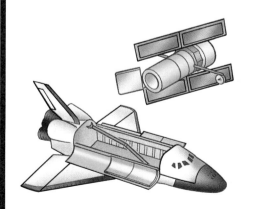

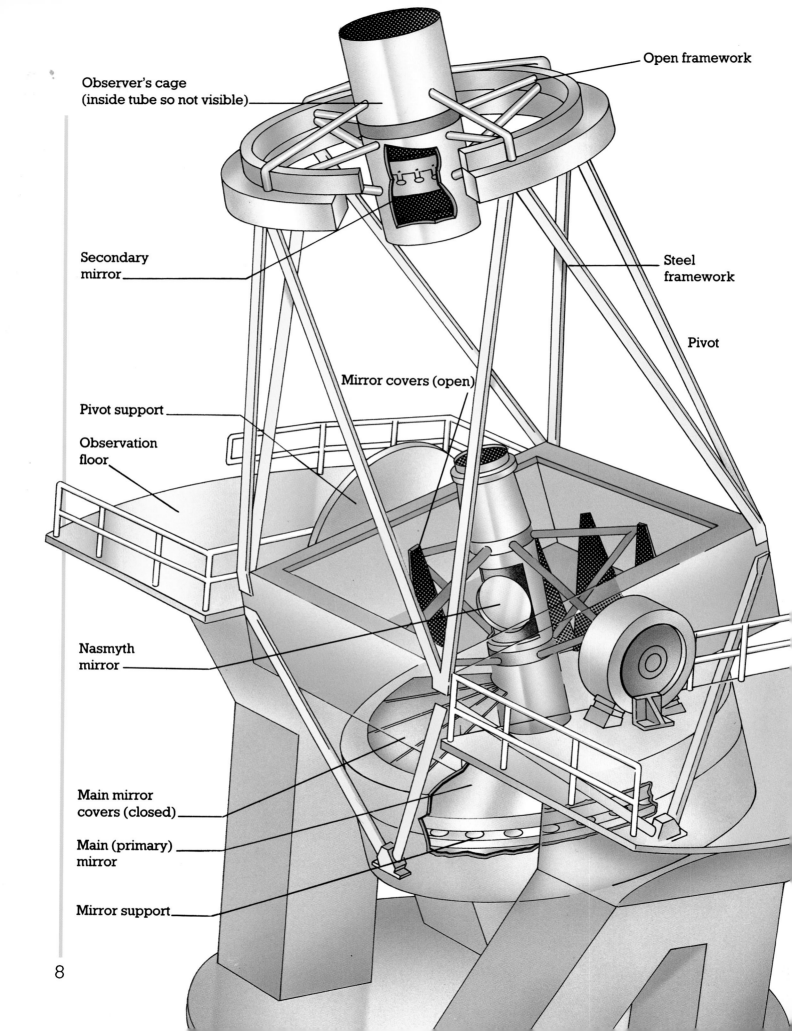

Open framework

Observer's cage
(inside tube so not visible)

Secondary
mirror

Steel
framework

Pivot

Mirror covers (open)

Pivot support

Observation
floor

Nasmyth
mirror

Main mirror
covers (closed)

Main (primary)
mirror

Mirror support

8

THE WORKING PARTS

On a clear night, away from the glare of city lights, it is possible to see thousands of stars in the sky. There are in fact hundreds of thousands of stars visible in the night sky, but most of them are too dim to be seen with the naked eye. Many of these can be seen by using binoculars or a telescope. The other planets in our star system, the Solar System, can also be studied in greater detail with binoculars or a telescope.

The telescope shown here is a reconstructed cutaway of an instrument used by professional astronomers to study the stars and planets. It is known as a "reflector" because it uses mirrors to collect and direct light by reflection.

Light rays enter the telescope through the open framework at the top. They travel down to the bottom of the structure where they are reflected upward by the main, or "primary," mirror. The curved main mirror also directs the light rays so that they will come together to form a sharply focused image.

The light rays then continue up to the top of the telescope where the image becomes visible. An astronomer can sit in a cage at the top to see the image. More commonly, the light rays forming the image are directed down again by a secondary mirror and then reflected out to the side of the telescope by an angled "Nasmyth" mirror onto an observation floor. Here, astronomers have more room to analyze the image with their instruments.

The main mirror is the telescope's most important and most expensive part. Its surface is protected by a safety cover when it is not in use.

The telescope is supported by a massive base to minimize unwanted vibrations that would otherwise make the image shake. The base, also called the telescope "mount," is constructed so that the telescope can be moved by electric motors to track or follow the stars. This is necessary to keep a star or a group of stars in view as the earth spins beneath them. The telescope is protected from the weather by a dome-shaped building (not shown) with a slot-shaped opening across the top. The dome rotates until the opening is above the telescope. Doors on the slot are then opened and observing can begin.

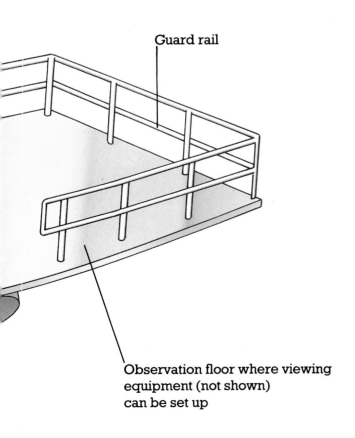

Guard rail

Observation floor where viewing equipment (not shown) can be set up

MIRRORS AND LENSES

Optical telescopes collect and focus light by using lenses or mirrors. Bending light rays with a lens is called refraction, and so telescopes that use lenses are called refractors. In all but the cheapest of models with plastic components, the lenses are made of glass. Bouncing light off a mirror is known as reflection. Telescopes that use mirrors instead of lenses are called reflectors.

If a telescope can collect more light, it can detect fainter and more distant objects. Larger lenses and mirrors collect much more light than smaller ones. However, it is difficult to make large lenses. They can only be supported around their thin rim and the weight of the lens causes it to sag, distorting the images it produces. Large mirrors are easier to make because they can be supported over their entire back surface. That is why the largest optical telescopes in the world today are all reflectors.

Scientists have devised several different ways of viewing the image produced by a reflector. The first practical one was the Newtonian developed by Sir Isaac Newton (right) in 1672. It uses a small flat mirror to reflect light out through an eyepiece in the side of the telescope. The next, named after the 17th century French astronomer Cassegrain, uses a small second mirror to reflect the light out through a central hole in the main mirror for easier viewing. In the Nasmyth type (far right), the light path is folded back on itself by one small mirror before it is brought out by another mirror through an eyepiece lens in the side of the telescope.

Refracting and reflecting
In a refractor, light rays from a distant object enter at one end, pass through a lens or several lenses, and the image is seen at the other end. In a reflector, the light path is folded back on itself by the main mirror. However, the image is focused in the path of the incoming light, where it is difficult to look at it. The problem is often solved by reflecting the image out to the side of the telescope by means of a small second mirror.

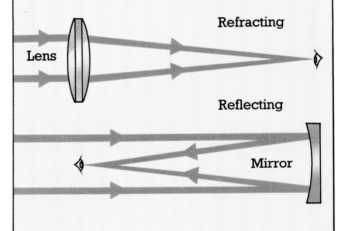

Refracting

Lens

Reflecting

Mirror

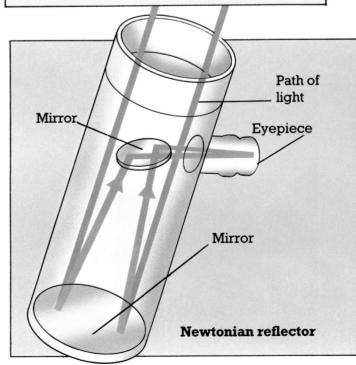

Path of light

Eyepiece

Mirror

Mirror

Newtonian reflector

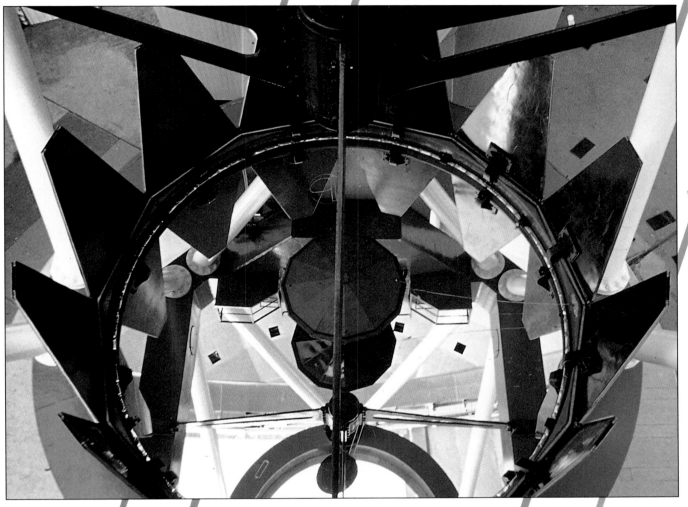

The 20-feet wide mirror inside the world's largest reflector telescope at Mt Semirodriki, USSR.

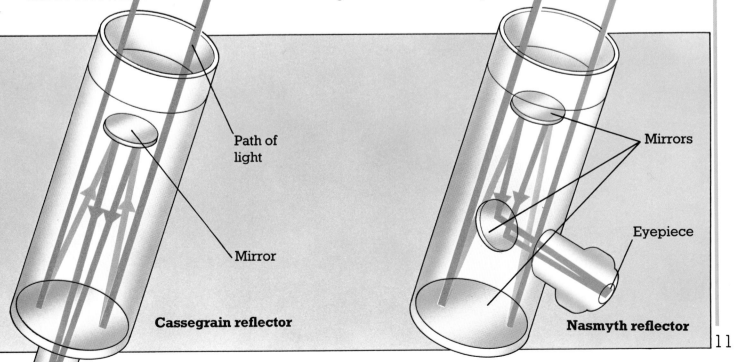

Path of light

Mirror

Cassegrain reflector

Mirrors

Eyepiece

Nasmyth reflector

FIELD OF VIEW

Whatever can be seen through a telescope is called its field of view. A more powerful telescope – one that seems to magnify, or increase, the size of an object the most – has a *smaller* field of view than a less powerful one.

Astronomers find their way around the sky by knowing the patterns of the stars. If only a few stars are visible in the field of view, it may be difficult to recognize any patterns and find the particular object that the astronomer is looking for. For this reason, such telescopes are fitted with a finder computer or a small wide-angle telescope called a "finder telescope." This is used to locate the general area of interest. When the object that the astronomer wants to find is positioned in the middle of this field of view, it can also be seen in the middle of the high-power telescope's smaller field of view.

Only one type of telescope, called a Schmidt telescope, can produce a detailed image of a large area. It is usually called a Schmidt camera because the first Schmidt instruments could only record their images on film.

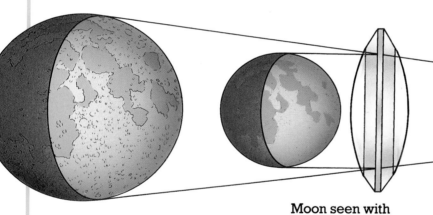

MAGNIFICATION WITH A LENS

Moon seen with naked eye

Moon seen through telescope

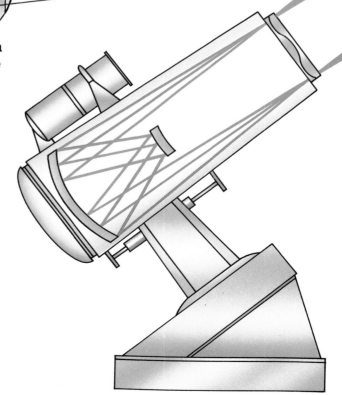

A convex (bulging outward) lens magnifies a distant object by bending, or refracting, the light rays traveling from it to the observer's eye. The refracted rays appear to come from a larger object.

The Schmidt camera (right) was specially designed in 1930 by Bernhard Schmidt to photograph a sharp image of a large field of view in a single image. It collects light using a 6-feet diameter mirror, but it also has a specially shaped lens to correct distortions in the image caused by the shape of the mirror.

The lens is 4 feet across.

Astronomers constantly hunt for interesting objects in the sky to study. If they were to only use a high-power telescope with a tiny field of view (small circle in diagram), it would take a very long time. So first they search through a photograph taken by a wide-angle telescope such as a Schmidt (outer area). If any interesting objects or areas show up on the Schmidt image, they can be checked further with a more powerful telescope. For instance, in the cluster of stars called the Pleiades, or "Seven Sisters," a Schmidt camera can record 150 main stars and 20,000 background stars as opposed to seven seen by the naked eye or one or two with a high-powered telescope.

13

ON LAND

Astronomical telescopes create images which are upside down. This does not matter, especially in astronomy, but it is a serious disadvantage when using astronomical telescopes for bird-watching, surveying or watching sports.

Telescopes intended to be used for non-astronomical purposes are often known as terrestrial telescopes, or field telescopes. They have an extra lens or lenses, called erecting lenses or prisms, that turn the image the right-side up. The telescope is made from two or more tubes that slide inside each other. The image is brought into sharp focus by sliding the tubes to bring the lenses closer to each other or farther apart. This arrangement has given us the adjective "telescopic," which can be applied to anything that extends in the same way even if it is not a telescope, a telescopic radio aerial for example.

The field telescope has two major drawbacks. The user has to look through it with one eye while keeping the other eye closed. This can quickly become uncomfortable. Secondly, it can be quite long and therefore awkward to use in confined spaces.

Both problems are readily solved by folding the telescope up into a shorter length and putting two of them together so that the user can keep both eyes open. The result is a pair of binoculars. They are as powerful as a pair of much larger telescopes but, being compact, the binoculars are much more convenient to use.

Binoculars provide the most convenient way of getting good close-up views of wildlife.

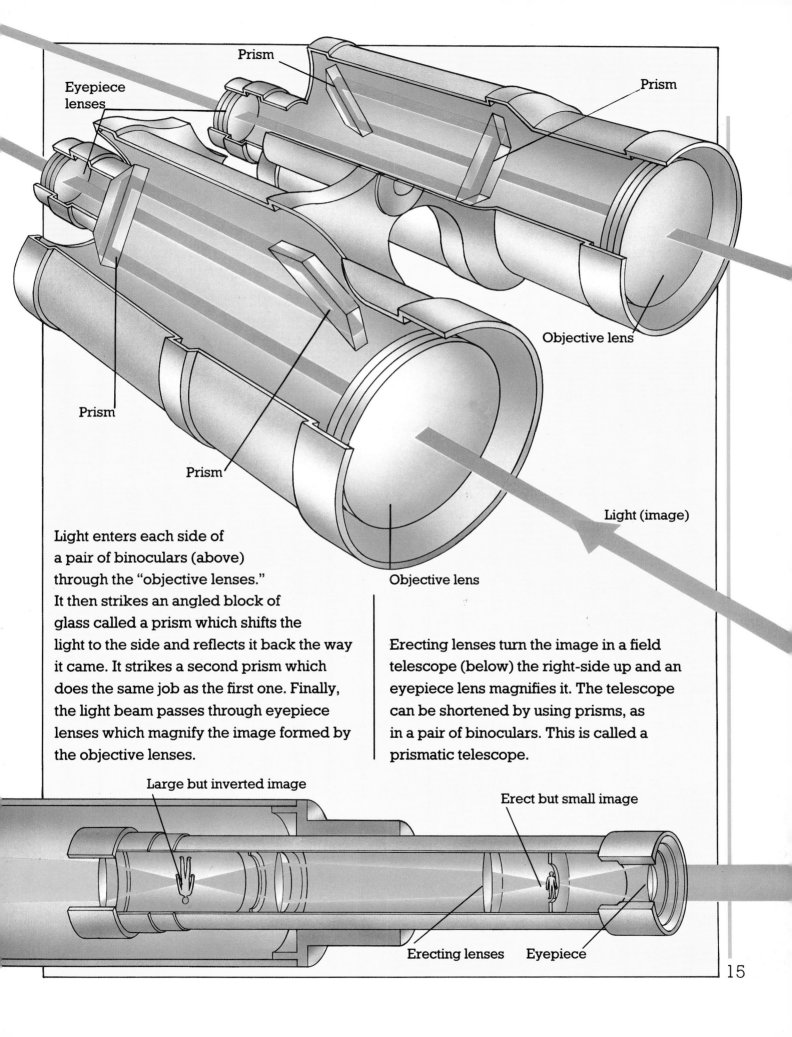

Prism

Prism

Eyepiece
lenses

Objective lens

Prism

Prism

Light (image)

Objective lens

Light enters each side of
a pair of binoculars (above)
through the "objective lenses."
It then strikes an angled block of
glass called a prism which shifts the
light to the side and reflects it back the way
it came. It strikes a second prism which
does the same job as the first one. Finally,
the light beam passes through eyepiece
lenses which magnify the image formed by
the objective lenses.

Erecting lenses turn the image in a field
telescope (below) the right-side up and an
eyepiece lens magnifies it. The telescope
can be shortened by using prisms, as
in a pair of binoculars. This is called a
prismatic telescope.

Large but inverted image

Erect but small image

Erecting lenses

Eyepiece

15

VIEWING THE SUN

No matter how much the stars are magnified by the most powerful of telescopes, they are so incredibly far away that they never appear larger than points of light. The one exception to this in the entire universe is our own star, the sun. It contains 99.9 percent of all the matter in the whole solar system. Its force of the nine planets, the asteroids and comets, and it provides the visible light and heat that sustains all life on earth.

Scientists study the sun to try to improve their understanding of its behavior and how it affects the earth and the other planets. An ordinary photograph of the sun reveals dark spots called sunspots and long fiery tongues stretching out into space from its atmosphere, the corona. They indicate magnetic disturbances. A special telescope, a coronograph, is used to study the corona.

The MacMath Solar Telescope at the Kitt Peak National Observatory in Arizona does not look like any other telescope. Only a tiny part of it is visible above ground. Sunlight strikes a mirror 5 feet across at the top. This mirror moves to keep the sun in view as the earth spins. The sunlight is reflected down to the end of a long tunnel, reflected back again and finally directed into the observing room. Here, an image of the sun measuring 33.5 inches in diameter can be projected onto a screen or studied by sensitive instruments. The instruments work at their best in the cool, even temperatures found deep underground, but there is an added cooling system.

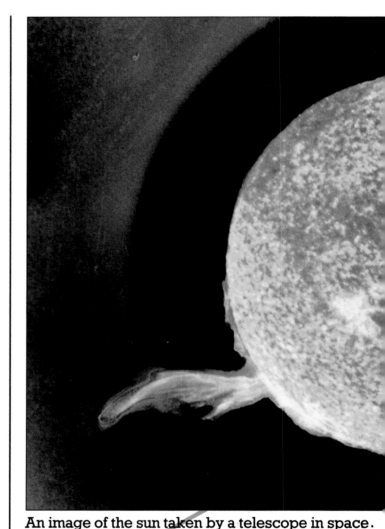

An image of the sun taken by a telescope in space.

Sunlight

Reflectors

Observing room

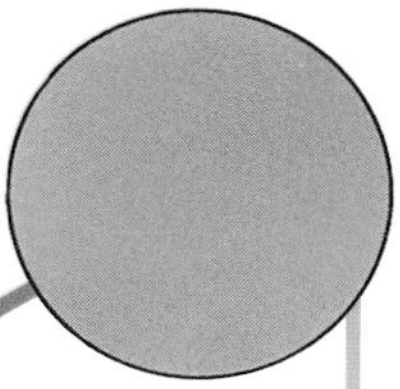
Sun

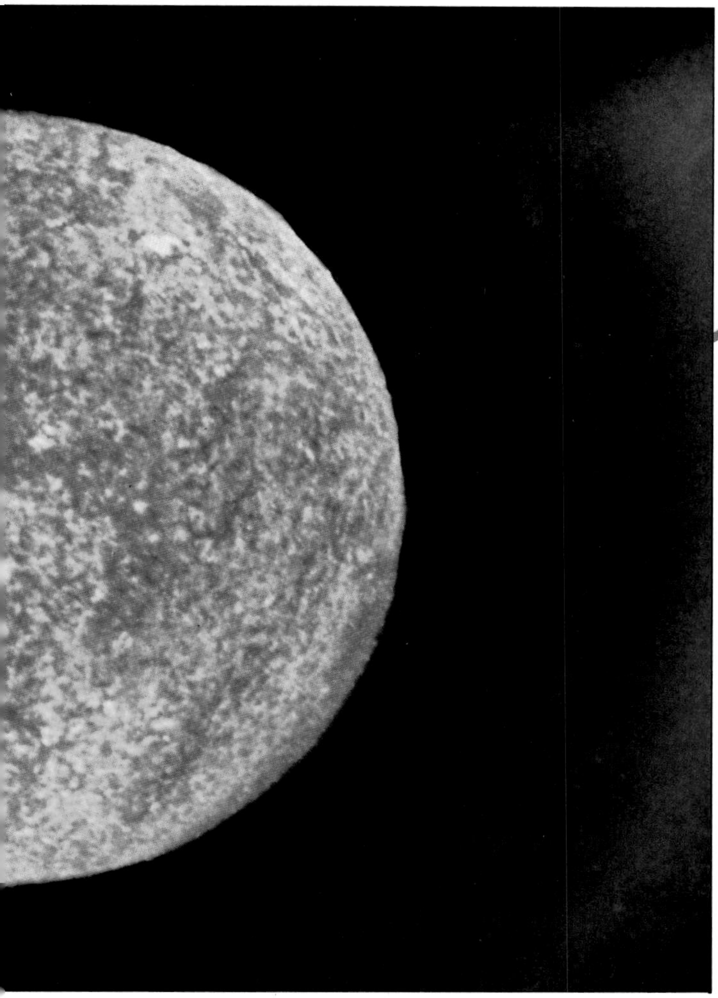

The image shows "sunspots" and a "flare."

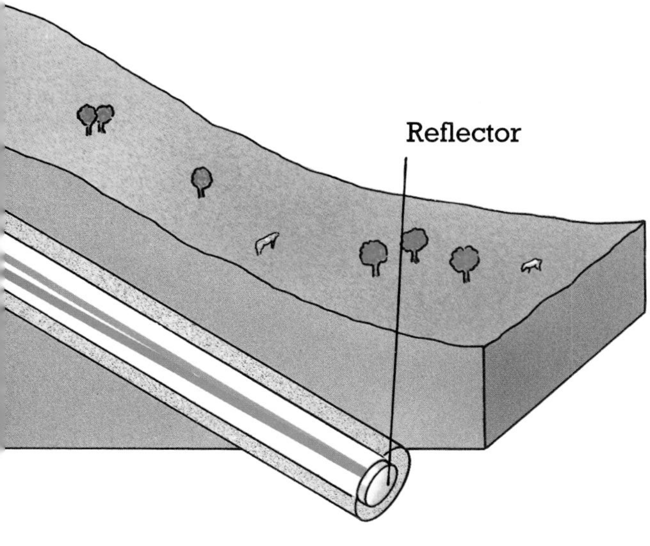
Reflector

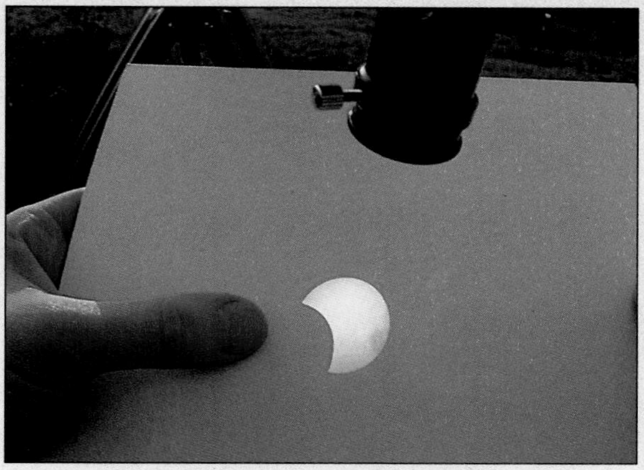

Projected image of solar eclipse

Viewing sunspots and solar eclipses
Sunlight is so intense that looking directly at the sun can permanently damage the eyes. The only safe way to observe the sun is to use a telescope to project it onto white cardboard held underneath, with black cardboard surrounding the eyepiece. The observer should aim and focus the telescope by looking for the sun's image on the cardboard, *never* by looking through the telescope. Any sunspots on the sun's surface will appear as dark spots on the bright disk.

WARNING: NEVER LOOK DIRECTLY AT THE SUN

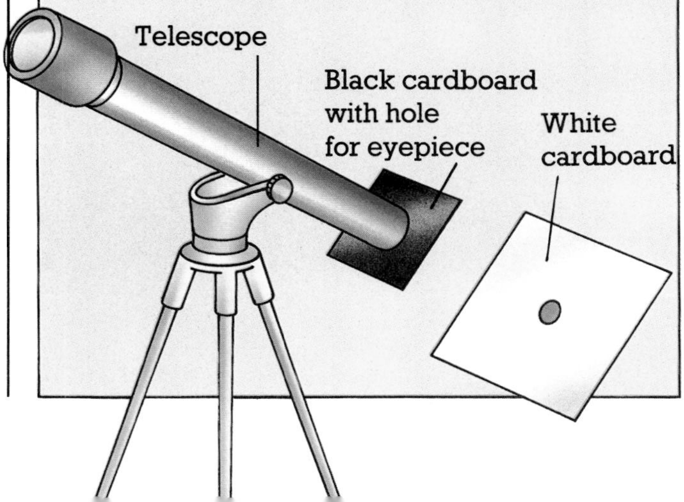
Telescope
Black cardboard with hole for eyepiece
White cardboard

COLORED LIGHT

In a clear night sky each star appears to have a color. They are always either blue-white, white, yellow, orange or red. The red ones may look hotter to us but they are at about 5,432°F, while the blue-white stars are around 45,032°F.

The best way to study a star's light is with an instrument called a spectroscope attached to a telescope. This splits the star's light into a band of separate colors by passing it through a prism. Black lines appear in several places on the "rainbow"-like spectrum of colors. These are caused by the star's atmosphere absorbing certain wavelengths of light, and they show which chemicals are present in the star's outer layers.

Most stars are rushing away from the Earth at an extraordinary speed, and the black lines in their light are shifted toward the red end of the spectrum. The size of this "red-shift" indicates how quickly each star is flying away. In the 1920s Edwin Hubble showed that the objects furthest away from the earth are moving the fastest - so that an object's red shift shows its distance as well as its speed.

Pictures can be made to reveal more information than is clear from an ordinary optical photograph (lower right). This is done by a process called computerized image enhancement. Different wavelengths of invisible radiation from space, such as radio or infrared, can be shown in "false" colors, as in a "radio map" photograph of a galaxy (top right). The brightest colors usually show where the most radiation at the chosen wavelength is being emitted.

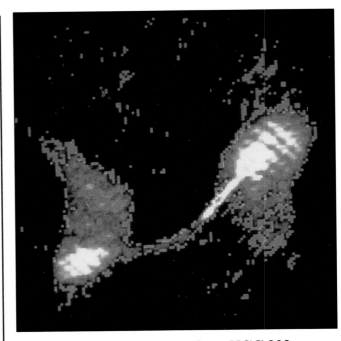

Image enhancement of galaxy NGC 326

Optical photograph of a spiral galaxy

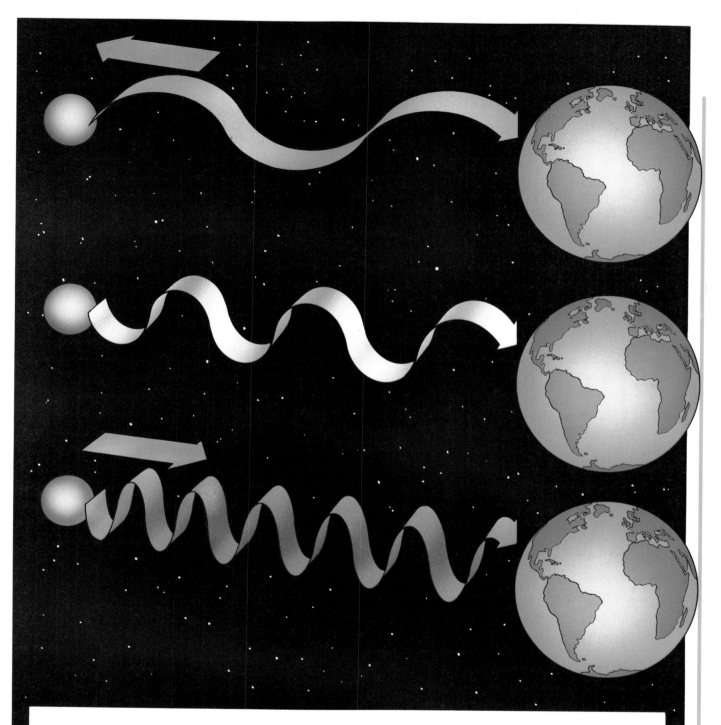

How colors show a star's movement

Astronomers can tell which way and how fast stars are moving in space by studying their light with an instrument called a spectroscope. This contains a prism which spreads the light into a rainbow-like band (a spectrum) with a pattern of thin black lines. When light waves coming from a star are of short wavelength, the black lines cluster near the color blue. This shows that the star is approaching us (bottom). If the star's light waves are long, the lines "shift" toward the red area of the spectrum. This shows that the star is moving away (top). When the lines are spread evenly and no shift occurs it means that there is no change in the distance between the star and earth (middle).

THE SPACE TELESCOPE

The Hubble Space Telescope (HST) is the largest space observatory ever built. The 43-feet-long 11-ton reflecting telescope was launched from the payload bay of the U.S. Space Shuttle in April 1990. It was designed to provide astronomers with images of objects such as galaxies that are up to 14,000 billion light years away at the edge of the universe or detailed pictures of the outer planets. From its position in orbit high above the earth's atmosphere, it can receive images that are ten times sharper than those picked up by any earth-based optical telescope.

While the HST was being tested in space, it was discovered that its main mirror, 8 ft across, had been made the wrong shape. The error was 2,000th of a millimeter, but that was enough to make the telescope's images hazy. In 1993 astronauts repaired the telescope by fitting new equipment designed to compensate for the mirror's faults. The mission was a complete success. They restored the space telescope to it's design performance, and it has since taken stunning pictures of very distant objects.

The telescope was launched from the Space Shuttle Orbiter using its robot arm. When the Orbiter was safely in space, the payload bay doors were opened (1). Then the robot arm grasped the telescope and lifted it out of the payload bay (2). Finally, the telescope's solar panels were unrolled and its aperture door opened to begin testing the telescope's instruments (3). The Hubble Space Telescope will have a lifespan of 15 years.

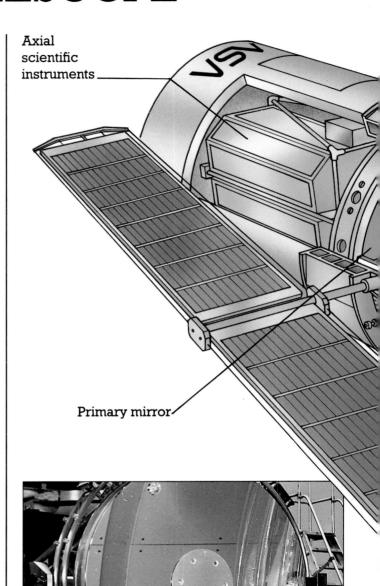

Axial scientific instruments

Primary mirror

Inspecting the main mirror before fitting

1.

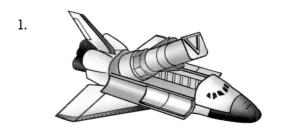

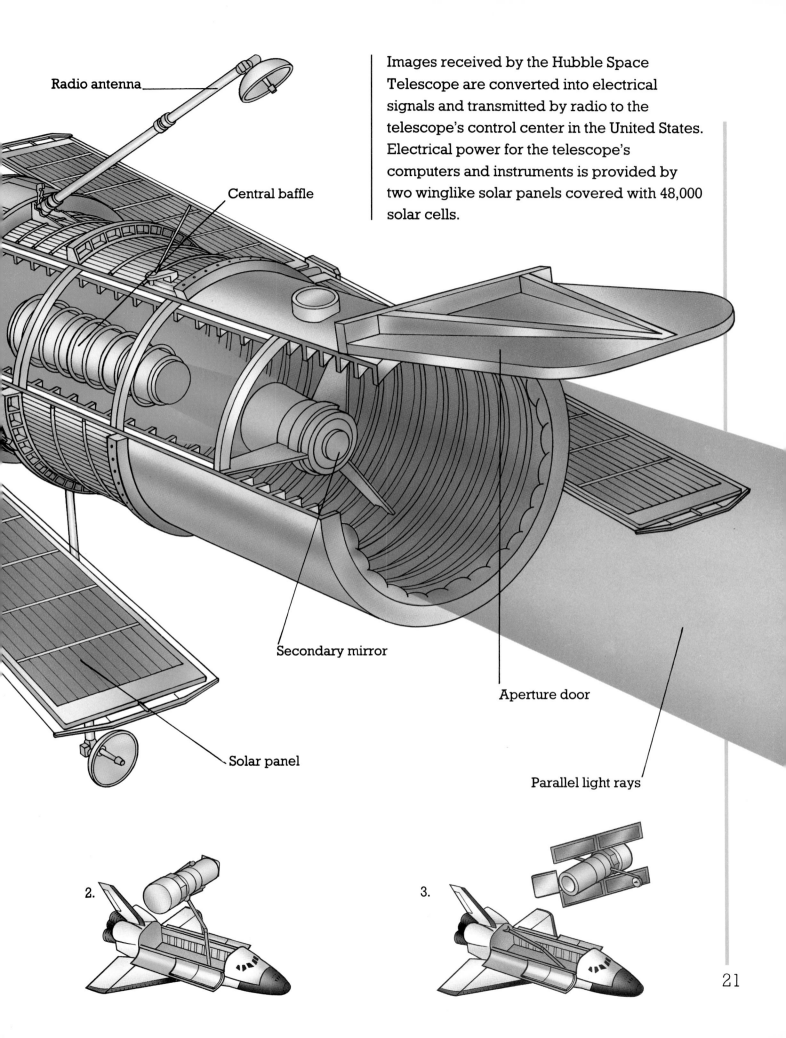

Radio antenna

Central baffle

Images received by the Hubble Space Telescope are converted into electrical signals and transmitted by radio to the telescope's control center in the United States. Electrical power for the telescope's computers and instruments is provided by two winglike solar panels covered with 48,000 solar cells.

Secondary mirror

Aperture door

Solar panel

Parallel light rays

2.

3.

21

SPECIAL TELESCOPES

Astronomers would like to build larger reflectors to gather more light and enable them to see faint objects more clearly. Large mirrors are distorted by changes in temperature and also by their own weight. One answer is to replace the large mirror with several smaller mirrors. The mirrors are controlled so that the image formed by each is directed to a central point, where they act together as one huge mirror.

Perhaps the strangest type of telescope is that which can only work deep underground. The photograph top-right shows part of one such "neutrino trap." This operates in a special chamber inside the Mont Blanc tunnel deep within the French Alps. Neutrinos are tiny particles produced by the nuclear fission in stars. Most of those that reach the earth come from the sun. Others have come to us from distant parts of the universe and have taken millions of years to get here.

The Multiple-Mirror Telescope (MMT) perches on top of Mount Hopkins in Arizona.

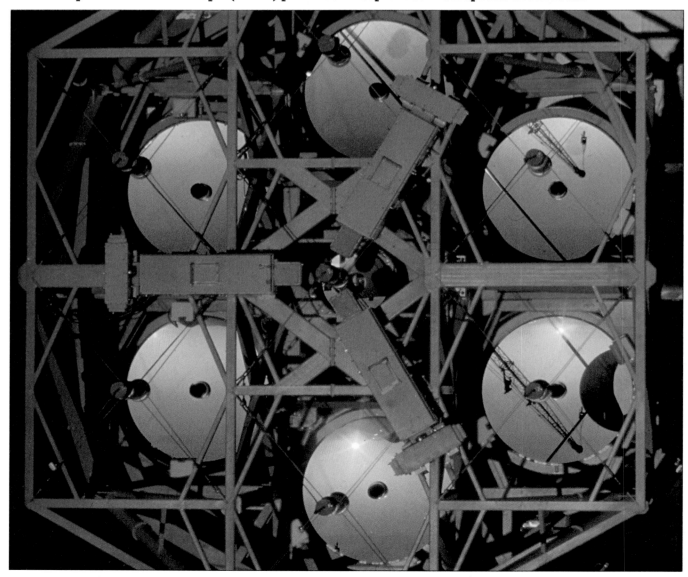

The light-sensitive equipment on an underground telescope.

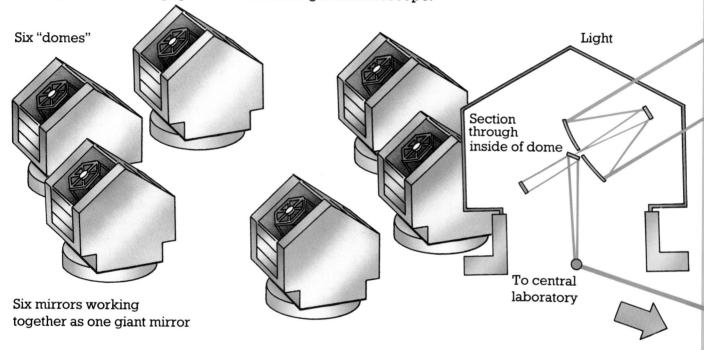

Six "domes"

Six mirrors working
together as one giant mirror

Light

Section
through
inside of dome

To central
laboratory

Neutrinos are even smaller than atoms, and they pass right through the earth. Other types of radiation make them very difficult to detect above ground. However, this neutrino trap is shielded by 19,685 feet of solid rock. It has metal tanks filled with a liquid similar to cleaning fluid. When a neutrino passes through these it emits a faint flash of light. Scientists studying these flashes say that some neutrinos have come from stars which no longer exist.

Each mirror in a multiple-mirror telescope is controlled independently so that the images formed by all the mirrors come together in a central laboratory. The Mount Hopkins Multiple-Mirror Telescope (left) consists of six mirrors, each 6 ft across, as good as a single mirror 15 ft across. Even larger multiple-mirror telescopes made from several dozen small mirrors arranged like the petals of a flower are being planned. They will be as good as reflectors of 33 ft across. Six together will act like a 82 ft-diameter mirror.

THE HISTORY OF TELESCOPES

The telescope is thought to have been invented in 1608 by a Dutch eyeglass-maker called Jan Lippershey. Within a year, news of Lippershey's invention reached the Italian astronomer, Galileo Galilei. Galileo soon made his own telescopes. They were tiny compared to today's giant instruments. The eyeglass lenses he used were at most 1 inch across. Even so, Galileo's telescopes enabled him to make a series of very important discoveries between 1610 and 1619. Some of his discoveries include craters and mountains on the moon, and moons orbiting the planet Jupiter.

Galileo, the earliest telescope-user.

The great English scientist, Sir Isaac Newton, tried to solve the refracting telescope's major problem. Its lenses split light into different colors which are focused at different points, blurring the image. Newton's solution was to use mirrors instead of lenses, because mirrors do not suffer from this color-smearing effect. Newton invented the reflecting telescope, or "reflector." He presented his invention to the Royal Society in London in 1671.

Sir William Herschel 1731-1814.

The German-born astronomer William Herschel built larger and larger reflectors. The biggest had a mirror 4 ft across. The third Earl of Rosse built an even bigger reflector in the 1840s. It had a 6 ft mirror. With it, Rosse was the first person to see the spiral shape of some galaxies.

In the 1930s Karl Jansky, working at the Bell Telephone Laboratories in the United States, discovered radio signals coming from the center of our galaxy. Astronomers were slow to realize its importance, but Jansky's discovery eventually developed into the modern science of radio astronomy and radio telescopes.

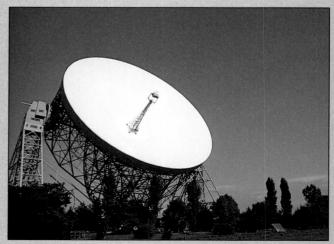

Jodrell Bank radio telescope, England.

The late 19th century and early 20th century was a very active period of telescope building. A refractor with a 3 ft-wide objective lens, built by Alvan Clark and George Hale, in 1897 near Chicago, is still the world's biggest refractor. Hale also built a reflector with a mirror 16 ft across at Mount Palomar in 1948.

Most telescopes built in recent years have been smaller, with mirrors of about 13 ft across. New electronic light detectors and computerized image processing enable these telescopes to outperform the larger ones. With modern communication links, astronomers operate telescopes at a distance.

A modern reflector on an island in Hawaii.

Astronomers are building large reflectors again. Mirrors more than about 26 ft across are distorted by their own weight. Reflectors in the 1990s will be bigger than this, up to 52 ft across, by linking together several small, individually steered mirrors. As most of the radiation from the universe is blocked or distorted by the earth's atmosphere, telescopes are increasingly placed in space where they can "see" further, with more clarity and detail.

Facts and figures

The most powerful optical telescope in the world is also the world's largest reflector. The telescope, on Mount Semirodriki in the Soviet Union, has a 20 ft mirror weighing 70 tons. It is so powerful that it could detect the light from a candle 15,000 mi away.

The largest refractor ever built was a 4 ft horizontal telescope built for the Paris Exposition in 1900. However, the instrument was so cumbersome that it was dismantled after the Exposition.

The largest successful refractor in the world is the 1.01m (40-inch) telescope built at the Yerkes Observatory near Chicago. Its lens weighs a quarter of a ton.

The largest radio telescope was built in a natural hollow in the earth, in Arecibo on the island of Puerto Rico. The dish, which measures 1,000 ft across, was built in 1963 and rebuilt in 1974 to improve its performance.

The first astronomical observatories in space were the U.S. Orbiting Solar Observatory satellites. They began to be launched in 1962. Since then, numerous American-, Soviet- and European-built telescope-carrying satellites have been put in orbit.

The largest telescope in space is the Hubble Space Telescope. The tube of this optical telescope measures 43 ft long by 14 ft in diameter. The whole craft weighs 11 tons.

Chapter Two

CAMERAS

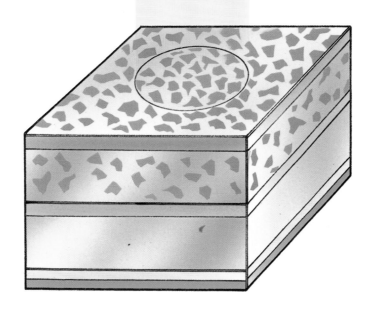

CONTENTS

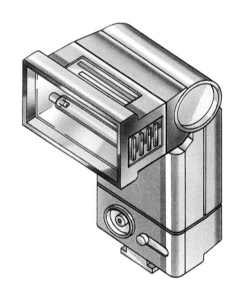

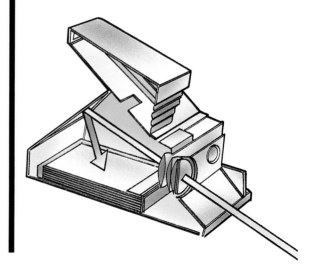

THE WORKING PARTS

A camera is a device designed specially to record images on light-sensitive film. There are many different types of camera, but they all work in much the same way. The Single-Lens Reflex, or SLR, camera shown here is an example of one of the most popular types.

A camera is basically a lightproof box. A lens is fixed to one side and film is positioned inside the box opposite the lens. Light is prevented from entering the box by a shutter, a type of blind, behind the lens. When closed, the shutter stops light passing through a hole, the aperture, in the camera body. Light entering the lens of an SLR is reflected upward by a mirror. At the top of this camera, a specially shaped block of glass called a penta-prism reflects the light out through the viewfinder. Other types of cameras have separate viewfinder and shutter-lens systems.

When a camera user wishes to take a photograph, or "shot," almost the exact image that will be recorded on the film can be seen in the viewfinder. At the right moment, the shutter is opened by pressing a button known as the shutter release. If the camera is an SLR, the mirror flips up out of the way, allowing the light to pass through the lens and reach the film. The lens bends the rays of light so that they produce a sharp image on the film. The amount the light rays have to be bent, or refracted, depends on how far away the objects are from the camera. Refraction is adjusted by rotating the focusing ring on the lens. Some cameras use a fixed-focus lens that is suitable for photo-

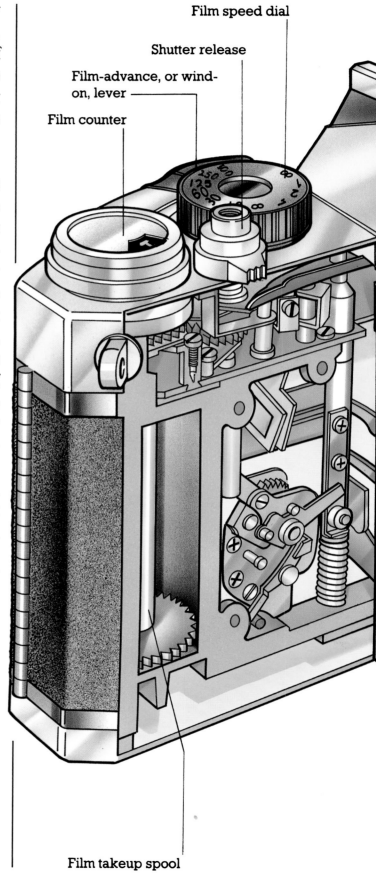

Film speed dial

Shutter release

Film-advance, or wind-on, lever

Film counter

Film takeup spool

28

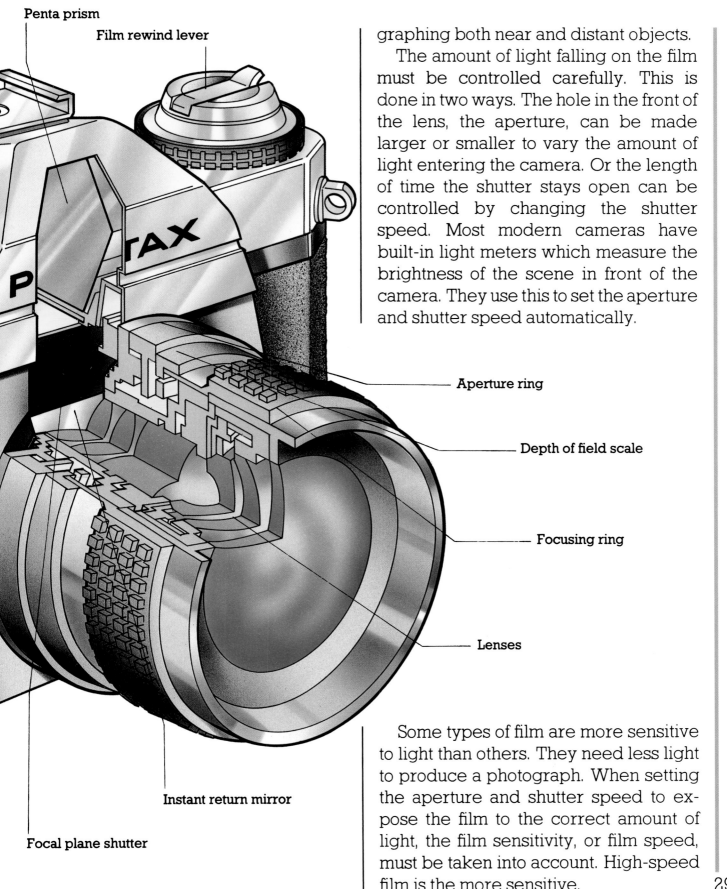

Penta prism

Film rewind lever

Aperture ring

Depth of field scale

Focusing ring

Lenses

Instant return mirror

Focal plane shutter

graphing both near and distant objects.

The amount of light falling on the film must be controlled carefully. This is done in two ways. The hole in the front of the lens, the aperture, can be made larger or smaller to vary the amount of light entering the camera. Or the length of time the shutter stays open can be controlled by changing the shutter speed. Most modern cameras have built-in light meters which measure the brightness of the scene in front of the camera. They use this to set the aperture and shutter speed automatically.

Some types of film are more sensitive to light than others. They need less light to produce a photograph. When setting the aperture and shutter speed to expose the film to the correct amount of light, the film sensitivity, or film speed, must be taken into account. High-speed film is the more sensitive.

29

LENSES AND FOCUSING

The basic job of a camera lens is to form a sharp image on the film. Without a lens, there would be no picture at all. The simplest camera lens is a single piece of glass or plastic, shaped like a magnifying glass. More advanced cameras use sophisticated lenses. These are made by combining closely several different simple lenses, or elements. Compound lenses produce clearer and brighter pictures because they allow more light to reach the film and they correct faults in the simple lens, particularly those that distort the colors or blur the edges.

The image is focused by rotating the lens's focusing ring. In the viewfinder of an SLR camera, the photographer sees the image become less and less blurred until it is sharply focused. Some cameras have interchangeable lenses. One lens can be taken off the camera and easily replaced by a different lens that makes objects appear larger or smaller.

A camera is usually supplied with a standard lens already fitted. Mostly, this has a focal length of about 50mm. This means that it will bend inward rays of light from a distant object so that they all meet 50mm from the center of the lens. Lenses that make objects appear smaller, but get in more of a scene, have shorter focal lengths. They are called wide-angle lenses. More "powerful" lenses with longer focal lengths make objects appear larger in the photograph. They are called telephoto lenses. A zoom lens allows the focal length to be varied from, say, 100mm to 200mm. It offers the photographer a greater range of photo compositions.

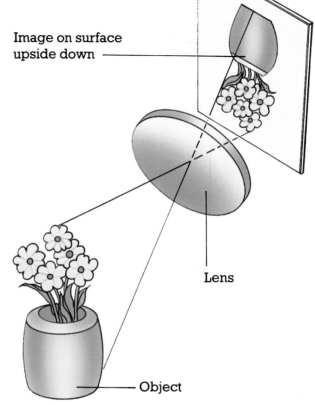

Image on surface upside down

Lens

Object

A single lens, also called a simple lens, will focus rays from an object to form an image on a screen. Because the light rays from the top and bottom of the object cross over at the lens, the image is upside down and reversed left to right compared to the object.

Wide-angle lens

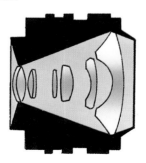

The view through a fish-eye lens. With its wide angle of view, a circular image is formed.

Standard lens

Telephoto lens

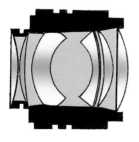

A fast shutter speed can "freeze" actions that would otherwise appear as a blur.

The diaphragm shutter, also called a leaf shutter, is a ring of metal segments, or leaves. When the shutter release is pressed, the segments rotate and move apart, opening up a hole, or aperture, through which light can pass to the film. While the diaphragm shutter opens up to expose the whole film, the focal plane shutter exposes a vertical window which passes across the film. The shutter is composed from two blinds, or blades. When the shutter release is pressed, the first blind snaps back, exposing the film. Then the second blind snaps across, covering the film again. The time separating the two blind movements is set by the shutter speed. This may be 1/2,000 of a second. The shorter the time, the narrower the gap between the two blinds. For speeds slower than 1/60 of a second, the first blind exposes all the frame.

The leaf shutter

A: Closed

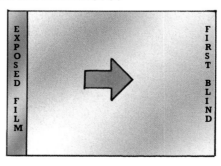

Focal plane shutter

A: 1st blind moves

EXPOSED FILM

FIRST BLIND

B: 2nd blind follows

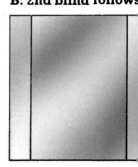

THE SHUTTER

A camera's shutter controls the length of time that light is allowed to fall on the film. Many cameras allow the photographer to choose a shutter speed ranging from as little as 1/2,000th of a second up to several seconds. Each speed is half of the one before. The range might be, say, 1/2,000th, 1/1,000th, 1/500th and so on. There may also be a 'B' setting that lets the photographer open and close the shutter manually to obtain exposures of several minutes or even hours. The shutter speed is selected either automatically by the camera's electronics or manually by rotating the shutter speed dial.

The shutter may be one of two types – the diaphragm shutter or the focal plane shutter. Most compact cameras are fitted with the diaphragm type of shutter. It is usually positioned within the lens, between the lens elements. If more advanced cameras fitted with interchangeable lenses used diaphragm shutters, each lens would have to have its own shutter mechanism, making the lenses very expensive. It makes more sense to build the shutter into the camera body. This is the focal plane shutter, so-called because it is placed just in front of the plane (a flat surface) where the image is focused on the film.

The diaphragm shutter opens to expose the whole film evenly at once. At shutter speeds shorter than about 1/30th of a second, the focal plane shutter opens to form a type of window which sweeps across the film.

B: Opening **C: Wide Open** **D: Shutting** **E: Shut**

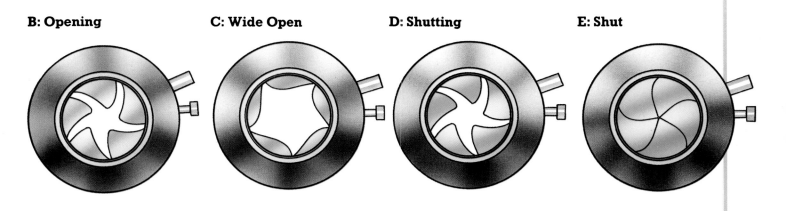

C: Exposure gap crosses frame **D: 2nd blind closing gap** **E: Exposure completed**

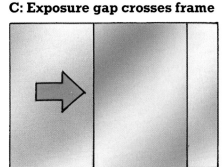
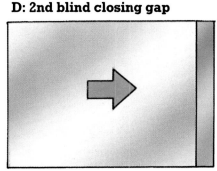
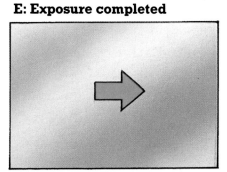

THE DIAPHRAGM

A camera's diaphragm works in the same way as the iris functions in the human eye. In bright sunshine, the iris closes down to reduce the amount of light entering the eye. In a darkened room, it opens up to let in more light.

A camera's diaphragm must therefore be opened up or closed down to control the amount of light entering the camera and falling on the film. It is necessary to control the amount of light in this way because exposing the film to too much light (known as overexposure) or too little light (underexposure) will spoil the photograph.

The diaphragm consists of a ring of overlapping metal blades. When the aperture ring around the outside of the lens is rotated by the photographer, the diaphragm blades swing around and a hole, or aperture, opens in the middle. The more the ring is turned, the bigger the aperture grows.

A lens's aperture is indicated by its f-number or f-stop. The f-number is calculated by dividing the lens's focal length by the diameter of its aperture. A 50mm lens with a 25mm aperture is therefore set to f2. Similar lenses set to the same f-stop will allow about the same amount of light through.

Print from underexposed negative film.

Print from overexposed negative film.

A camera's aperture ring usually has a number of click-stops so that it can be set to a series of known apertures. The click-stops are chosen so that each allows twice the amount of light through compared to the previous one. The higher the f-number, the smaller the aperture. So f11 is half the brightness of f8 and twice that of f16.

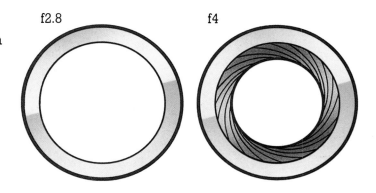

f2.8   f4

34

Depth of field

When a camera lens is focused on something, some objects closer to the camera and some that are further away are in focus too. The distance between the closest and furthest objects in focus is referred to as the depth of field.

Smaller apertures produce a greater depth of field than larger apertures. Short focal length lenses have a greater depth of field than long focal length lenses. Depth of field can be used, for example, to make an object stand out from blurred surroundings by choosing a wide aperture with a small depth of field.

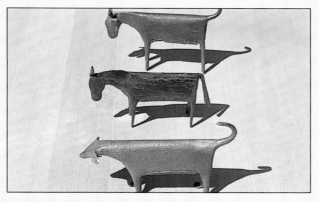

At f16, all three objects are in focus.

At f2, only the middle object is in focus.

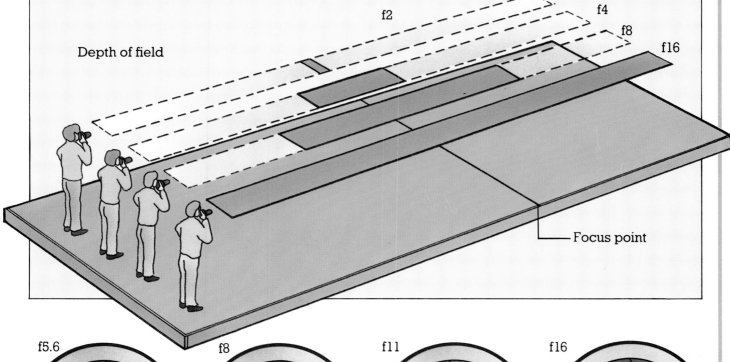

Depth of field

Focus point

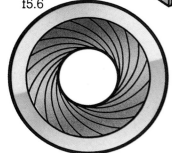

f5.6

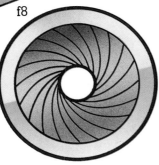

f8

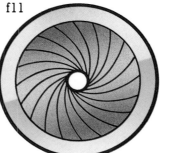

f11

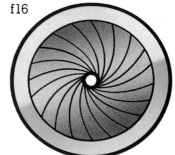

f16

TYPES OF FILM

Color film has a more complicated structure than black and white film. It resembles three black and white films sandwiched together. Each layer is made sensitive to a different main, or primary, color. For films, there are three primary colors – red, green and blue. (For paints, the primary colors are red, blue and yellow.) If all three are mixed together equally, they combine to produce white light. By varying the amounts of these three colors in the mixture, any color in the rainbow can be made. By making the three layers, or emulsions, of a color film sensitive to the three primary colors, the film can record images in full color.

There are two types of color film. One produces a negative when it is developed and this is used to make prints. The second type, called reversal film, produces color slides or transparencies, when developed.

Most color films are manufactured so that they produce realistic colors in natural daylight conditions. Some are specially produced for photographing in artificial light, as in a studio.

Each layer of color film reacts to a different color (A). The top layer records blue, the middle green and the bottom red. Other colors are recorded in more than one layer. White light activates all three as it is made up of all the colors of the rainbow.

The film is developed in a similar way to black and white film in order to change exposed silver halides to silver (B). Colored dyes are activated where silver forms. The negative image is revealed when the silver is dissolved away chemically (C).

A.

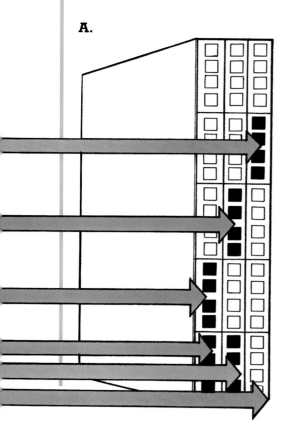

B.

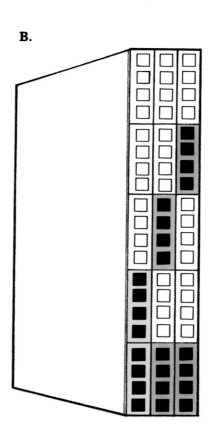

C.

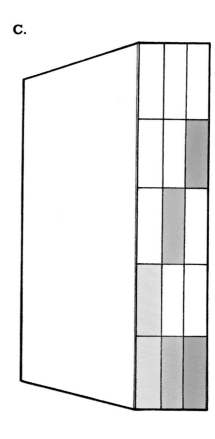

Instant pictures

Light passes through the lens of this instant picture camera and bounces off a mirror onto the film. Each exposed frame of film is automatically pushed out of the camera between a pair of rollers which squeeze together the film, chemical developer and fixer. The image then forms in daylight after about a minute.

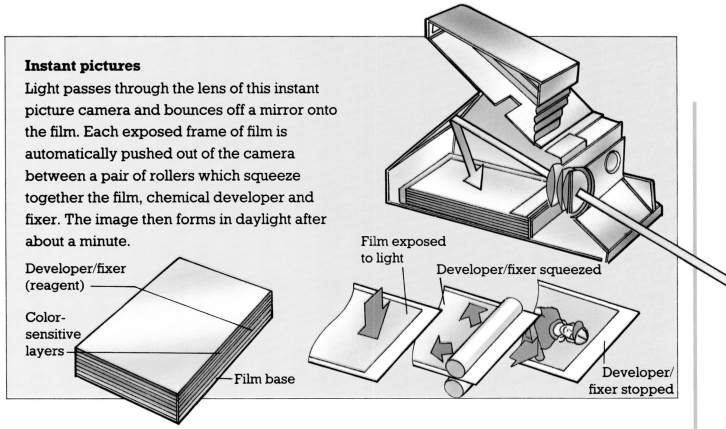

Developer/fixer (reagent)

Color-sensitive layers

Film base

Film exposed to light

Developer/fixer squeezed

Developer/fixer stopped

To make a photographic print, the negative is loaded into an enlarger and projected onto a sheet of photographic paper (D). The f-stop and exposure time for the paper are adjusted to the brightness of the negative – a dark negative needs longer exposure.

Photographic printing paper is similar to color film and it is developed in a similar way (E). During development, the unnatural negative colors are transformed chemically into the original lifelike colors so as to reproduce the scene (F).

D.

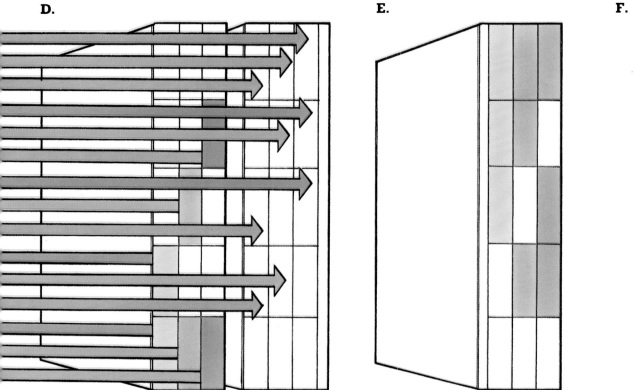

E.

F.

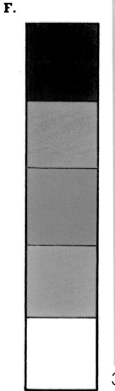

TAKING A PHOTO

Taking a photograph is a curious mixture of science and art. The science is in operating the camera and its systems correctly. The art is in deciding what parts of a scene should be included in the photograph, where objects should be in relation to one another, the length of the exposure, and choosing the right moment to take the photograph.

Every time a camera's shutter release button is pressed a photograph may be taken. But merely pointing a camera at something of interest and pressing the shutter release would probably give rather disappointing results.

The photographer has to think about where to take the photograph from. A low viewpoint might give better or more interesting results than a high viewpoint. A close-up might be better than a long shot taken from further away.

If the camera has interchangeable lenses, the choice of lens is important too. The image should fill the viewfinder. It might be necessary to use a more powerful telephoto lens to magnify the image sufficiently.

The choice of shutter speed and f-stop is important. If a slow shutter speed is used to photograph a fast-moving object like a running horse, the horse may appear blurred in the picture because it was moving while the shutter was open but a fast shutter speed will "freeze" the action. With slow shutter speeds, camera shake is more likely.

The photographer loads the camera with a fresh roll of film and sets the film speed dial (1) to the speed printed on the film cassette, usually given as an ASA or ISO number.

The shutter speed (2) and lens aperture (3) are set. The camera may do these automatically or the photographer may set them manually.

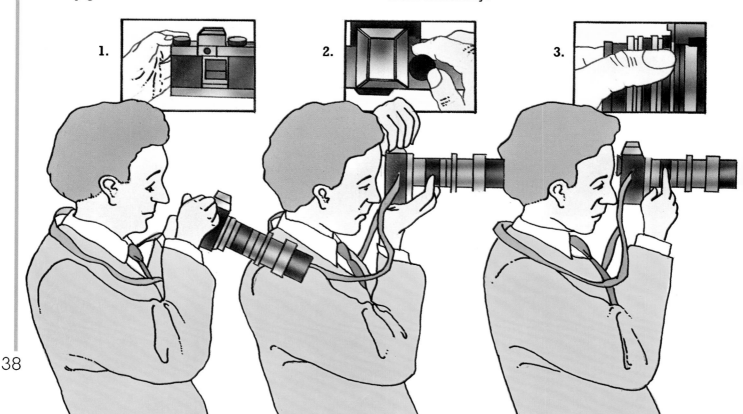

1. 2. 3.

It is important to hold a camera steady to avoid shaking it and blurring the photograph.

The photographer aims the camera at the scene to be photographed and focuses the lens (4) until the image in the viewfinder is clear and sharp.

The shutter release button is slowly pressed to take the photograph (5). The film wind-on lever is operated (6) to move a fresh piece of film into place for the next photograph.

4.

5.

6.

FLASH AND LIGHTING

The word photography comes from two Greek words, phos and graphos, meaning light and drawing. Photography is drawing with light. Most photographs are taken in natural sunlight. But there are times when daylight does not give satisfactory results. The sky may be overcast. Even on a bright day, the subject may be in deep shadow or the film may not be light-sensitive enough for the conditions.

The answer is to provide artificial light. In the studio, professional photographers use a range of flood and flash lights, spotlights and reflectors to create the desired effect. Outside, photographers use electronic flashguns as a compact and lightweight source of light. The flashgun is connected to the camera so that a flash of light occurs when the shutter is fully open. This is called synchronized flash. As a focal plane shutter exposes only part of the film frame at a time when using fast shutter speeds, cameras with this system are usually synchronized with flash at a setting of 1/60th of a second or below.

▶ An electronic flashgun converts the low voltage from a battery pack into a very high voltage. When the camera's shutter opens, the high voltage is switched to a gas-filled flash tube. The surge of electricity causes tiny particles in the gas to be boosted with energy. They race to either of two metal plates (electrodes). Collisions between the particles result in some of their energy being released in a burst of intense light.

A scene is captured on film with flash.

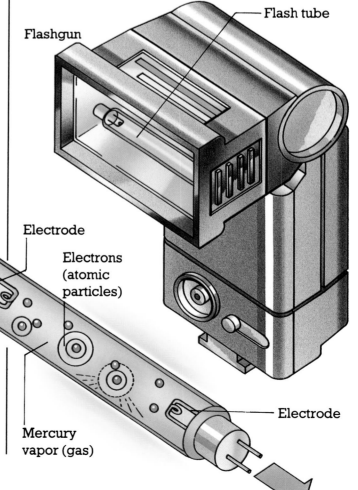

Flashgun

Flash tube

Electrode

Electrons (atomic particles)

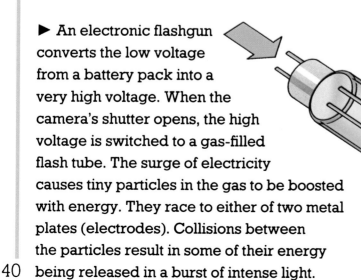

Mercury vapor (gas)

Electrode

40

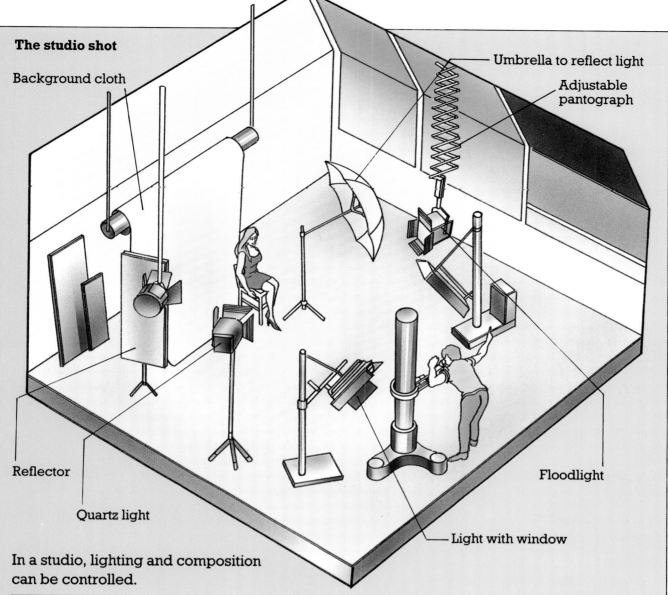

The studio shot

Background cloth

Umbrella to reflect light

Adjustable pantograph

Reflector

Quartz light

Light with window

Floodlight

In a studio, lighting and composition can be controlled.

Studio Lights
Within a studio, a photographer will use a range of light reflectors and lamps to create the desired lighting. Large reflectors used with "diffused" glass bulbs give soft, general illumination. Reflectors with polished surfaces used with small, clear glass lamps give hard lighting with sharp-edged shadows. Spotlights are fitted with various hoods and blinkers to concentrate their light onto a small area. Lights are supported on stands or suspended from the ceiling. The direction and strength of each light's illumination can be adjusted as required.

SPECIAL CAMERAS

Some cameras are very specialized. They may be designed to do only one particular type of photographic work. They do exactly the same thing as the family snapshot camera in that they capture images on film, but at least one aspect of the camera is highly developed. Some have very advanced lenses to process the image in a unique way, as in the panoramic camera. Another type may be attached to additional instruments to obtain images from inaccessible places.

In medicine, cameras are often used to record images from inside the human body. X ray cameras use large sheets of film sensitive to both visible light and X rays. Instant picture cameras are used to take photos from ultrasound equipment (scanners) used to monitor the progress of unborn babies. The TV-type screens of computers and views through microscopes are often photographed to record experimental results.

By using rotating mirrors or lenses, panoramic cameras can record up to a full circle of view, or a long row, in a single photograph (top). The view through a medical instrument such as an endoscope (middle), used to look inside the body, can be photographed by attaching a camera to it. Cameras on board aircraft photograph the ground in order to prepare maps or even to spy on enemy airfields and harbors. Those on diving equipment can photograph underwater life (right). Stereo cameras (far right) take two photographs from slightly different views. When the photos are looked at together in a special viewer, a three-dimensional effect is created.

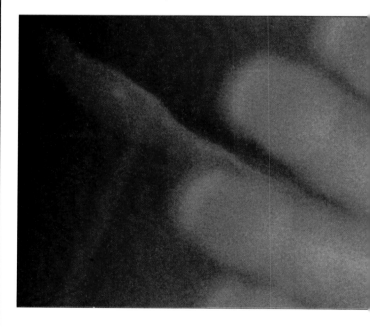

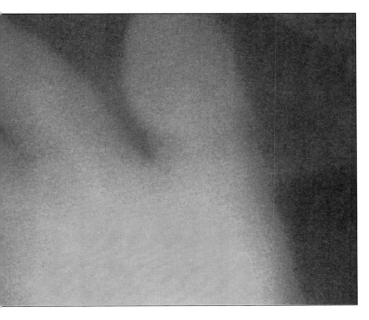

Holograms

All photographs taken with conventional cameras show scenes where everything appears flat. A special type of photograph called a hologram, made using the intense beam of light from a laser, shows three-dimensional scenes. You can look around objects in the foreground and see what is behind them. Holograms can be produced only with highly specialized and expensive equipment. They cannot be taken with ordinary cameras.

An illusion created by a hologram.

THE HISTORY OF CAMERAS

The word camera comes from the Latin "camera obscura" which means "darkened room." For hundreds of years people knew that an image of a bright scene could be projected through a tiny aperture onto a wall in a darkened room. However, it was not until 1827 that Joseph Niepce claimed to be able to "fix the images from a camera obscura." Using an asphalt varnish as his light-sensitive material he captured the view through his window – but the picture needed an eight hour exposure!

A camera obscura has an upside down and reversed image, as in a pinhole camera.

In 1837 Parisian Louis Daguerre, produced "daguerreotypes." These one-off positives needed 15-30 minutes of exposure. In England, William Henry Fox Talbot made tiny negatives, after half-hour exposures, in cameras which his wife called "mousetraps." New lenses, by the Hungarian Josef Petzval, improved exposure times greatly. Soon Fox Talbot made negatives in less than a minute, and then multiple prints from each which he called calotypes.

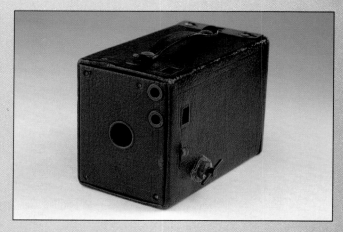

The popular Kodak box camera.

These inventions became obsolete when a process called wet-plate collodian came out in 1851, but a photographer still needed to be something of a chemist to take a successful picture. In 1888 American George Eastman introduced the light and portable kodax box camera which took 100 exposures on a roll of film, but the camera itself had to be sent back to the factory to process the film. By 1900 the Kodak "Brownie" was on sale to the general public at a cheap price, and films could be loaded separately. Popular photography was born.

An early Leica camera.

The first precision 35mm camera, the Leica, was made in Germany in 1925. It paved the way for a revolution in photography. The development of tiny electronic circuits led to cameras with built-in light meters and exposure control systems. In recent years the demand for simple "point-and-shoot" cameras produced the fully automatic 35mm compact, the smaller 110 pocket, and the slim, easy to load, disc cameras. The development of miniature electronic motors has allowed for built-in film winders.

A Nikon SLR, an electronic camera.

Video and computer-based imaging are beginning to rival film. By the end of the 1990s, movie studios will have begun to change over from film to high-definition video. Computers can store pictures in the form of a stream of numbers on a magnetic disc. Filmless cameras like the Sony Mavica work in this way. Developments in computerized imaging systems are advancing rapidly, as the enormous computing power needed to process high-quality images continues to become less costly.

FACTS AND FIGURES

The first negative photo was taken in 1835 by William Henry Fox Talbot, 18 years after Niepce captured the first photographic image.

The films used now are so sensitive that they can capture images in exposures that are 20 million times shorter than those used by the earliest photographers like Daguerre and Fox Talbot.

The first photograph taken from the air was taken from a balloon over Paris in 1858 by Gaspard Félix Tournachon.

A 35mm color negative contains the equivalent, in computer terms, of 72 million bits of information.

The fastest camera in the world is an electronic camera used for laser research at London's Imperial College. It can record images at the rate of 33,000 million every second.

The largest theater screens in the world are found in IMAX cinemas. The screens can be 18 meters high and 25 meters across. To obtain sharp images this size, IMAX cameras use a huge film format. The frame is ten times the size of a 35mm frame used in normal camera films.

The earliest process for adding sound to a movie was developed by Eugene Augustin Lauste in 1906. He produced a working system in London in 1910.

Chapter Three
TELEVISION AND VIDEO

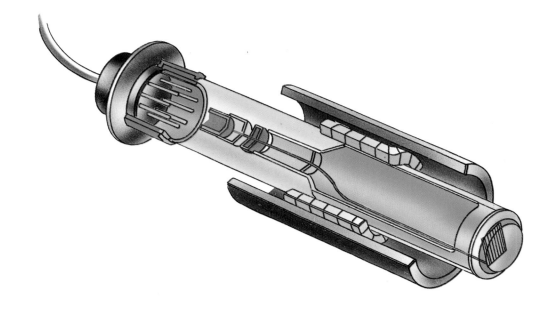

CONTENTS

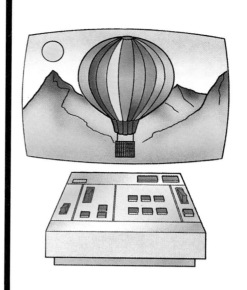
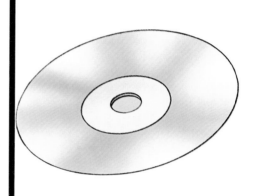
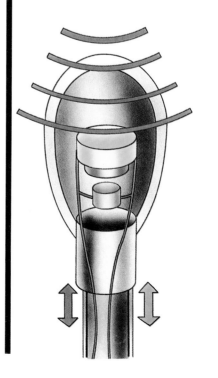

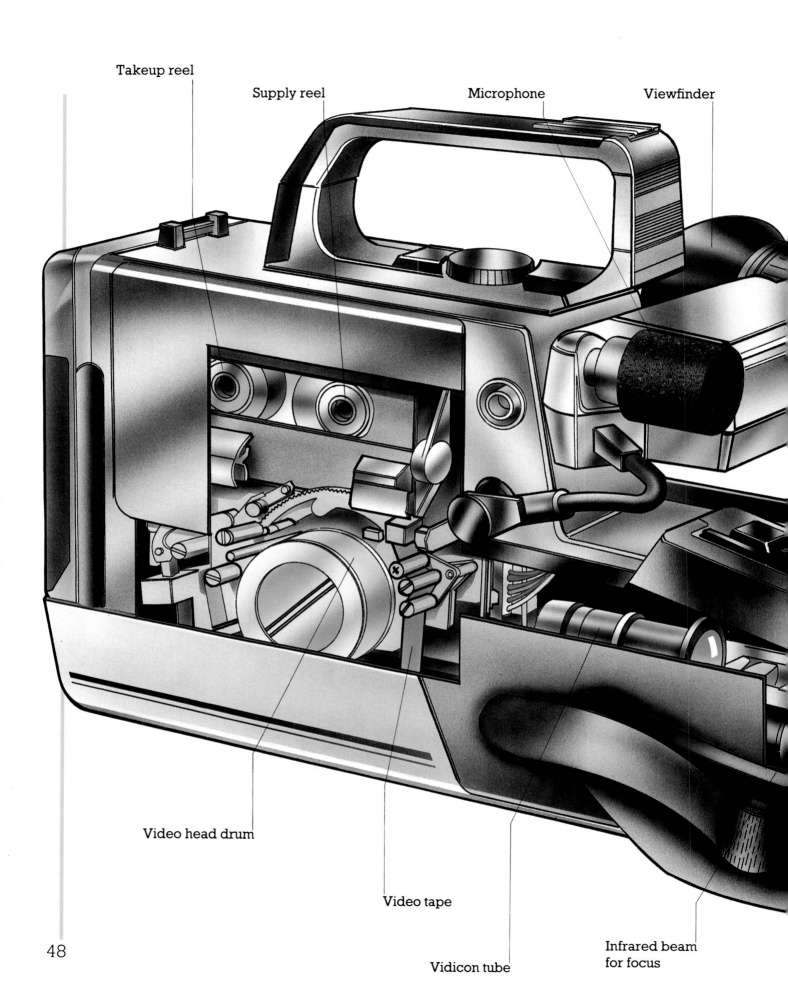

Takeup reel

Supply reel

Microphone

Viewfinder

Video head drum

Video tape

Vidicon tube

Infrared beam
for focus

48

THE WORKING PARTS

A camcorder is a portable video camera and a video tape recorder combined in a single piece of equipment. It is designed to record full-color moving pictures and sound on magnetic tape.

The image entering the lens is seen by looking through the viewfinder. This is actually a television tube, or monitor, with a tiny. wide screen. Power zoom controls on the camcorder's hand-grip operate a motorized system for changing the lens's angle of view. In effect, this changes the lens focal length enabling both telephoto and wide-angle pictures to be recorded from the same position. Many camcorders also have an automatic focusing system. Infrared beams sent out from and detected by devices on the front of the camcorder measure how far away objects are and control a motor that focuses the lens to produce a sharp picture.

The lens in the camcorder shown here focuses the image onto a "pickup" tube. The tube converts the image into an electrical signal. The latest camcorders use a small sturdy device called a Charge Coupled Device, or CCD for short, instead of the larger, fragile glass pickup tube. Both devices do the same job. An image enters at one end and an electrical copy of the image comes out of the other end.

Once the image has been converted to an electrical form, it can be fed to the recorder part of the camcorder. At the same time, sound picked up by a microphone is also sent to the recorder. There, the two signals are stored on magnetic tape in the same way that, for example, pop music is recorded on cassette tapes. The recording can be played back at any time using the camcorder or another video recorder. To see and hear the recording, the camcorder or recorder is connected to an ordinary television set.

Power zoom controls

Lens group

THE TV SET

A television, or TV set, is a device for converting television signals back into the pictures that originated the signals. It relies on the fact that any color can be produced by mixing three basic, or primary, colors – red, green and blue – in different quantities. Three electron beams produced by electron "guns" continuously sweep across and down the inside of the screen. This is coated with stripes of materials known as phosphors, which glow red, green or blue when struck by electrons.

A perforated sheet of metal called a shadow mask ensures that each electron beam lands on a slightly different area of the screen. One beam strikes only red phosphors, one strikes only blue and the third strikes only green. The colored dots are so tiny and so close together that our eyes see them merged together into a complete full-color picture.

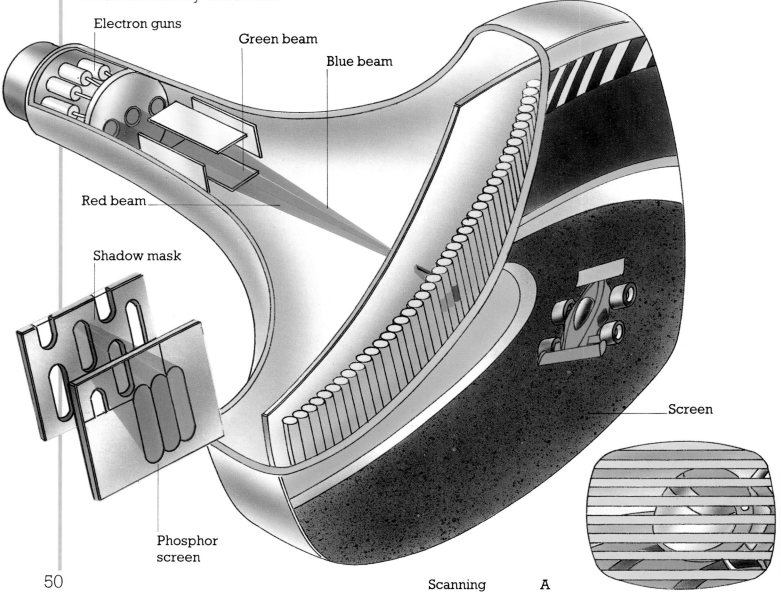

Electron guns

Green beam

Blue beam

Red beam

Shadow mask

Phosphor screen

Screen

Scanning   A

The complex interior of a TV set, with the tube to the right in this photo.

Electrical signals consist of streams of tiny particles known as electrons. When the TV is switched on, the electron guns each produce a narrow beam of electrons. As the three electron beams scan the screen through the shadow mask, the phosphors they fall on glow (right) and give the impression of a lifelike image. The beams do not start at the top of the screen and trace out one complete picture at a time. First, the odd-numbered lines are scanned (A). Then the spaces between these lines are scanned (B) to fill them up (C). All this happens many times a second.

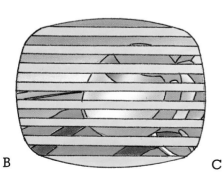

B

C

Video cameras are smaller than ever now thanks to the use of miniature pickup tubes.

Light from an image entering a TV camera lens is focused through a glass block onto three pickup tubes at the same time. One tube is sensitive to red light, one to blue and the third to green light. Inside the tube, an electron beam is swept across the target by a variable magnetic field provided by electromagnets around the tube.

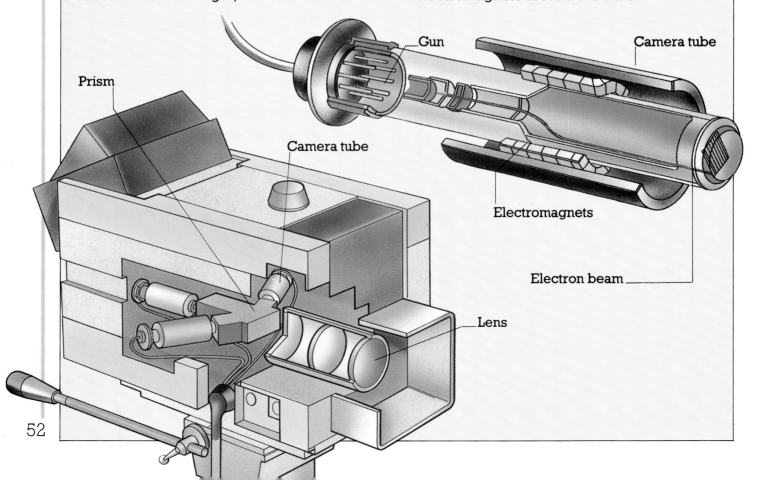

Prism

Camera tube

Gun

Camera tube

Electromagnets

Electron beam

Lens

THE TV AND VIDEO CAMERA

The process of bringing television pictures into your home begins with the television camera. It converts the scene in a television studio, or at an event such as a football match, from a mass of light rays into a stream of electrical signals.

Television cameras rely on the ability of some materials to react to light by releasing electrons. These are vital for the operation of the camera's most important component, the pickup tube.

Color television cameras have three pickup tubes, one for each of the primary colors – red, blue and green. One end of the tube, called the faceplate, is coated with the light-sensitive material. This is referred to as the target. Different types of tube use different target materials. One common type is a compound containing the elements selenium, arsenic and tellurium. Once the image has been transformed into an electrical signal, it can be processed and stored by other equipment.

The light-sensitive target at the front of a pickup tube is charged up to a low voltage of around 30 volts (1). An electron beam scans the target (2). Light enables the charge to leak away (3). The brighter the light is, the more charge leaks away. An image focused on the target is transformed into a pattern of electric charges. As the electron beam scans the target, it soon restores each point to its fully charged state. The size of the charging current depends on how much light has fallen on the target at that point. A brightly lit point requires a much higher charging current (4) than a dimly lit point (5). The video signal is formed from this charging current.

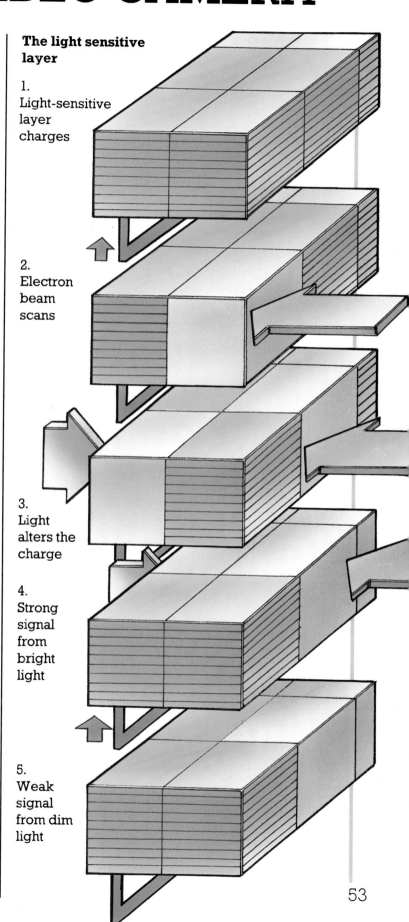

The light sensitive layer

1. Light-sensitive layer charges

2. Electron beam scans

3. Light alters the charge

4. Strong signal from bright light

5. Weak signal from dim light

PICTURE SIGNALS

Television picture signals may be obtained from any one of several sources. They may be received from a transmitter or relay satellite using an antenna, or directly from a broadcasting studio via an underground cable. They may come from a video tape playing in a home video recorder or a camcorder. They could originate from a video game player or a home computer.

Wherever the signals come from, they must be processed so that they can be fed into the television tube, the main image-forming component. TV sets are designed to receive television pictures in the form of a high-frequency radio signal. This incorporates a carrier wave used to transport the picture signals through space. It is added to the picture at transmission and removed by the TV set. Video recorders and game machines have a device called a modulator whose job is to add the picture signals to a carrier wave, a process known as modulation. Many TV sets now have direct video connections for video recorders, eliminating the unnecessary modulation process.

For many years the television set was a self-contained device for receiving broadcast television programs picked up by a rooftop antenna (above far right). Today, the TV set is becoming a display unit for pictures received from a wide range of sources including the video recorder (far right) or graphics unit (right), and also the computerized images created by TV games. Some games allow players to interact with the changing images on the screen (above right).

Recording on tape

A video head, the device responsible for recording pictures on video tape, is a tiny electromagnet made from an iron core with a coil of wire wound around it. When a video signal flows through the coil, it creates a magnetic field in the head. A narrow gap in the head interrupts the field. If magnetic tape is positioned close to the gap, the field can complete its magnetic circuit by flowing through the tape. Magnetic particles in the tape are magnetized by the field. A recorder's video drum normally uses two video heads. Each revolution of a head produces one field (half-section) of the picture. So each spin of the drum produces a complete frame. Stopping the tape results in a still picture.

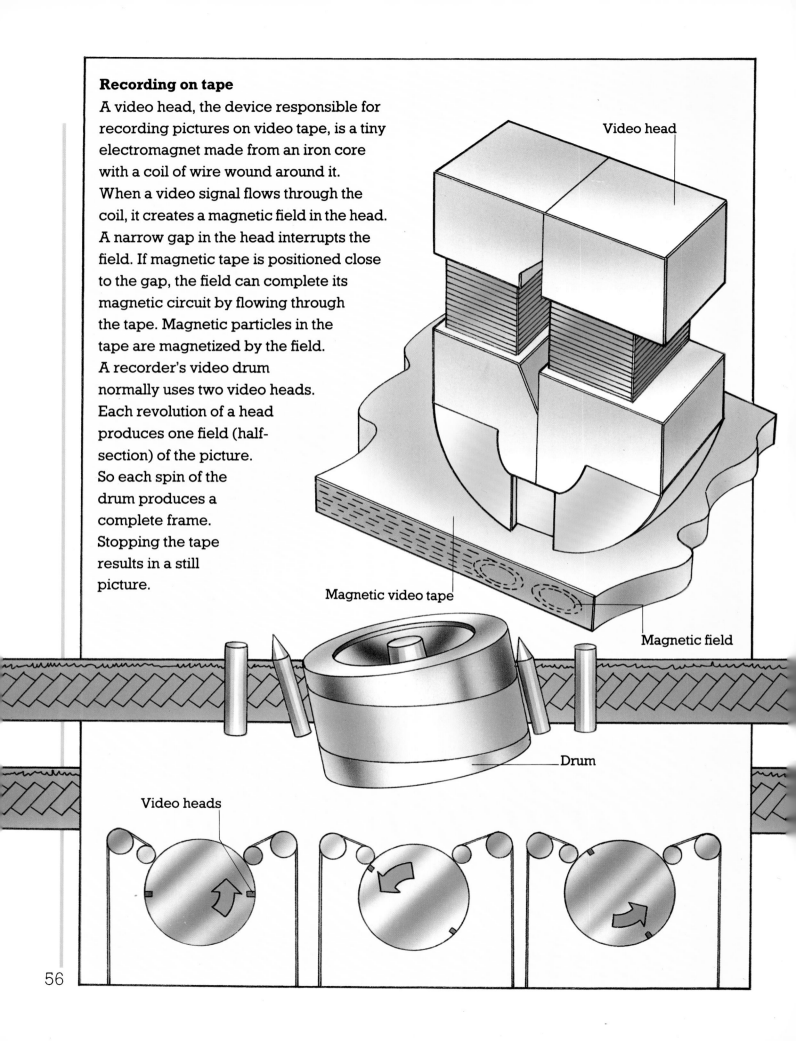

Video head

Magnetic video tape

Magnetic field

Drum

Video heads

VIDEO TAPE AND RECORDERS

Recording television pictures on magnetic tape requires a high tape-speed because a vast amount of information must be stored quickly. The tape would have to travel at 5 meters a second (5 m/s), – over 100 times faster than the speed of audio tape. This is impractical. The tape speed is kept down to just over 2 cm/s by a special scanning technique. The video heads that transfer the picture signals onto the tape are mounted in a spinning drum. In VHS, the most popular home video system or format, the drum spins at 1,500 revolutions per second in the opposite direction to the direction of tape travel. The drum is set at an angle and the tape is wrapped around more than half of the drum. The path of the video heads along the tape traces out a spiral shape, and this helps to provide the required video "writing" speed of almost 5 m/s.

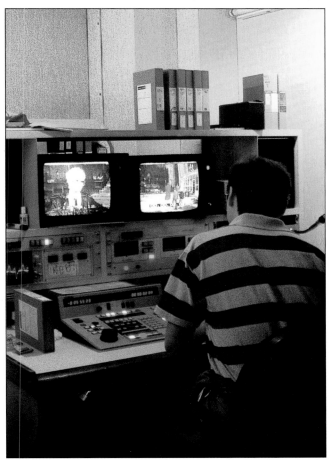

A video editor at work.

Tape to be edited

Part of tape not wanted

Edited tape

Video recordings are rarely made to the same length of time or in precisely the same order as they are required to appear in the final program. The process of shortening and rearranging sections into the desired time-span and order is called editing. Unlike film, which is edited by cutting it up and sticking it together again in a different order, video recordings are edited electronically. Chosen sections of the program material are recorded in the correct order from the original tape onto a new tape.

Television programs are distributed around the country by a network of main transmitters. The signals from these are picked up by relay stations and are distributed to network stations that have the network affiliate. Growing numbers of viewers receive their programs by satellite or from cable television stations. Satellite and cable offer additional channels to those put out (broadcast) by many TV studios.

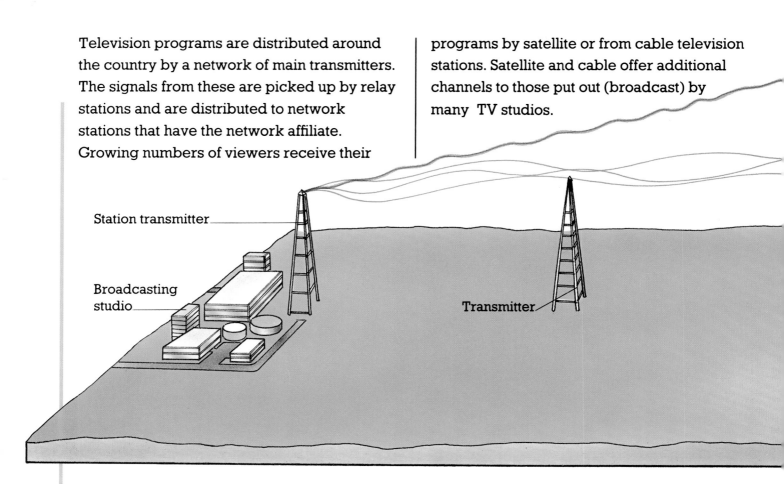

Station transmitter

Broadcasting studio

Transmitter

TRANSMITTING SIGNALS

When electrons vibrate, some of their energy forms electrical and magnetic effects, an electromagnetic field. If they vibrate quickly enough, the field can become separated from the circuit the electrons are flowing through and travel through space. This principle is used to transmit television signals. The low frequency picture signals are combined with a high-frequency radio wave called a carrier wave. This provides the necessary conditions for the signals to spread outward from the transmitter.

Television signals flow around us all the time. They are received by pointing an antenna at the transmitter. The electromagnetic waves produce tiny voltages as they flow around the antenna. There are boosted in strength (amp-lified) and, in the television tube, converted back into the pictures and sounds that produced them.

Most television antennas resemble metal trees with a central trunk and branches. All the branches are usually lined up in the same direction to match the direction of signal being transmitted. There are now small dish-shaped antennas too. These are designed to concentrate the television signals relayed by a satellite in space onto a small pickup suspended above the dish. Cable transmission does not require an antenna. A central cable TV station collects all the signals from ground transmitters, satellites and other sources, and feeds them into homes along metal or fiber optic cables buried underground.

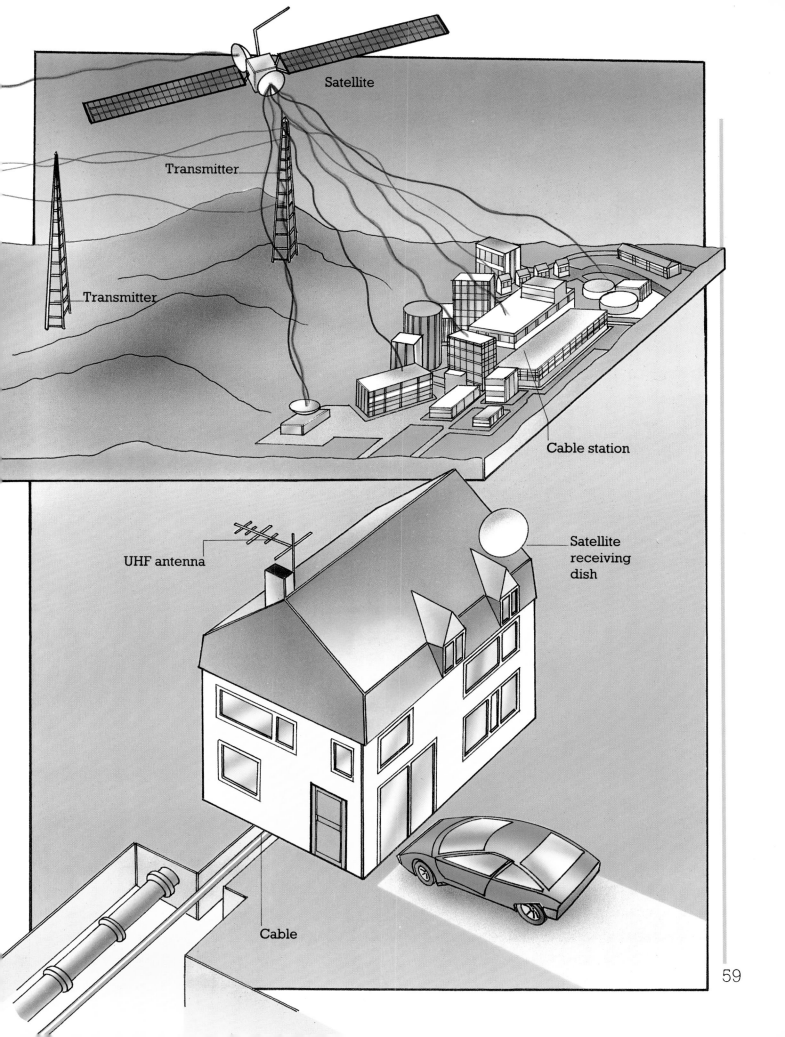

Satellite

Transmitter

Transmitter

Cable station

UHF antenna

Satellite receiving dish

Cable

59

SPECIAL EFFECTS

By processing a video or television signal electronically, the picture that appears on the screen can be altered to produce a range of special effects. Simple effects include changing the overall color of the picture or turning it from a positive to a negative image, but considerably more ambitious and sophisticated effects are possible.

Multiple images and moving images may be created. The picture might be stretched, squeezed, spun around or flipped over. It can be distorted so that it changes from the flat screen shape into a rolling cylinder. Several images can be brought together to form a tumbling cube with a different image on each face. A picture may be exploded into a million tiny specks that blow around the screen like dust in the wind and then reform as a totally different image.

The availability of inexpensive yet powerful computers has given rise to a new branch of special effects based on computer generated images and computer-enhanced video images. Many TV adverts are now made using these.

The shape, color and size of a television picture can be changed quite easily. The picture can be split up into any number of segments and each segment altered using a computer graphics system (below). Within such a setup, the segments can be juggled around, some of them can be repeated at the expense of others, and segments from different programs can be mixed together. Computer graphics can also form part of an ordinary TV broadcast (right) or the basis for a TV advert (below right).

One very useful special effect is called chroma-key. An object, in this case a hot-air balloon, is viewed against a blue background by camera 1 (see A). Camera 2 shows an outdoor scene (B). The two images are mixed together (C) and the blue backing is removed so that the balloon appears to be flying through the mountainous scenery. Here, the three images for just one frame are shown, but the technique can be used for a sequence.

A.

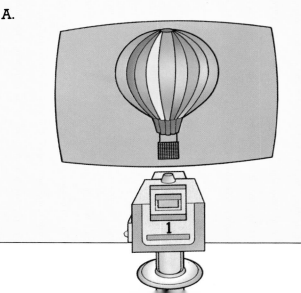

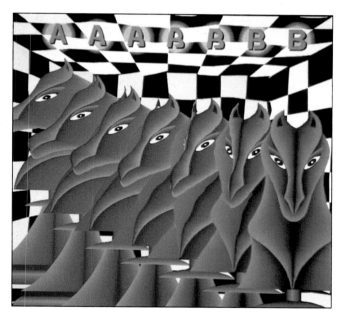

B.

C.

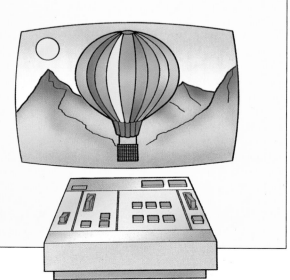

61

LASER DISCS

Television pictures can be recorded on discs as well as on tape. The laser disc stores information as microscopic pits burned into the disc. The pits form a track spiraling out from the center of the disc. The disc is played by bouncing a narrow laser beam off it as it spins at up to 1,500 revolutions per minute. The beam is reflected strongly by the disc's silvery surface, but not by the pits. The flashing reflections are converted into an electrical signal which is then decoded into pictures and sound.

The laser beam does not have to follow the track all the way from beginning to end. It can be made to jump to any point on the disc within a second or so. This makes laser discs ideal for educational uses. Each student can choose a quite different combination of lessons and tests by responding to questions shown on the screen.

The BBC's Domesday Project in 1986 demonstrated the enormous amounts of information that laser discs can store and present in useful ways. The equivalent of over 300 books of maps, still and moving pictures, statistics, text and sounds about Britain are stored on just two 12 in laser discs. The Domesday discs are read by a laser disc player controlled by a computer.

The Domesday Project took two years to complete. One million people supplied data.

To record onto a laser disc, television pictures and sound information are converted into electrical signals which control a laser. The laser beam burns pits in the disc in a pattern that matches the changing strength of the signals. To play the disc, it is scanned from underneath by a laser beam. The pits are tiny and there are billions of them on each disc. Tracking such pits on a disc spinning 1,500 times per second requires great precision.

The reflective surfaces of laser discs.

The video disc system

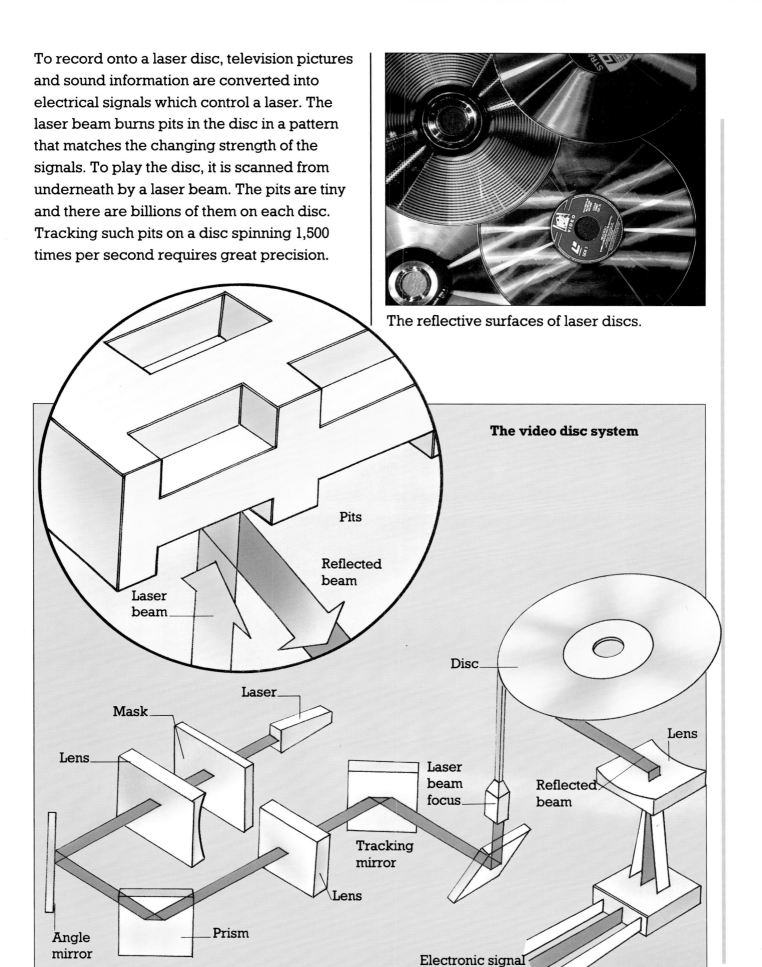

Pits

Reflected beam

Laser beam

Disc

Laser

Mask

Lens

Laser beam focus

Lens

Reflected beam

Tracking mirror

Lens

Angle mirror

Prism

Electronic signal

SPECIAL SYSTEMS

Video and television technology is often combined with other types of equipment to produce specialized systems. Linking a video camera to a communications system enables video images to be sent from wherever the camera is to a more convenient place for viewing them. It enables dangerous places such as nuclear reactors to be monitored at a distance. Images are sent by cable from the camera to a viewing room where they can be looked at in safety. Linking video cameras to an industrial robot results in a robot that can see. By combining video and telephone technology, it is possible to make phones that enable callers to see each other.

The latest area of development, known as multimedia, involves the combination of video and home or office computer systems. With the right equipment and computer programs, video recordings can be mixed with computer text and graphics on a computer screen. Some multimedia systems enable live television pictures to be shown in a small panel, called a window, on a computer screen while the rest of the screen continues to run a computer program. Other systems enable live action and video stills from a laser disc to be incorporated in a computer game.

A mobile giant TV set shows adverts while on the move.

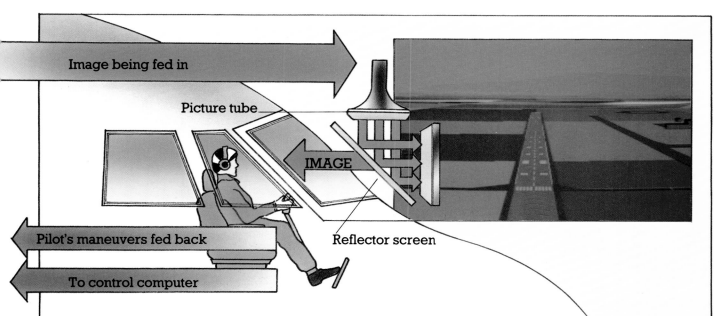

Image being fed in

Picture tube

IMAGE

Reflector screen

Pilot's maneuvers fed back

To control computer

Flight simulators enable pilots to practice maneuvers safely and without taking aircraft out of service. The pilot sits in a mock-up of the flight deck surrounded by moving computer-generated images of the land and sky. Hydraulic rams move the flight deck according to the pilot's actions and sound effects make it sound realistic too. The pictures can be changed to copy the layouts and flight paths of many different airports.

A closed circuit TV (above) allows a security guard to monitor a doorway. Pictures of goods in a store, or text describing them, can be sent from a videotape or laser disc by telephone to a home computer (above right). The goods can be ordered and paid for by keying in a credit card number. A video camera mounted on a military robot (right) is used to look for bombs. A digitizer (left) converts images into digital code – a series of on/off or strong/weak signals – for processing by computer.

65

HISTORY OF TV AND VIDEO

The invention of the telephone in 1876 inspired scientists and inventors to look for ways of sending pictures by electricity. There were many suggestions as to how to do it, but the technology of the day was not able to turn them into working systems.

In 1907 in the Soviet Union, Boris Rosing used a cathode ray tube (CRT) to display crude outlines of shapes. A mechanical device changed the image into an electrical signal. This controlled a beam of electrons that made the CRT screen glow dimly. A British engineer, Alan Campbell Swinton, suggested using a beam of electrons to turn pictures into an electrical signal as well as to change it back into pictures in the CRT.

The first TV set designed by John Logie Baird.

The first successful television system was made by the Scottish inventor John Logie Baird. He transmitted the image of a Maltese cross to a tiny screen in February 1924 in Hastings, England. The world's first regular television broadcasts were made experimentally from Alexandra Palace, London, by the BBC in 1929 using Baird's system.

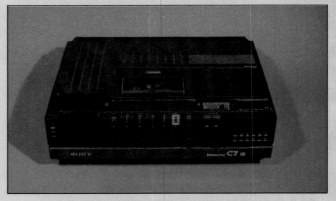

A Betamax video recorder, now obsolete.

The experimental service ended in 1935. In 1936 the Baird scan system, with its picture boosted from 30 lines to 240 lines per frame, was operated on alternate weeks with an all-electronic television system developed by the British EMI and Marconi companies. The EMI-Marconi system offered a better quality 405-line picture and more reliable cameras. Within three months the Baird system was discontinued.

All early TV broadcasts had to be live because there was no way of recording them. In America in 1956 the Ampex Corporation first recorded pictures and sound on two inch magnetic tape.

A 1980s TV set with remote control unit.

When the first communications satellites were launched in the 1960s, transatlantic broadcasts became possible. As the satellites became more powerful and could relay more television channels, transatlantic broadcasts became quite commonplace.

Satellites in orbit now transmit such powerful signals that these can be received by dish antennas only 1½ feet across. With a suitable antenna and receiver, every home can now watch programs beamed down from space.

A modern compact lightweight camcorder.

Home video recorders first became available in the early 1970s. Different manufacturers created several different systems or formats. The Video Home System (VHS) developed by JVC became the most popular. Portable video equipment enabled people to make their own movies, but the equipment was heavy. The camera and recorder were separate units. By miniaturizing the equipment, camera and recorder were combined in a single lightweight unit, a camcorder.

Chapter Four
COMPUTERS

CONTENTS

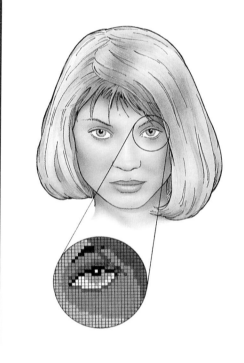

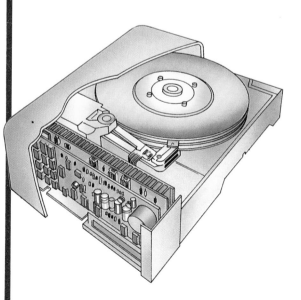

THE WORKING PARTS

A computer is an electronic device designed to process information according to a set of instructions called a program. The computer itself, and any of the working parts that go with it, is called the "hardware." The program, which tells the computer how to process data, is known as "software." The data is information that could be the result of a scientific experiment, a company's sales figures, a video game or even personal files.

Computers have few moving parts. Their work is performed by complex electronic circuits hidden inside the plastic casing. The most complex, the microprocessor, is the computer's master control circuit. Data typed into the computer by means of the keyboard can be viewed on the screen. Both the keyboard and screen are connected to the computer's main processing unit in a variety of different ways depending on the kind of hardware.

Besides the keyboard, a device called a "mouse" is often used to communicate with a computer. The mouse is used to move a pointer called a "cursor" around on the screen and controls the computer program. The processor, screen, and disk drive of the computer shown on the right are combined in a single unit for convenience.

The computer uses two types of electronic memory for storing data. RAM stores the computer user's data temporarily until the computer is switched off. ROM is a permanent store for programs and other data needed by the computer.

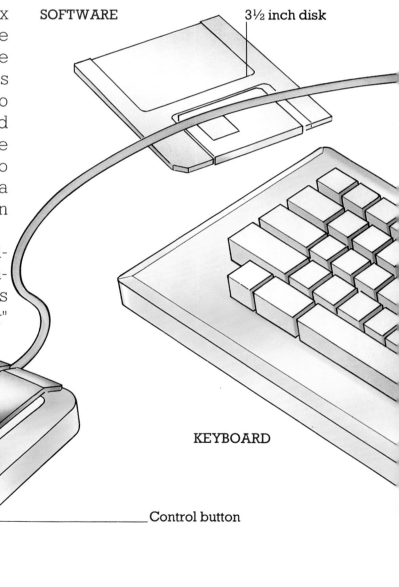

SOFTWARE

3½ inch disk

Optical sensor

Rotating ball

KEYBOARD

Control button

70

MOUSE

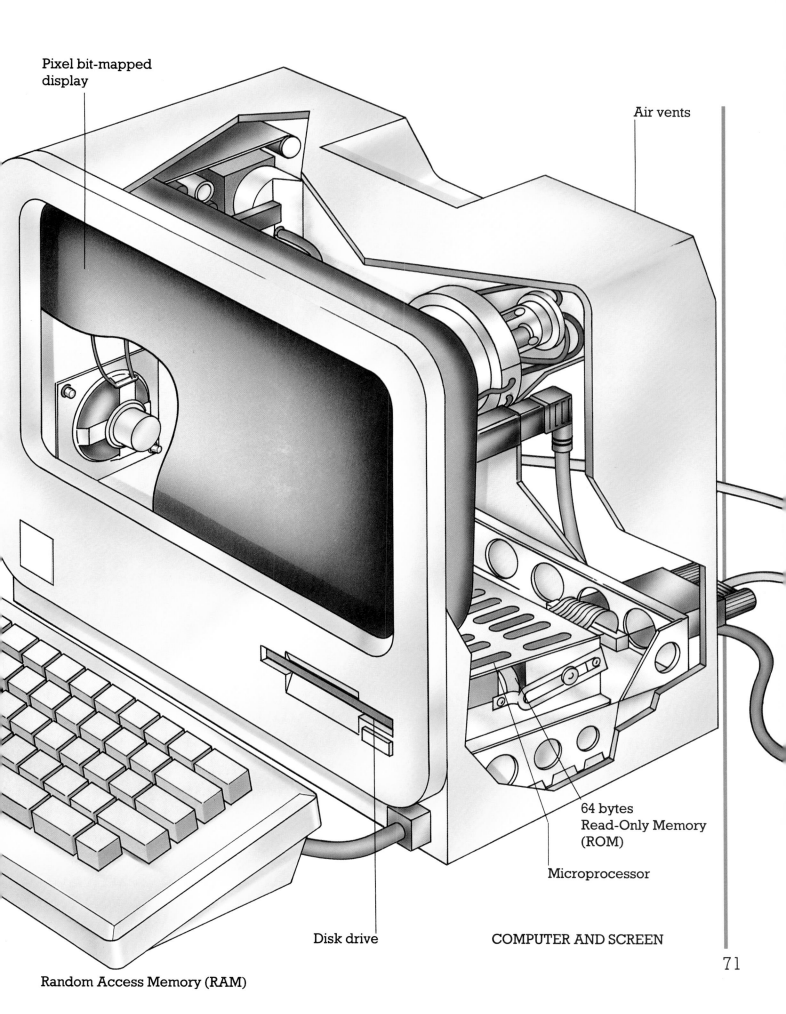

Pixel bit-mapped
display

Air vents

64 bytes
Read-Only Memory
(ROM)

Microprocessor

Disk drive

COMPUTER AND SCREEN

Random Access Memory (RAM)

71

THE COMPUTER

A computer is basically a very sophisticated calcutating machine. The simplest pocket calculator and the most advanced computer have much in common. Both have an input unit to feed information in - the calculator's numerical keypad and the computers keyboard. Each also has a memory unit for storing data. The calculator's memory is very small, but adequate, for the few numbers that must be stored to carry out simple calculations. A computer's memory is much bigger. A typical home or office computer has a memory big enough to hold 2,000,000 three digit numbers or 1,000,000 words.

The calculator and the computer both have a processing unit which controls the system and carries out all the calculations. Each has an output unit – the calculator's liquid crystal screen, and the computer's monitor. The monitor is often referred to as a visual display unit (VDU), a display, or simply a screen.

The major difference between a calculator and a computer is that the computer can be programmed to carry out a wide range of complex tasks, whereas the calculator is normally limited to simple calculations. However, some scientific and programmable calculators are now available and these manage to bridge the gap between computers and calculators.

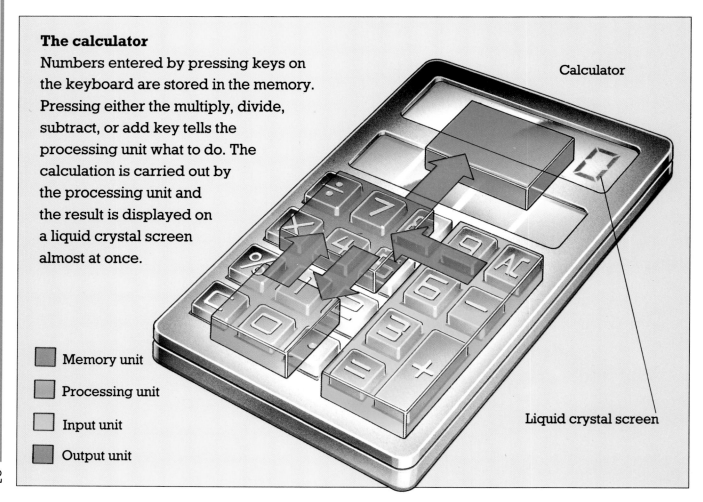

The calculator
Numbers entered by pressing keys on the keyboard are stored in the memory. Pressing either the multiply, divide, subtract, or add key tells the processing unit what to do. The calculation is carried out by the processing unit and the result is displayed on a liquid crystal screen almost at once.

Calculator

Liquid crystal screen

■ Memory unit
■ Processing unit
□ Input unit
■ Output unit

The computer

The main part of a computer contains a processing unit and a memory unit with Random Access Memory (RAM) for storing the user's programs and data, and Read-Only Memory (ROM) for storing the computer's essential data. When a program is needed, a copy of it is transferred into the computer's memory from the disk where it is stored. The program might be on a floppy disk inserted in the computer's disk drive, or it could come from a hard disk sealed inside the computer. Once the program is run the results will be stored temporarily in RAM. They may also be displayed on the monitor, or stored more permanently on disk, either floppy or hard. These results can be sent to a printer connected to the computer. Other output devices include speakers for sounds or music, or plotters which can produce detailed blueprints. Any printed matter produced by a computer is also called "hard copy."

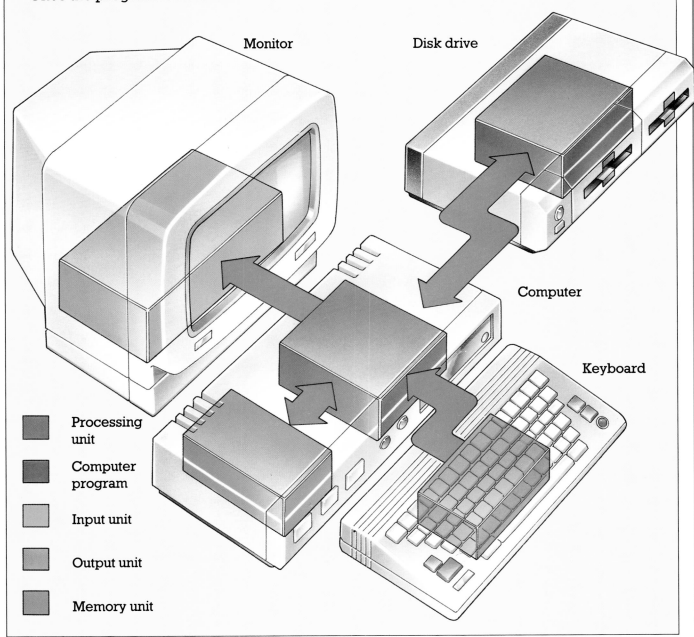

Monitor

Disk drive

Computer

Keyboard

Processing unit

Computer program

Input unit

Output unit

Memory unit

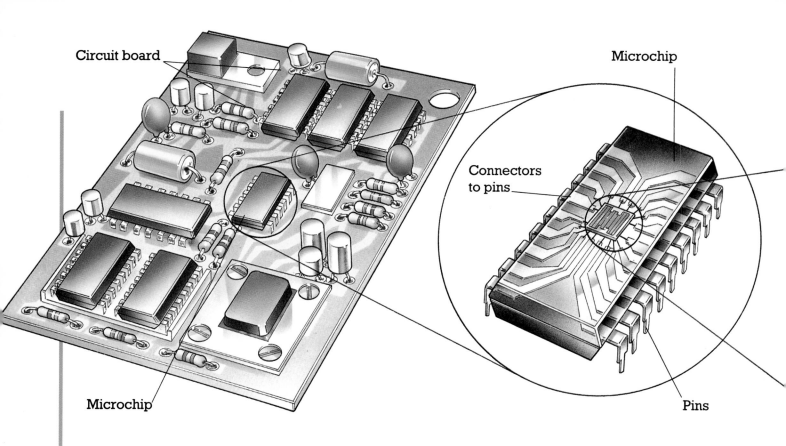

Circuit board

Microchip

Microchip

Connectors to pins

Pins

Inside a computer, electronic circuits are formed from components mounted on circuit boards (see above left), which are linked together by metal tracks on the boards. Many of the components are microchips (see above right). Each of them contains a tiny chip of silicon and this itself contains circuits composed of thousands of microscopically small components (see diagrams opposite).

THE MICROCHIP

Computers process information by first changing it into pulses of electric current that are then directed through complex electrical pathways or circuits. The majority of the electronic components on the computer's circuit boards are microchips. Most of them look like blocks of black or gray plastic with a row of metal pins along each side (see above right). The plastic block is to protect the chip which is buried inside, its metal pins connected to the metal tracks in the circuit board. The chip itself is often no bigger than a fingernail, although some are smaller. It is made from a slice of pure silicon on which intricately shaped layers of chemicals are added to form thousands of individual components. Silicon is one of a group of materials called semiconductors. Its resistance to an electrical current decreases as its temperature rises. This electrical resistance can also be changed by a process called "doping." This involves adding small amounts of different materials to the silicon. Some provide extra charged particles called electrons, forming n-type silicon. Others create a shortage of electrons forming p-type silicon.

Chips are made by adding specially shaped layers of different materials, such as aluminum, to a slice, or very thin wafer, of silicon. Each layer creates pathways for electric currents to flow through the chip. In the transistor illustrated on the bottom right of this page, a positive charge fed to the polysilicon gate attracts electrons from the p-type silicon base. This turns the transistor on as current only flows from the source to the drain when a gate current is applied. A negative charge at the gate repels electrons and turns the current and transistor off. Transistors commonly consist of three layers of silicon, either p-n-p or n-p-n.

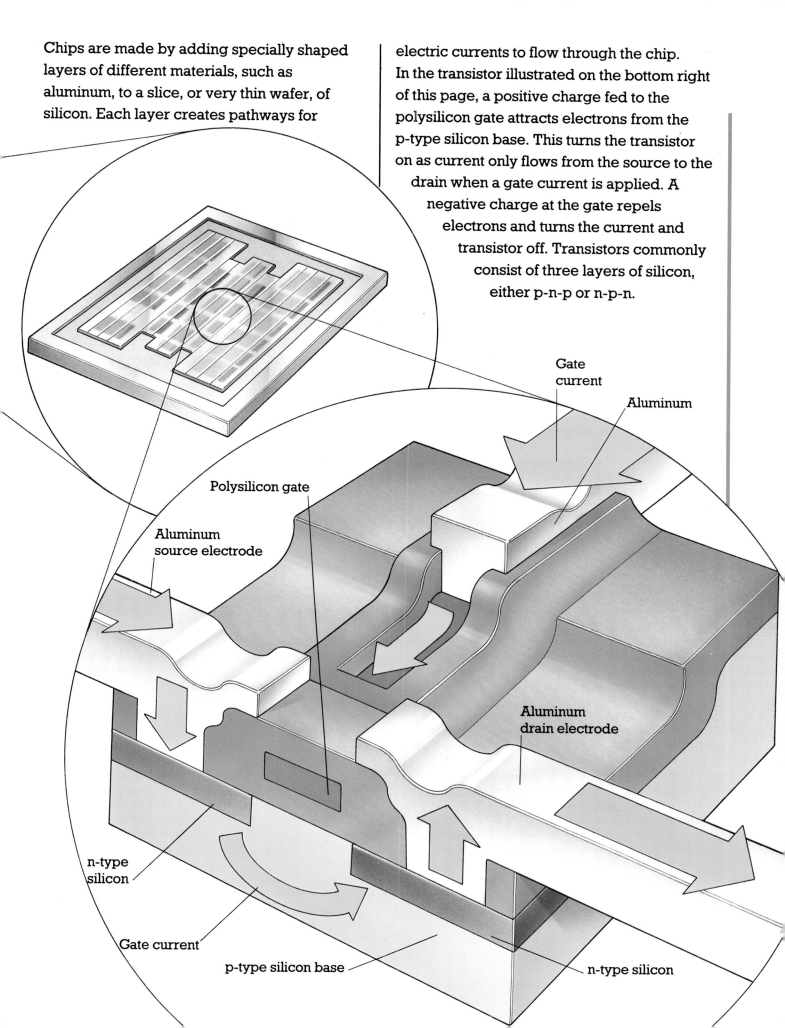

Gate current

Aluminum

Polysilicon gate

Aluminum source electrode

Aluminum drain electrode

n-type silicon

Gate current

p-type silicon base

n-type silicon

MEMORY UNITS

When a computer is programmed to carry out a task, the program and the data it generates are stored in Random Access Memory (RAM). It is called "random access" because the computer can print out any part of this memory without searching the bulk of the system first. RAM is gridlike in structure with each square holding one bit of information. To match the size of RAM commonly used by computers today, the grid would need more than half a million squares! Each square has an address, a number, so that the information stored in it can be found again. The presence of an electrical charge at an address represents a one, while no charge represents a zero. A second type of memory called Read-Only Memory (ROM) also has a gridlike structure, but its contents are permanently wired in place and cannot be changed.

A magnetic disk is another form of memory. Firstly, an electric current passes through a read/write head to produce a magnetic field. This magnetizes two bands on the spinning disk representing one bit of data (1). The next bit is recorded on the spinning disk with the magnetic field reversed to separate it from the first bit (2) and so on (3) until the disk is full.

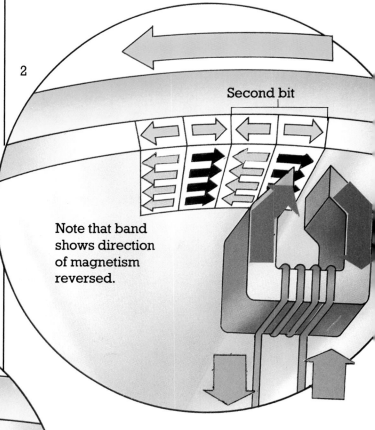

2

Second bit

Note that band shows direction of magnetism reversed.

1

First bit

Disk

Magnetic bands

Magnetic coating

Read/write head

Bits and bytes

A computer converts all the programs and data it receives into a simple code with only two numbers, zero and one, called binary digits or "bits." Groups of 8, 16, or 32 bits are called "bytes." Computers use binary numbers because the electronic circuits needed to process them only have two states: current flowing on (represented by one) and current off (represented by zero).

76

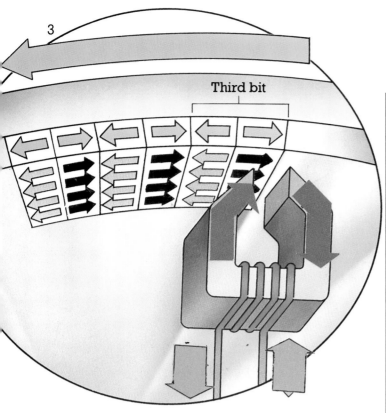

3

Third bit

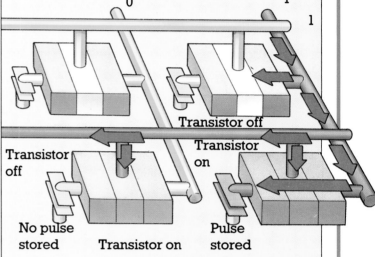

Random Access Memory (RAM)

To store the binary number 01 in RAM address number two, 01 is applied to the first two data lines and current flows along address line two. Only one transistor is switched on and supplied with a pulse to be stored (lower right).

0   1

1

Transistor off

Transistor off

Transistor on

No pulse stored

Transistor on

Pulse stored

Read-Only Memory (ROM)

To read the contents of ROM address two, address line two is activated. Current flows to an output only where diodes link the two (see below). The pattern of diodes is built into the ROM chip when it is made.

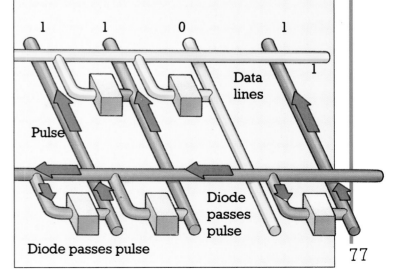

1   1   0   1

1

Data lines

Pulse

Diode passes pulse

Diode passes pulse

A magnetic tape reel placed in a computer.

COMPUTER PROGRAMMING

A computer cannot do anything without a program to direct it and data to process. The program is stored in the computer's memory. It tells the computer how to process the data and what to do with the results of the processing. These may be displayed on the computer's screen and also stored in the computer's memory. They may be sent to a more permanent storage device, such as a disk drive, or to a printer connected to the computer.

We understand what we say to each other because we speak the same language with the words linked together according to the same set of rules. In the same way, a computer program will only work if it is written in a language that the computer has already been programmed to recognize. Many different languages are spoken around the world and there are also many different computer languages. BASIC, Pascal, COBOL, Fortran, and C are just a few examples of computer languages. BASIC is very popular with amateur programmers because it is one of the easiest to learn and use, while scientists favour Pascal, Fortran, and C.

The languages that most programmers use to write computer programs are called high level languages. They use words and phrases that resemble English, to make them easier for people to use. Before a computer can operate or "run" such a program, it must first translate the high level language into a form that it can process. Called machine code, this is composed of only zeros and ones that are read electronically by the hardware.

```
10   MODE 2: X=640: Y=512
20   VDU 23,224,32,32,0,136,0,32,32
30   INPUT TAB(0,5) "BACKGROUND" B
40   COLOR 128+B: CLS: VDU 28,1,31,19,28
50   VDU 5: GCOL 0,0: MOVE 0, 140: DRAW 1279, 140
60   X=X+8*(INKEY(-26)-INKEY(-122))
70   Y=Y+4*(INKEY(-42)-INKEY(-58))
80   GCOL 3,7: MOVE X-12, Y+16: VDU
90   IF INKEY(-99) GOTO 120
100  GCOL 3,7: MOVE X-12, Y+16: VDU 224
110  GOTO 60
120  VDU 4: INPUT "HOW MANY SIDES ?" S
130  INPUT "DIAMETER ?" D: R=D/2
140  IF S=0 OR D=0 CLS: GOTO 120
150  INPUT "COLOR (0-15) ?" C
160  AN=PI/S-PI/2
170  VDU 29,X;Y;: MOVE R*COS(AN), R*SIN(AN)
180  FOR J=1 TO S: AN=AN+2*PI/S
190  MOVE 0,0: GCOL 0,C
200  PLOT 85, R*COS(AN), R*SIN(AN)
210  NEXT: CLS: VDU 29,0;0;5: GOTO 80
```

Computer programs written in BASIC.

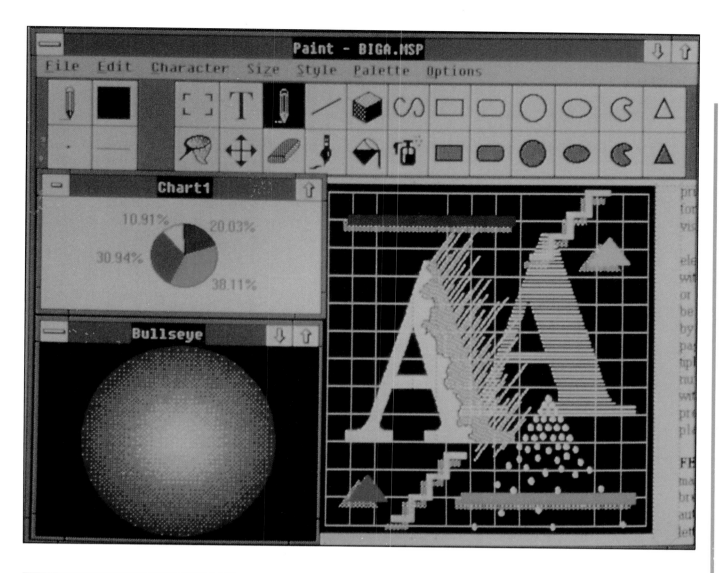

The computer's menu, illustrated in the photo above, is a guide to the functions that an individual program offers a user. Every computer can be programmed to take a range of software and each program will have a different menu to display.

The voice activated computer illustrated in the photo on the left is programmed to respond to its users' voices. This impressive new technology is still being developed. It is hoped that voice activated computers will someday be so sophisticated that they will do away with the need for the normal input devices such as the keyboard or the mouse. At present they are mainly used in security systems since each voice is as unique as a set of fingerprints. However, one new system helps the deaf learn speech.

79

COMPUTERS IN THE HOME

Microprocessors – computers on a chip – are now common in the home, although we are not always aware of them. For example, a cassette recorder is controlled by pressing buttons, but they may not operate the recorder directly. They may be connected to a tiny computer and this in turn controls the machine. If carrying out the user's wishes might damage the delicate recording tape, the computer can be programmed to block the action or carry it out safely. For example, if the tape is winding forward at great speed and the fast rewind button is pressed, reversing the tape's direction instantly at such high speed could damage it. Instead, the computer can direct the recorder to slow the tape, stop it, switch to rewind and then increase its speed safely in the opposite direction.

Many stereo systems, television sets and electrical appliances now contain similar control computers. As the operation of the machine is controlled by the computer, more features can be added to the machine by reprogramming the computer to control different operations. This ability to change what a machine does by changing its program is particularly useful for making electronic games. The same machine can be made to play lots of different games by plugging in different cartridges, each containing a different game program. The possibilities are enormous.

Teleshopping (photo below) is made possible when computers are linked by telephone.

Computers have made the appliances in our homes more reliable, easier to use and more versatile. A washing machine (right) can be preprogrammed by the manufacturer with the washing requirements of many different types of materials. The machine's user selects the appropriate wash program on the machine's control panel. Computer games (above) use a computer's ability to process sounds and pictures according to a set of rules, combined with its facility to be programmed with the rules of many different games. Different game programs are stored in ROM chips inside cartridges that plug into the console. CD players can be programmed to play musical tracks in any order on a disk.

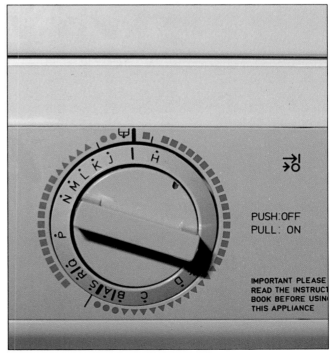

PUSH:OFF
PULL: ON

IMPORTANT PLEASE
READ THE INSTRUCT
BOOK BEFORE USIN
THIS APPLIANCE

COMPUTERS AT WORK

Over the past decade, computers have affected almost every business and industry. Some types of work have disappeared altogether and new types have been created. Businesses that rely on collecting and processing information, such as financial institutions and newspapers, use computers extensively to improve their efficiency. Computers can also analyze information much more quickly than people. In scientific research, this is invaluable for interpreting the results of experiments. All sorts of machines are now controlled and monitored more efficiently by computer than by a human machine-tender.

Computers are also changing the way in which people work. They enable people who work with information to work at home. Home workers can send

An office computer may be used on its own or it may be connected to other computers in a group called a network (see below). All the computers in the network share data and programs held in a central store. Powerful network "servers" boost linked computers' performance.

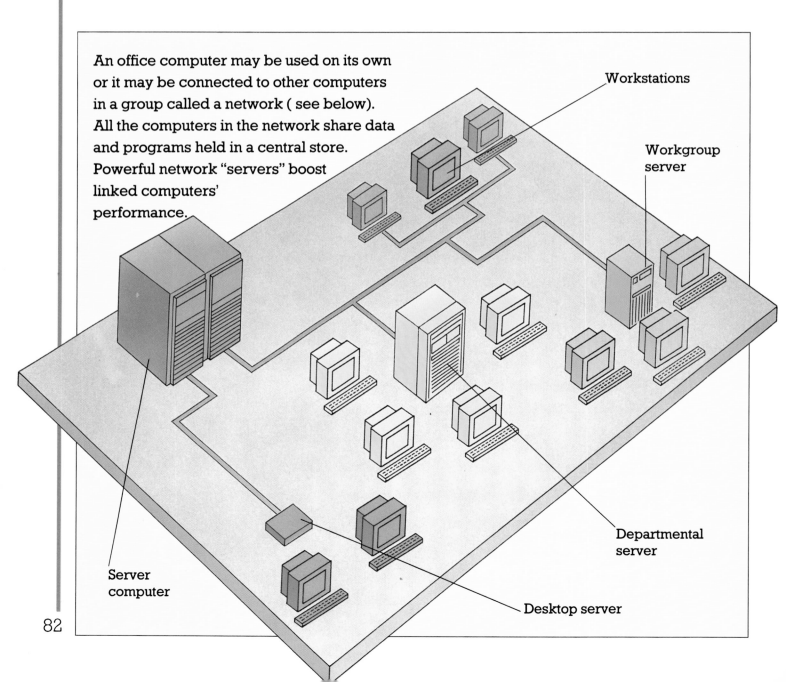

Workstations

Workgroup server

Departmental server

Desktop server

Server computer

their results to the office by linking their home and office computers by telephone. Small battery powered computers are used where never before. "Laptop" computers which sit comfortably on a person's knees, and even smaller "notebook" computers, that fit in your palm, are being used in increasing numbers by people who have to travel around to do their work.

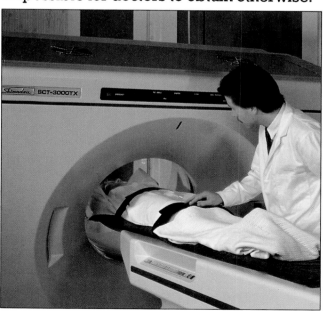

Computer Aided Design (CAD) systems are used to help design complex structures, ranging from microchips to skyscrapers.

The Computerized Axial Tomography (CAT) scanner links X-ray images in a picture impossible for doctors to obtain otherwise.

WISARD

Computers could tackle more jobs if they could see. It is easy to feed pictures from a television camera into a computer, but it is very difficult to program the computer to recognize what it sees. Wisard (Wideband System for Acquiring Data), a system built at Brunel University in London, England, can recognize people it has seen before. However, computer vision is still very crude compared with the human eye and brain.

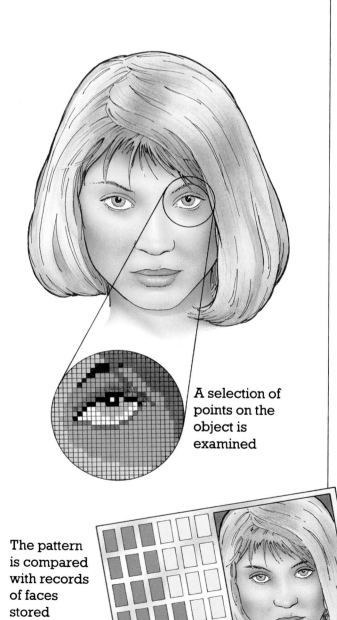

A selection of points on the object is examined

The pattern is compared with records of faces stored

THE FUTURE

Current trends in computer technology indicate how computers may develop in future. Scientists continue to look for ways of squeezing more components into a chip. As a result, computers will become increasingly smaller. Smaller computers can be made to work faster because data has less distance to travel inside the computer from chip to chip. The fastest way to move data from one place to another is by sending it along a beam of light instead of a wire. An experimental chip made in the United States in 1989 using a combination of electronic and optical components could process data at a rate of one billion bits per second. It is thought that such optical computers will not be generally available for many years.

One exciting development is "virtual reality." To participate in this imaginary adventure the user or player wears a helmet containing a video screen. This shows a 3-D image of a world created by the computer. If the player turns to the right or left or up and down, the image on the screen also turns. The player can move around in the imaginary space, play games there or fly over its imaginary landscape. By wearing a special glove linked to the system, the player can grasp imaginary objects or operate illusionary controls. Virtual reality systems can educate and entertain.

Satellites need computers to help fly them accurately and safely on course.

The world of a "virtual reality" system exists only in its computer's memory.

A "smartcard" is used in the same way as a conventional credit card.

Credit cards store information on a magnetic stripe along the back of the card. In the future, smartcards will have a built-in microprocessor and some memory. The card may store, for example, the user's medical history. Its advantage over conventional cards is that its memory holds a great deal of information, which can be updated regularly.

The smartcard

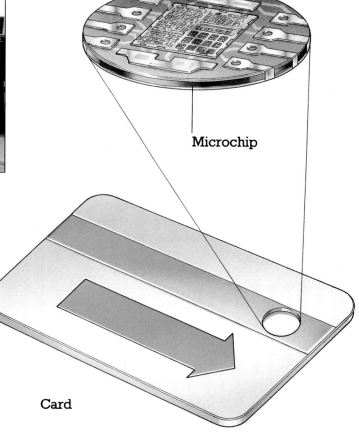

Microchip

Card

85

The HISTORY OF COMPUTERS

Until the middle of the twentieth century, all calculating machines were mechanical. The simplest device, called an abacus, is still in widespread use in many countries. It consists of rows of beads strung along a series of wires. Numbers are added together by moving the beads, which represent the numbers, from one end of each wire to the other. More complicated adding machines were made from interconnected gear wheels turned manually. The first of these was made by the French scientist Blaise Pascal between 1642 and 1644.

Charles Babbage's Analytical Engine.

In 1833, the English inventor and mathematician Charles Babbage designed a new type of calculating machine. Babbage's Analytical Engine as he called it could perform a series of calculations according to instructions supplied by the operator. It had the basic parts of a modern computer, but in a mechanical form. However, Babbage was unable to build his Analytical Engine because the engineers of his time could not make the parts accurately enough. In 1991, a working modern version of the Analytical Engine was built with contemporary construction techniques at the Science Museum in London. Babbage's Analytical Engine was in fact the first computer.

ENIAC

The invention of the first electronic components, called valves or tubes, at the beginning of the twentieth century made a new type of computer possible, the electronic computer. The first of these, called Colossus I, was built amid great secrecy during World War II in England. It was used to help Britain read messages written by the enemy in secret codes. More powerful computers were built in the United States at the same time. In 1946, a computer called ENIAC (Electronic Numerical Indicator And Calculator) was built at the University of Pennsylvania to calculate the paths of artillery shells so that they could be fired more accurately.

Computers built using valves were unreliable. In the late 1940s, a new

A computer "notebook."

device called the transistor was developed. It was smaller and more reliable than the valve and needed much less power. Computers immediately shrank to a fraction of their previous size and increased in reliability. Scientists began combining more transistors and other components in a single device called an integrated circuit or chip. Nowadays, a chip containing more than 100,000 components is little bigger than a single transistor. Chips have resulted in powerful, fast, and reliable computers that can be used by anyone.

A modern personal computer.

FACTS & FIGURES

The Mark 1 electronic computer built at Harvard University in the United States in 1944 weighed five tons and occupied a large room. It could perform roughly three calculations per second.

In 1945, the world's most powerful computer was the Automatic Computing Engine (ACE) built in England. It could carry out up to 30 additions or 1,000 multiplications per second.

Nowadays, the world's most powerful supercomputers can carry out more than 10 billion calculations per second. ENIAC, a computer built in the United States in 1946, contained 18,000 valves and needed so much electrical power that the lights in a nearby town failed when it was finally switched on!

ENIAC's memory was large enough to store 5,000 bits of information, which is equivalent to about 100 English language words. Supercomputers in production now have memories that can store over 16 billion bits of information.

Each of the microscopic electronic components contained in a single modern chip, the size of a fingernail contains thousands of microscopic components each of which performs the task of a valve used in one of the first computers. If each microscopic component was actually the size of a valve, the chip would cover an area the size of a football field.

Chapter Five
LASERS AND HOLOGRAMS

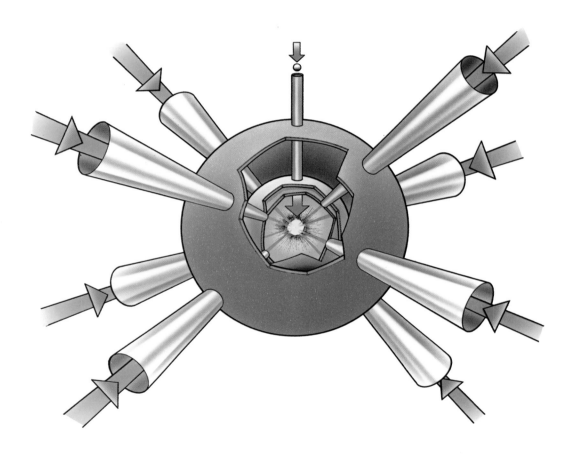

CONTENTS

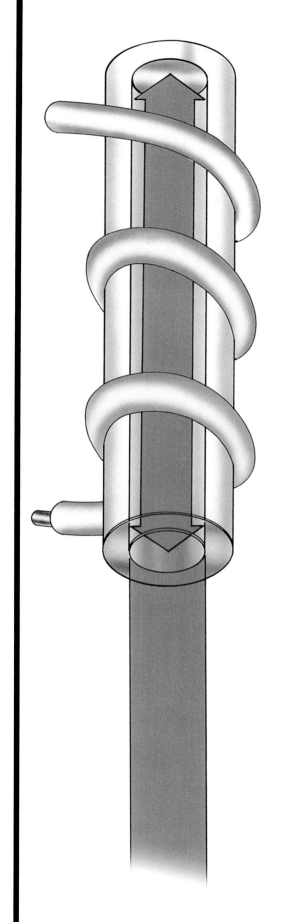

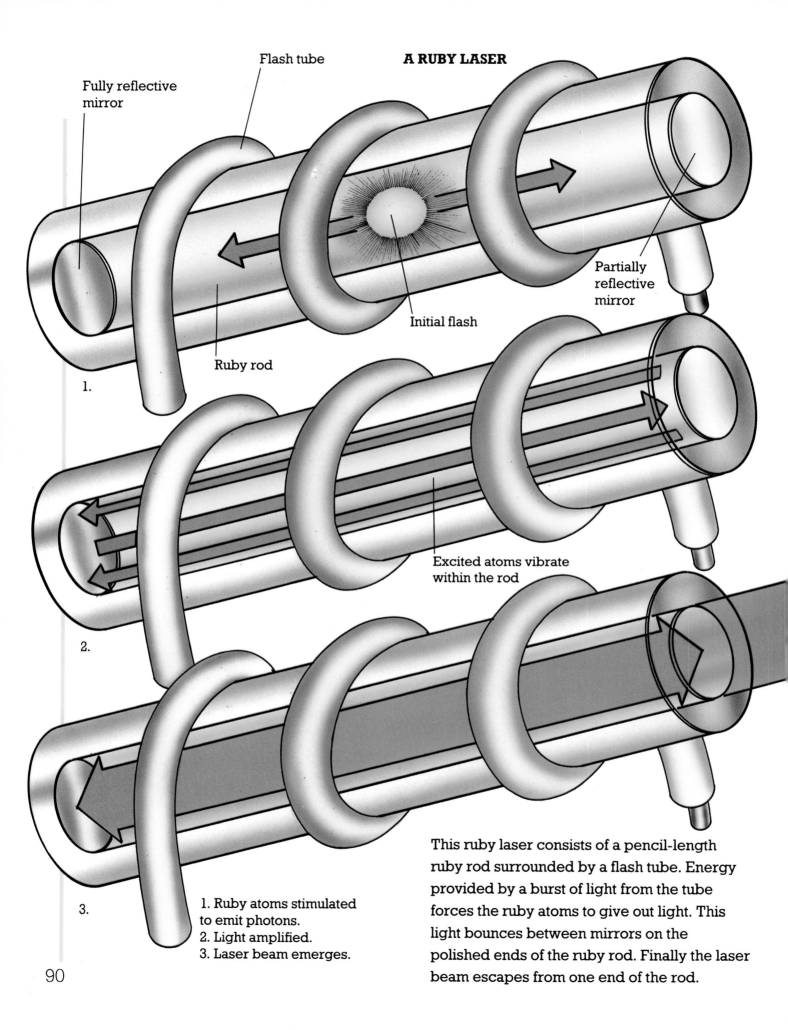

Fully reflective mirror

Flash tube

A RUBY LASER

Initial flash

Partially reflective mirror

Ruby rod

1.

Excited atoms vibrate within the rod

2.

3.

1. Ruby atoms stimulated to emit photons.
2. Light amplified.
3. Laser beam emerges.

This ruby laser consists of a pencil-length ruby rod surrounded by a flash tube. Energy provided by a burst of light from the tube forces the ruby atoms to give out light. This light bounces between mirrors on the polished ends of the ruby rod. Finally the laser beam escapes from one end of the rod.

HOW LASERS WORK

The name LASER comes from the first letters of the words which describe how it works – Light Amplification by Stimulated Emission of Radiation. A laser is a device which excites atoms, the smallest particles of the Universe, so that they give out energy as light in a special way. Follow the illustrations on the left and you can see how this happens. The laser shown here consists of a rod made of ruby crystals. This rod is set inside a cylinder with a mirror at either end. One mirror is fully reflective, but the other is only partially silvered and so a very strong light will to be able to pass through it.

A flash tube is coiled around the cylinder. When this fires a flash of light the ruby atoms inside the tube become excited and produce tiny bursts of light called photons. These photons strike the atoms, exciting them to produce more and more photons until the tube is filled with them bouncing back and forth from mirror to mirror. Soon the amount of photons is so great that they pass right through the partially reflective mirror. This is the laser beam itself.

Laser beam

A laser in action.

Ordinary light (below) consists of a random mixture of different wavelengths traveling in different directions. Laser light (below right) consists of a beam of parallel waves with their peaks and lows lined up with each other.

Ordinary light

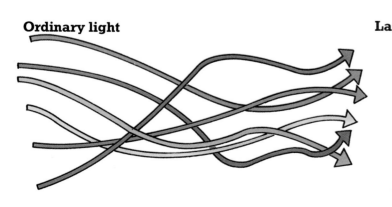

Laser light

CUTTING AND WELDING

Several types of laser are powerful enough to cut or drill through a wide range of materials. One advantage of using a laser is that there is no metal blade or drill bit to wear out or break. Paper, cloth, plastics, ceramics and metals can all be cut by laser. Some materials that can be heated by laser to their melting points can also be joined by melting their edges together. This process is called laser welding.

The carbon dioxide gas laser is often used in industry to cut and weld steel. A jet of oxygen is sometimes directed along the laser beam to the metal. Reactions between the hot metal and the oxygen enable the laser to cut or make holes through the metal more quickly. If materials are to be cut by laser, they must be able to absorb energy from the laser beam. Materials with smooth reflective surfaces, like glass, can be cut by laser if their surface is first coated with a layer of a substance like carbon which is black and so absorbs, but does not reflect, laser radiation.

Electronic components are often connected to each other by a process called soldering. The parts to be joined are held together and a metallic material known as solder is melted around them to make a good electrical connection. Soldering is usually done with a hot soldering iron, but it can also be done by a carbon dioxide laser.

Gas lasers, like this one cutting cloth, are replacing ordinary cutting machines in industry.

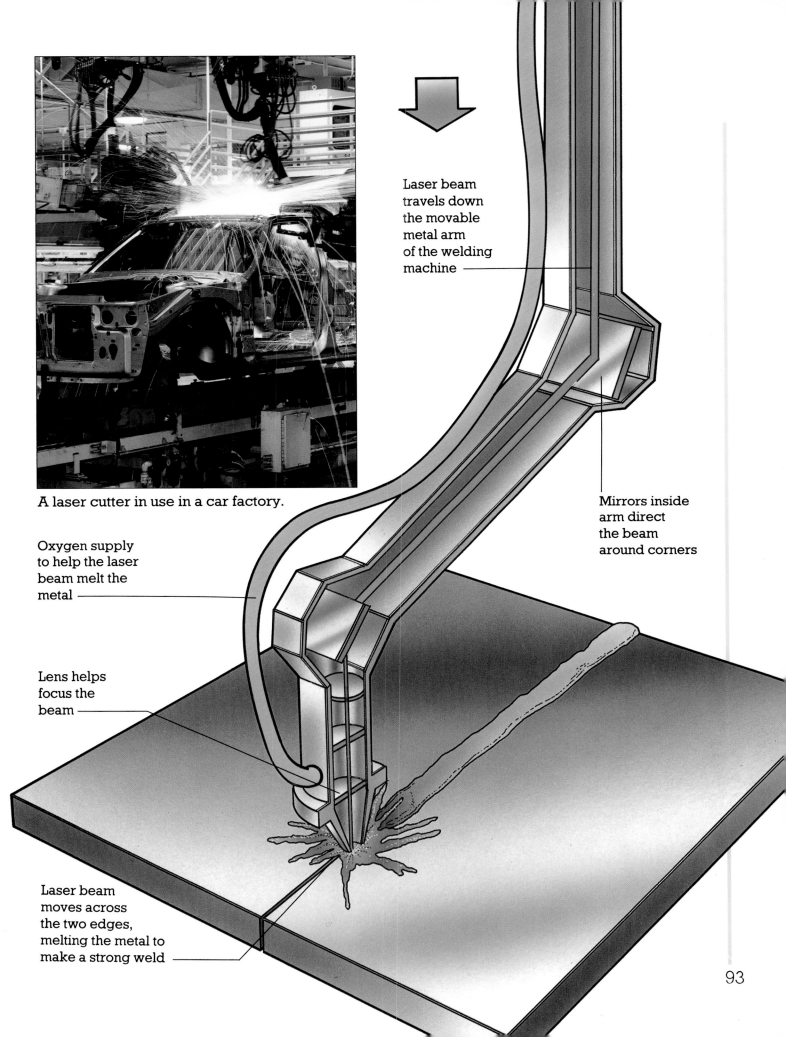

A laser cutter in use in a car factory.

Laser beam travels down the movable metal arm of the welding machine

Mirrors inside arm direct the beam around corners

Oxygen supply to help the laser beam melt the metal

Lens helps focus the beam

Laser beam moves across the two edges, melting the metal to make a strong weld

93

STRAIGHT AND TRUE

A laser beam travels in a straight and narrow line. Scientists and engineers make use of this "collimation" in two ways. The rodlike beams can be used to guide machinery in a straight line or to measure distances.

To measure distance, a short burst of light from a laser is directed at a target some distance away. The burst, or pulse, "bounces" back from the target like an echo. The time it takes the pulse to travel to the target and back to the

laser is measured. The distance to the target, also called its range, is given by multiplying half of this time by the speed of the pulse, which travels at the speed of light (186,000mp/sec). The time is halved because the pulse travels twice the required distance.

In the building industry, lasers are used like plumb lines, spirit levels and rulers to check structures are vertical or horizontal. In forestry, laser range-finders help to measure tree height. As

A laser beam trained on fixed points ahead and behind guides this tunnel-boring machine.

an aircraft carrying a laser flies over a forest, laser pulses are fired downward. They are reflected back by the tree tops and the ground. The difference in time between the returning pulses indicates the tree height.

A laser rangefinder can also be used to detect changes in the distance between itself and its target. They have been used to register movements in the earth's surface that occur before an earthquake or volcanic eruption.

A satellite called LAGEOS helps to study the movements of land masses in the hope of predicting earthquakes, such as along the San Andreas Fault in California. Laser beams are directed at LAGEOS from points around rock faults (points A, B, C). The beams are reflected back to adjoining targets. Any changes in position of the three points reveal dangerous land movements.

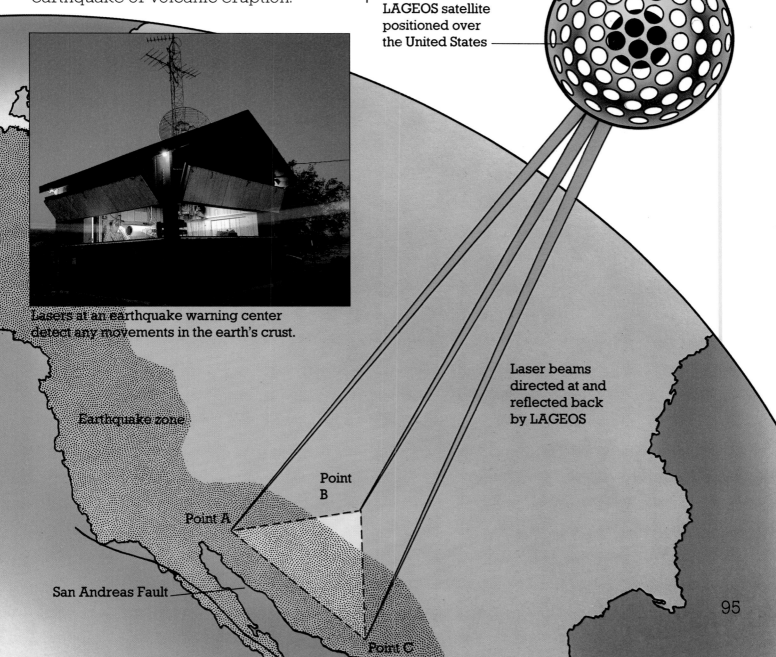

Lasers at an earthquake warning center detect any movements in the earth's crust.

LAGEOS satellite positioned over the United States

Laser beams directed at and reflected back by LAGEOS

Earthquake zone

Point A

Point B

Point C

San Andreas Fault

95

LASERS IN MEDICINE

Medical lasers are used in three ways: to cut like a scalpel, to destroy cells by heating, and to join cells together. When a cut is made with a scalpel, the open ends of blood vessels bleed into the cut. The advantage of using a laser instead of a scalpel is that the laser beam seals blood vessels as it cuts through them and the cut remains dry. Carbon dioxide lasers can be used for this and also for destroying harmful cancer cells by heating them quickly so that they burst or turn to vapor.

Several types of laser are used for medical welding, called "coagulation." The blue-green light from an argon laser passes through clear watery cells without any effect, but it is absorbed by brown skin cells or red blood cells underneath. Wounds can be healed without using bandages and stitches.

An Nd-YAG laser, a solid-state laser, produces light in the near-infrared. This is absorbed by most dark cells whatever their color and so it can treat cells that cannot be treated by an argon laser. A carbon dioxide laser beam is powerful and full of heat-energy so it affects *all* the cells it strikes.

Laser surgery

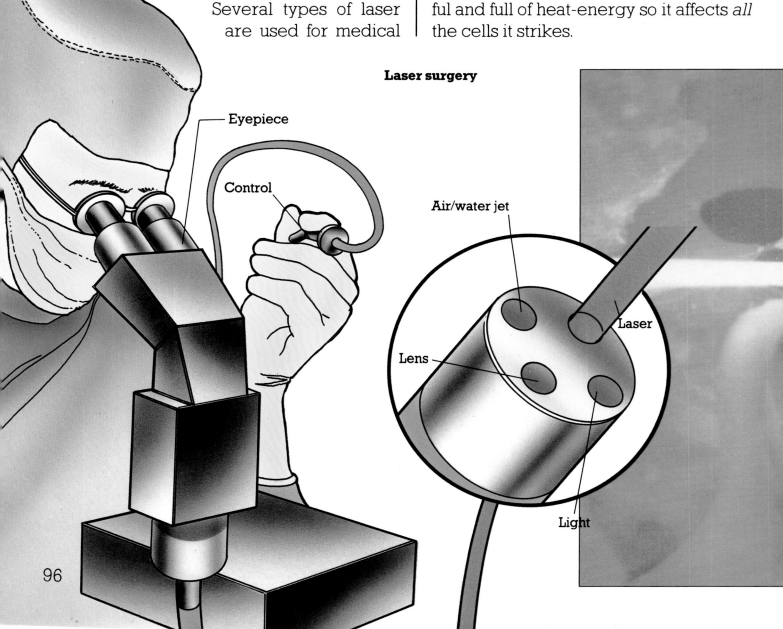

Eyepiece

Control

Air/water jet

Laser

Lens

Light

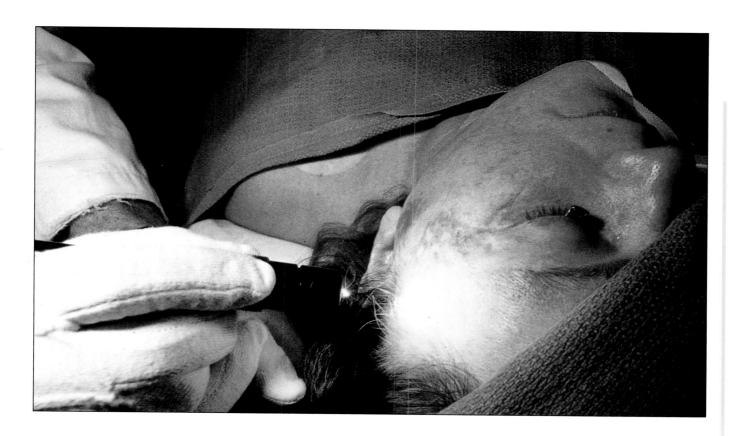

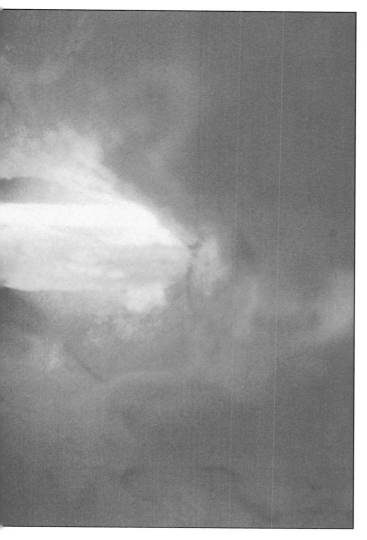

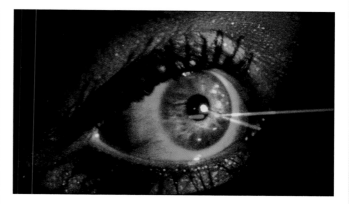

(Left) Laser surgery can be carried out inside the body. The laser beam is sent along a flexible fiber optic cable passed down the patient's windpipe.

(Top) Argon lasers are used to remove red marks on the skin called port-wine stains. The beam destroys the cells of the birthmark and seals the surrounding cells.

(Above) Leaking blood vessels inside the eye that may blur vision or cause blindness are sealed by laser surgery. If the light-sensitive part of the eye, the retina, becomes torn, the patient's sight can be saved by welding the retina in place by laser.

97

VISION AND SOUND

Visual information about an object can be obtained by firing a laser beam at the object and studying the reflection coming back from it. The fact that there *is* a reflection shows that an object lies ahead. The time taken for the reflection to arrive gives the object's range. The bright and dark pattern of the reflection contains information about the object's size and shape. This can be used to reject unwanted items from objects moving along a factory conveyor belt.

Information can be stored on a disc as a spiral track of shallow pits burned into the mirrored disc. If a laser beam is bounced off the disc, it is reflected by the shiny surface but not by the pits. The reflections picked up by a detector form a series of pulses which are converted back into the original information used to make the disc. One type of laser disc, called a compact disc, uses this method to store high-quality music. Another type, a video disc, stores visual information – photographic images and maps.

Objects passing along a conveyor belt (right) can be sorted by a laser system. A laser is positioned above the belt. Objects that pass along the belt are illuminated by the beam and reflect it up to a scanner. Identical objects should produce identical reflections. The system can be programmed to reject objects when the scanner does not receive the correct pattern or strength of reflection. Objects can be removed from the conveyor belt by triggering an electrically operated push rod or by a puff of high-pressure air to shift the object sideways off the belt. Such automatic sorting systems are used in factories.

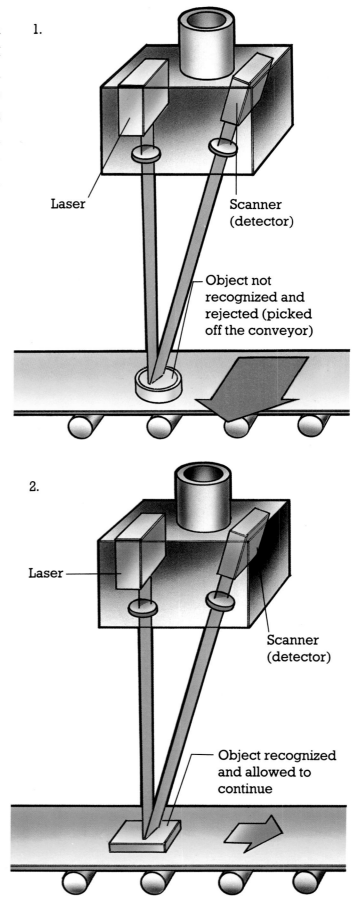

1.

Laser

Scanner (detector)

Object not recognized and rejected (picked off the conveyor)

2.

Laser

Scanner (detector)

Object recognized and allowed to continue

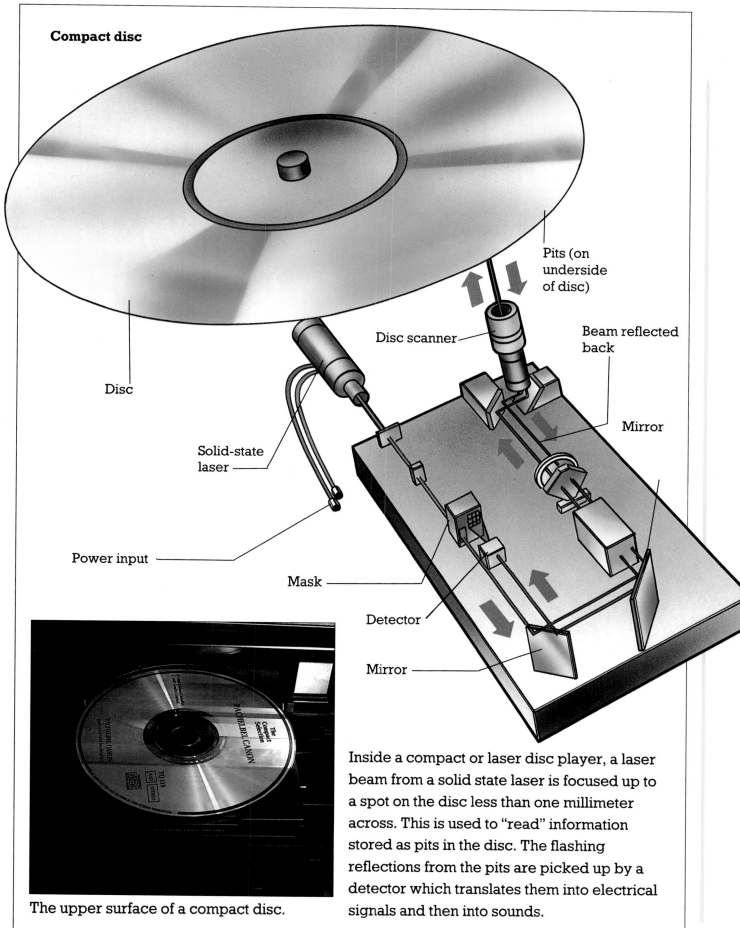

Compact disc

Disc

Solid-state laser

Power input

Pits (on underside of disc)

Disc scanner

Beam reflected back

Mirror

Mask

Detector

Mirror

The upper surface of a compact disc.

Inside a compact or laser disc player, a laser beam from a solid state laser is focused up to a spot on the disc less than one millimeter across. This is used to "read" information stored as pits in the disc. The flashing reflections from the pits are picked up by a detector which translates them into electrical signals and then into sounds.

IN SPACE AND WAR

Space lasers and military lasers are now used for rangefinding, identifying targets and communications. They are to be found as rangefinders for tanks and guns and bombs to indicate precisely how far away targets are. Scientists have even used lasers to measure the distance between the earth and the moon.

Some missiles are designed to fly toward laser radiation. If a laser beam is trained on a target, a missile can pick up the beam's reflection and fly along it toward the target. Secret military messages are transmitted using lasers, because it is very difficult to listen in to a laser beam carrying messages or computer data without being detected.

There have also been plans to use large high-power lasers as weapons, but there are problems with this. Experiments show that the air around the beam heats up, spreading the beam and reducing its effectiveness. When the beam strikes, say, a tank, a small area of metal turns to vapor and forms a cloud that prevents the beam from getting through to cause more damage.

The crews of American spacecraft Apollo 11, 14 and 15 each positioned a laser reflector on the moon. Each consisted of 100 individual reflectors arranged in a square frame 46 centimeters (17.9 inches) across. They reflected laser pulses fired from ruby lasers at the Lick Observatory, California, and the McDonald Observatory, Texas. Lasers are also used as rangefinders on a variety of weapons, from rifles to 60-ton tanks (far right). These are usually miniature battery-powered infrared lasers.

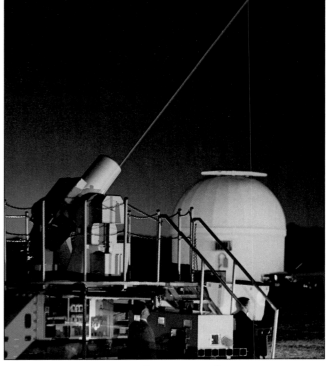

A laser aimed at a reflector on the moon.

A laser rangefinder mounted on a field gun.

A group of soldiers (below right) has discovered an enemy tank. They fire their portable laser at it and call up a missile launcher by radio. From a hidden position it fires a laser-guided missile. High above the battlefield, the missile detects laser radiation being reflected up into the sky from the target (inset). It turns and descends toward the target. The missile follows the target as long as the soldiers illuminate it with their laser. The beam travels in a straight line from the laser to the target, so there is no danger of the missile attacking the soldiers firing the laser. However, the enemy tank may "see" with its sensors that it has been made a target by the beam. It can call up forces to wipe out the soldiers or even to send up an antimissile missile.

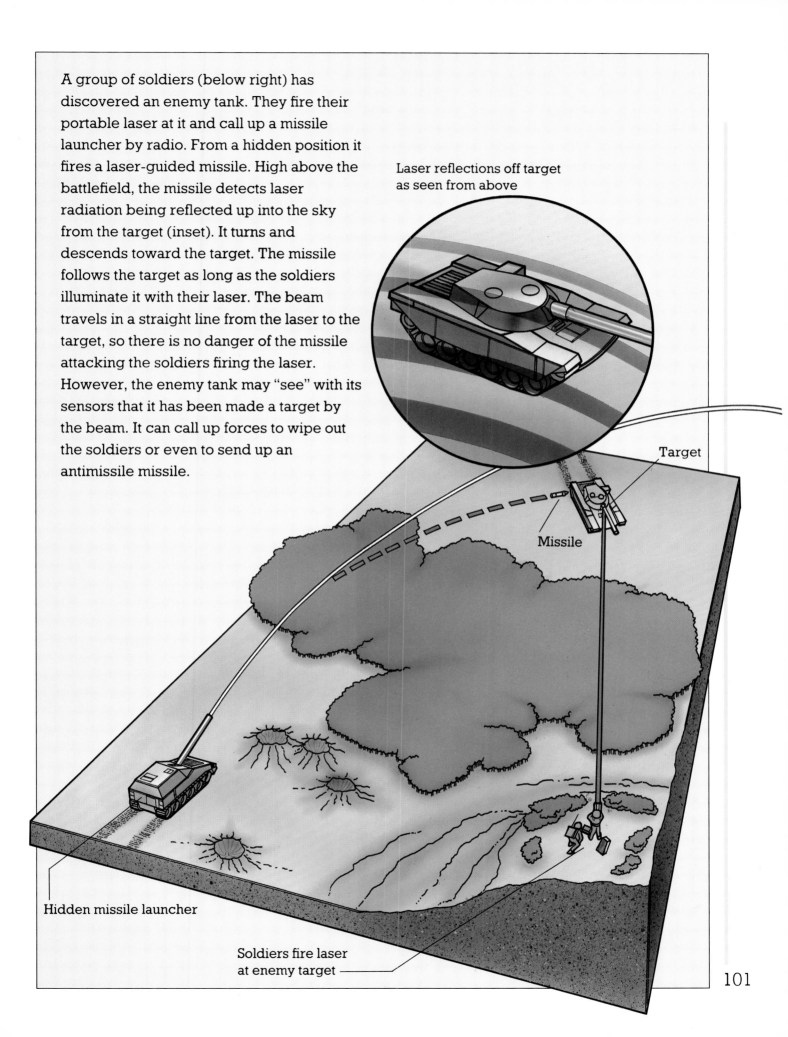

Laser reflections off target
as seen from above

Target

Missile

Hidden missile launcher

Soldiers fire laser
at enemy target

HOLOGRAPHY

Laser light allowed a new type of image to be invented. Holograms, as they are called, are three-dimensional (3-D) images, quite different from the two-dimensional (2-D) pictures we see in a photograph or painting. Holograms look more "real" because you can see the sides or even the back of the object shown if you move in front of it. In a 2-D image, everything is flat and looks much the same from every angle. There are two ways to make holograms. The first, called a "transmission" hologram, is lit from behind and can only be viewed in laser light. The "reflection" type of hologram is an improvement. It uses a laser to light the subject from the front, and then it can be seen in ordinary light.

Now you see it, now you don't

The two pictures (top right) show how a hologram can store surprises. (These are reflection holograms.) Looked at from the front you see a magician's hand. Move to one side and balls appear between the fingers. The hologram is really two pictures in one thanks to the shutter mechanism which allowed them to be recorded one after the other on the same plate by the laser's light.

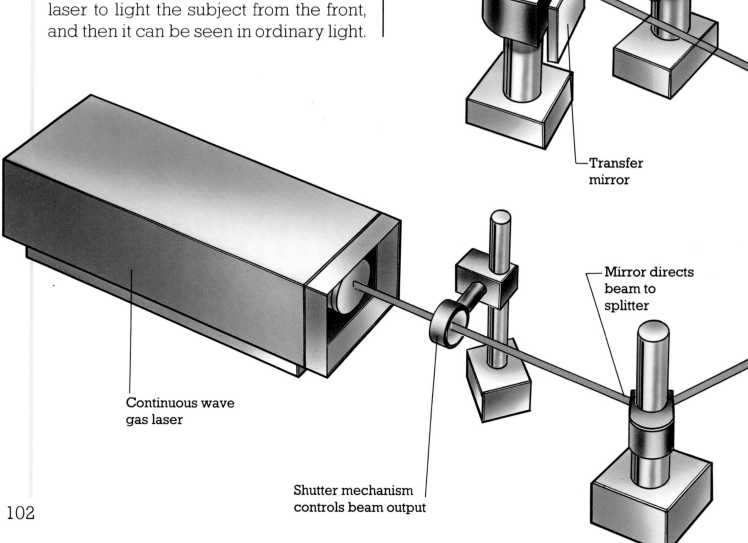

Beam spreader

Transfer mirror

Mirror directs beam to splitter

Continuous wave gas laser

Shutter mechanism controls beam output

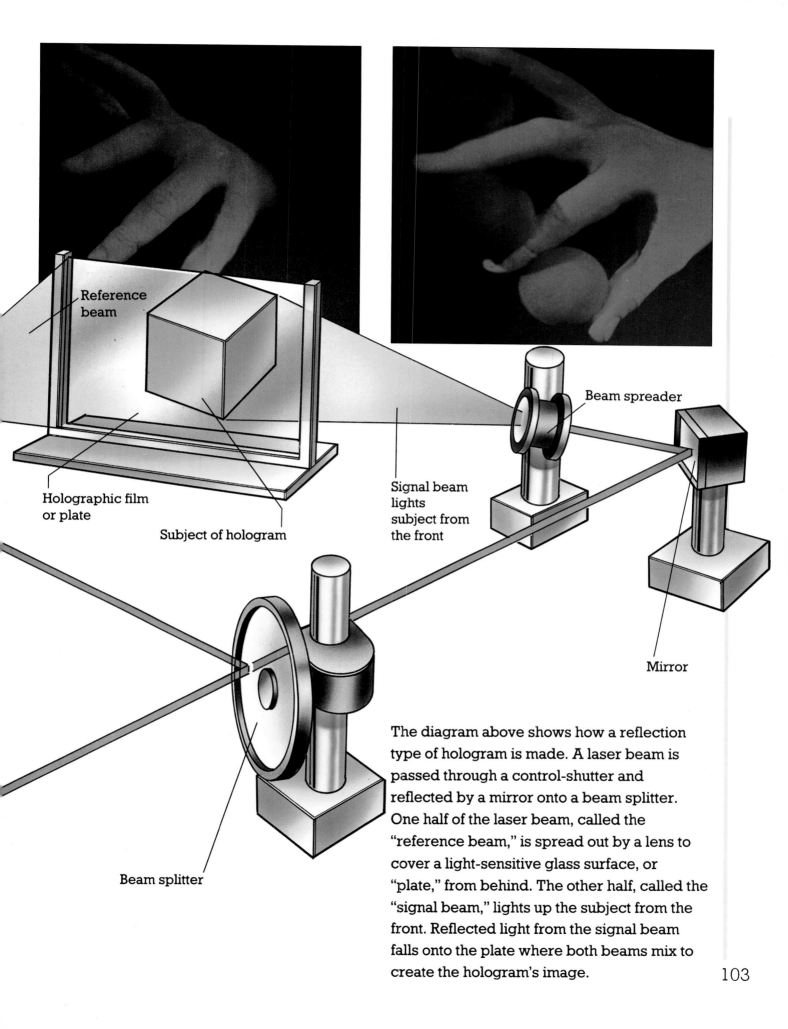

Reference beam

Holographic film or plate

Subject of hologram

Signal beam lights subject from the front

Beam spreader

Mirror

Beam splitter

The diagram above shows how a reflection type of hologram is made. A laser beam is passed through a control-shutter and reflected by a mirror onto a beam splitter. One half of the laser beam, called the "reference beam," is spread out by a lens to cover a light-sensitive glass surface, or "plate," from behind. The other half, called the "signal beam," lights up the subject from the front. Reflected light from the signal beam falls onto the plate where both beams mix to create the hologram's image.

USING HOLOGRAMS

Holograms are used in three main ways: as an art form, to record information, and as a security measure to prevent something being copied. Some shops now specialize in selling holographic works. Holograms have even been added to the exhibitions of painting and sculpture in major art galleries.

One of the most important uses of holograms in the future will be to store information. The 3-D image in a hologram contains much more detail than a normal photograph. It can be turned to show parts of the image that are normally hidden and to reveal how different objects or parts of objects relate to each other in space. Information can also be recorded in a hologram in the on-off binary code computers use.

Until recently, holograms were only made in laboratories in small numbers and they could only be viewed in laser light. Today, holograms can be made in large numbers and they can be seen in daylight. Because of this, holograms will become common in packaging, store windows and street signs.

Although holograms can be made more easily now by specialist companies, they are still almost impossible to copy. This is why they are printed onto security items, for instance credit and identity cards. In this way, holograms help to prevent fraud.

Holograms like this bird are often printed on credit cards to make it difficult to copy them.

Science has helped to create the new visual art forms of our age – photography, movies, television and now holography (as seen in the gallery above). Holograms are increasingly being used to record 3-D images of complex objects. Designers and architects can now produce holograms which show how their work will look from computer programs, and dentists can keep holographic records of patients' teeth or dental plates (below).

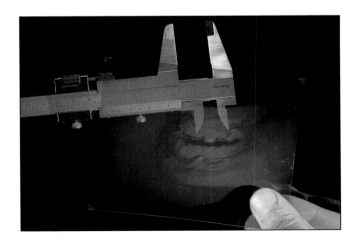

Information stored as holograms

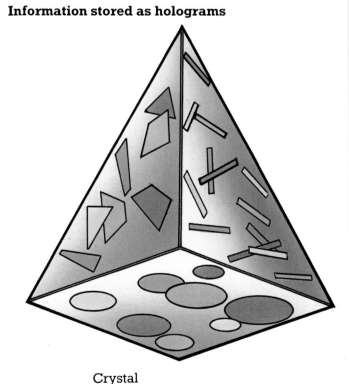

Crystal

Crystals are materials with a regular geometrical shape formed from sheets (or planes) of particles. Some crystals can store a different hologram on each plane. In 1969, the

U.S. Bell Laboratories found that 1,000 holograms could be stored in a crystal of lithium niobate. As the crystal is tilted, the hologram on each plane appears.

105

HISTORY OF LASERS

Between 1910 and 1920 discoveries made by scientists, including Albert Einstein, suggested that atoms could be made to give out radiation under certain conditions. Every atom emits light of its own particular wavelength, which is determined by the structure of that atom.

In 1953, while working at Columbia University in the United States, Dr. Charles Townes built a device called a maser. Its name was formed from the first letters of Microwave Amplification by Stimulated Emission of Radiation. Townes' maser produced an intense beam of radio waves from ammonia gas. More masers were built in the 1950s.

Albert Einstein studied light and atoms.

In 1958, Charles Townes and Arthur Schawlow suggested that masers could be made to produce light instead of radio waves. The first of these devices was made in 1960 by Theodore Maiman. It used a ruby rod surrounded by a flash tube. A burst of light from the flash tube produced an intense pulse of light from

Theodore Maiman with one of his lasers.

the ends of the rod. After the ruby maser came development of the helium-neon gas maser in 1961. Other gas masers followed. Scientists then began looking for ways of making solid-state masers from semiconductor materials. The first of these, the gallium arsenide maser, was developed in 1962.

All these new types of light-producing devices were called optical masers until 1965. Since then, they have been known as lasers from the first letters of Light Amplification by Stimulated Emission of Radiation.

The laser provided the pure, intense light needed to produce holograms.

Portrait – in a mirror and a hologram.

The first holograms had been made in the 1940s, but they were small and dim since a sufficiently powerful light source with the special properties of a laser beam was not available. The laser made it possible to make much larger and clearer holograms. Interest in holograms grew. Scientist Emmeth Leith in the United States made the first holographic movie in the 1960s. Full-color holograms were produced soon after.

When the laser was invented, it was thought to be merely an interesting scientific oddity with no practical use.

Development of new laser technology.

Since then, important uses have been found for lasers. These include industrial cutting, welding and drilling, eye surgery, cancer treatment, communications, pollution monitoring and nuclear fusion research.

In 1988, the world's first transatlantic optical fiber cable began service, carrying 40,000 simultaneous telephone messages by laser between Britain and France and the United States. In 1991, laser-guided missiles were first used on a large-scale by the coalition forces and Iraq in the Gulf War.

FACTS AND FIGURES

The first commercially built laser was made in 1961 by Trion Instruments in the United States and sold to the U.S. company Texas Instruments.

The first hologram was made in 1948, long before lasers were available, by the Hungarian-born scientist Dennis Gabor while carrying out research for the Rugby Electrical Company in Scotland. His light source was a mercury lamp. He received the Nobel Prize for Physics for his work.

The first laser holograms were made in 1961 by Emmett Leith and Juris Upatnieks at the University of Michigan.

Lasers were first used in surgery in 1963.

The first hologram of a human being was made by L. D. Siebert of the U.S. Conductron Corporation in 1966.

Lasers were used to cut cloth for the first time when in 1973 the British clothing manufacturer, John Collier, used a carbon dioxide laser to cut out cloth to make suits.

The brightest artificial light was produced by a laser at the U.S. Los Alamos National Laboratory in New Mexico in 1987.

The first compact disc to sell one million copies was *Brothers in Arms* by the rock group Dire Straits in 1986.

Chapter Six
TRUCKS

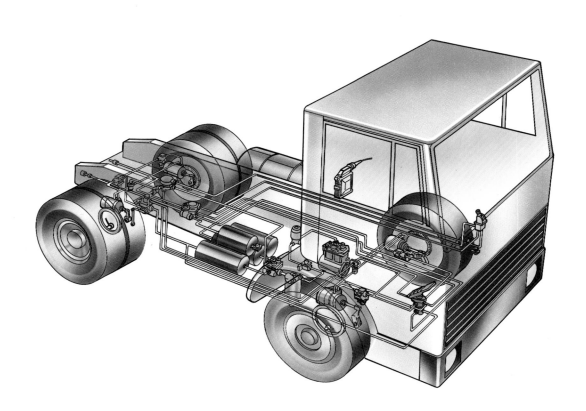

CONTENTS

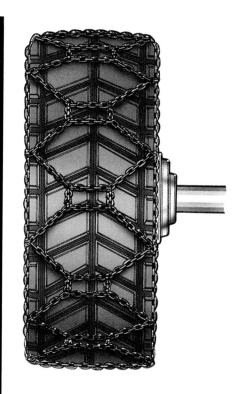

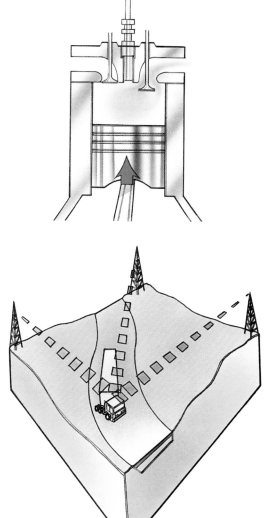

WORKING PARTS

A truck is a motor vehicle designed to transport heavy goods. The tractor unit at the front of the truck shown here contains the engine and the driver's cab. Behind it, a platform or trailer carries the cargo or load.

Most trucks are powered by diesel engines, because they are more powerful than an equivalent gasoline-fueled engine. The diesel fuel they use is also less expensive than gasoline. Engine power may be boosted by the addition of a turbocharger to increase the pressure inside the engine.

Trucks use many of the same kinds of parts as cars or any other road vehicles. However, because a truck carries heavy loads, its basic framework, called its chassis, must be much stronger than a car's chassis. Its engine must be more powerful than a car's and its brakes must be able to stop the truck safely with its maximum load on board. Its wheels and tires must be able to support the weight of the heaviest load it can carry. A truck usually has many more wheels than a car in order to evenly distribute the weight of its load. The springs in its suspension system must be much sturdier than a car's to provide a smooth ride over a bumpy road surface.

Today, most goods carried by trucks are either packed into standard sized containers or tied on to standard wooden platforms that are called pallets. Pallets are specially designed to be lifted and moved by powerful vehicles called forklifts.

The shape of a truck is important in keeping down fuel costs. A lumpy,

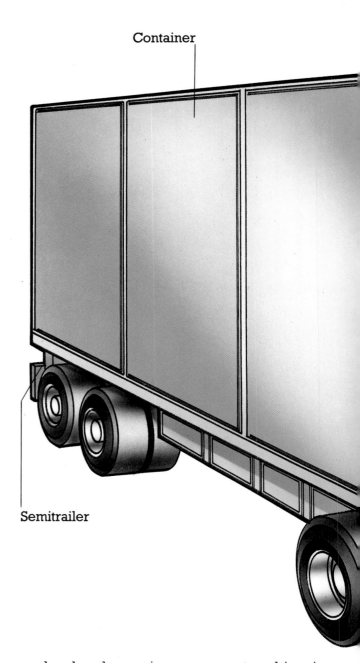

Container

Semitrailer

angular load can increase a truck's air resistance, slowing it down and resulting in more fuel being burned to overcome that effect. By packing the load inside smooth-sided containers or covering it with smooth plastic sheets, air resistance is minimized. The driver's cab may also have rounded contours and a specially shaped roof to direct air smoothly over the top of the load and reduce air resistance.

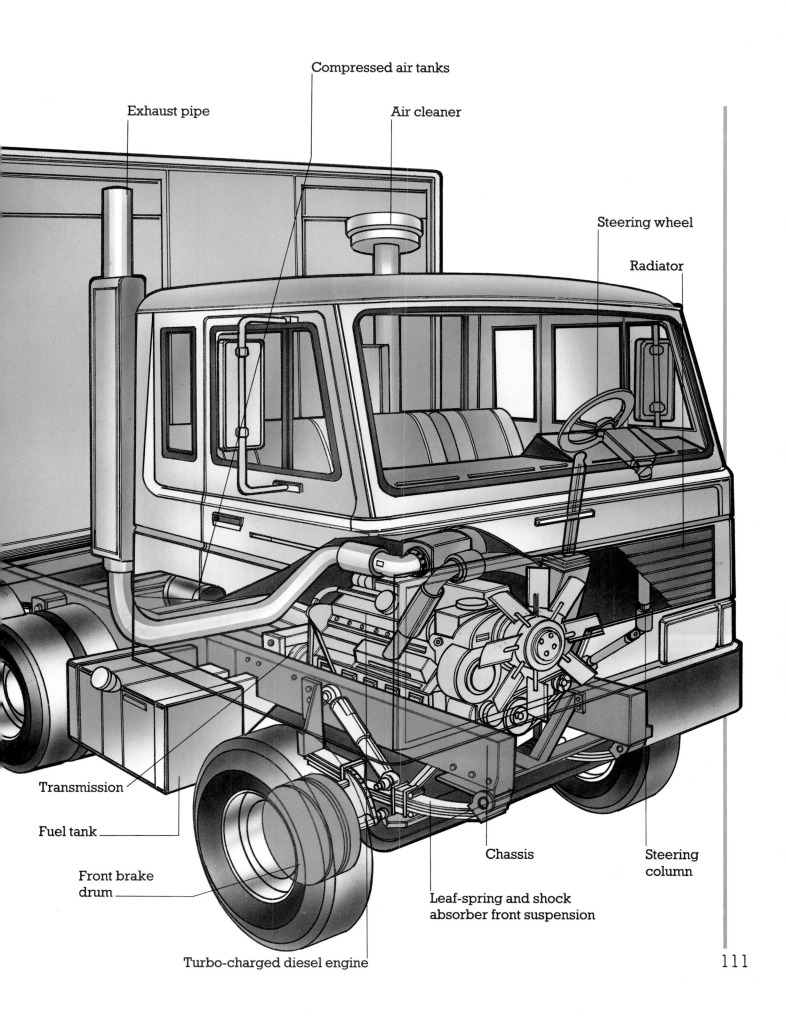

Compressed air tanks

Exhaust pipe

Air cleaner

Steering wheel

Radiator

Transmission

Fuel tank

Front brake drum

Chassis

Steering column

Leaf-spring and shock absorber front suspension

Turbo-charged diesel engine

111

DIESEL ENGINE

Modern trucks are fitted with diesel engines. These are similar to the type of gasoline engine used by most cars. Both use pistons to convert the energy stored in the fuel into mechanical power to turn the wheels. They use different fuels. Most cars use gasoline. Diesel engines use a heavier fuel called diesel oil, which in Britain is also called DERV (Diesel Engine Road Vehicle).

The fuel is burned in different ways in the two types of engines. In a gasoline engine, a fine mist of the fuel is sucked into each cylinder. The mixture of fuel droplets and air is compressed by a piston and then ignited by an electric

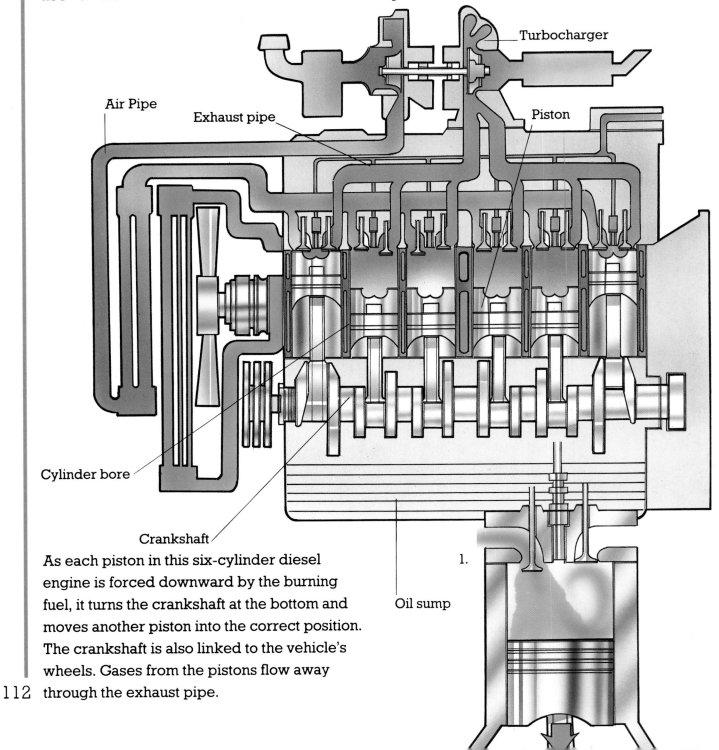

As each piston in this six-cylinder diesel engine is forced downward by the burning fuel, it turns the crankshaft at the bottom and moves another piston into the correct position. The crankshaft is also linked to the vehicle's wheels. Gases from the pistons flow away through the exhaust pipe.

Turbocharger

Before fuel will burn, it must be mixed with air. Without the oxygen in the air, burning cannot take place. All engines suck in air from the atmosphere for this purpose. If more oxygen were available, the fuel would burn more efficiently and the engine would be more powerful. A turbocharger achieves this by compressing the incoming air before it reaches the cylinders where it is compressed again by the pistons.

The propeller-like turbine that compresses the air is powered by a second turbine. This is driven by the hot exhaust gases that rush out of the engine. Some ordinary family station wagons are now fitted with turbochargers similar to those used in trucks.

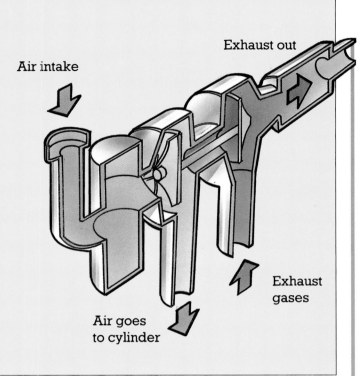

Air intake

Exhaust out

Exhaust gases

Air goes to cylinder

spark. This is called spark ignition. In a diesel engine, air is sucked into each cylinder and compressed. Squeezing the air into a much smaller space like this heats it to over 930°F. When the diesel fuel is sprayed into the cylinder at this temperature, it ignites and burns without the need for a spark. This is called compression ignition.

The four-stroke cycle. On the intake stroke (1), the falling piston reduces pressure in the cylinder, sucking in air through the inlet valve. The piston rises, compressing the air (2). The exhaust valve is closed, preventing the air escaping. Fuel sprayed into the hot air burns, expands and drives the piston downward (3). The piston rises again and pushes waste gases out through the exhaust valve (4).

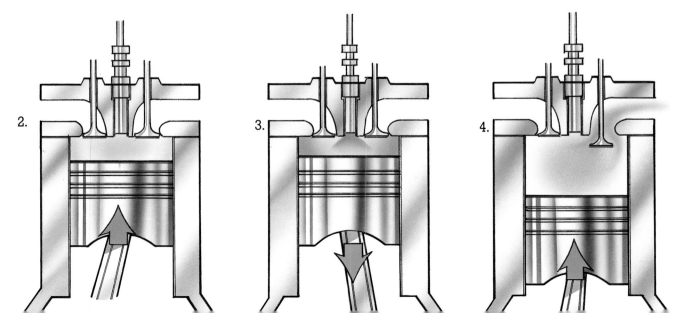

2.

3.

4.

WHEELS AND SUSPENSION

A truck's wheels and suspension system serve several important purposes: they support the weight of the truck; the wheels and tires transmit the power of the engine to the road; and the suspension system smooths out bumps in the road that could make the truck difficult to handle, uncomfortable to drive, and damage a delicate load.

The oldest type of suspension system uses springs. If the truck drives over a bump, the wheel bounces up over it. This compresses the leaf- (not a coiled) spring above the wheel, preventing the violent movement from reaching the rest of the truck. Most trucks still use spring suspension.

A newer type of suspension system uses "air springs." The front of the truck has normal metal springs, but the rear is supported by a special air suspension system.

Air springs are bags filled with air, like a football. If the truck hits a bump in the road, the bag is flattened slightly as the air is compressed. Then it bounces back to its original shape. Dump trucks that ride over rough ground may also be fitted with solid rubber springs.

Suspension

Air suspensions are beginning to replace metal spring systems. Some air suspensions can be pumped up or down to raise or lower the truck for easier loading. Metal springs are also beginning to be replaced by composite springs. Composites are plastic and glass fiber materials that are lightweight and also extremely strong.

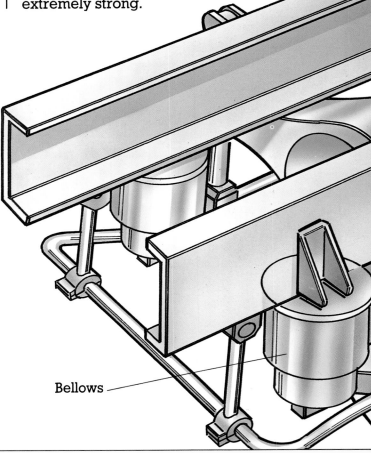

Bellows

Wheel layouts

Trucks are classified not only by whether they are articulated or rigid, but also by their wheel arrangement. Tractor units may have four or six wheels with two-, four- or six-wheel drive. Trailers may have wheels on one, two or three axles. In some countries, more than one trailer may be pulled by a tractor to form what is popularly called a road-train.

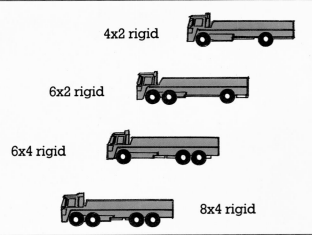

4x2 rigid

6x2 rigid

6x4 rigid

8x4 rigid

Cut-away of bellows

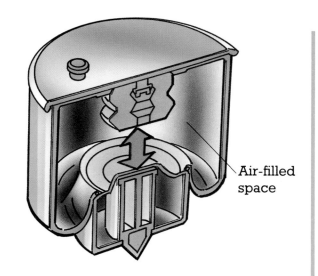

Air-filled space

Bellows

The air-filled bags used in air suspensions are called bellows. The air pressure inside the bellows controls the system's performance.

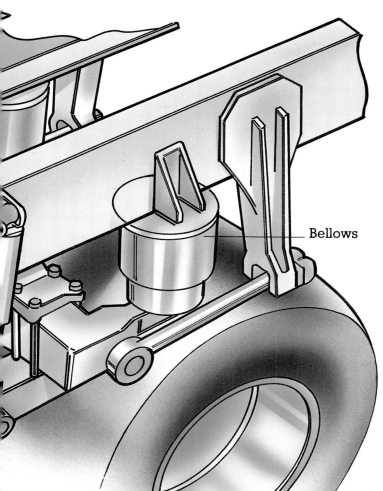

Bellows

Part of a leaf-spring on a truck.

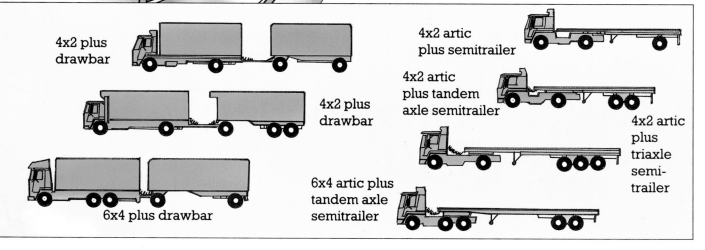

4x2 plus drawbar

4x2 plus drawbar

6x4 plus drawbar

6x4 artic plus tandem axle semitrailer

4x2 artic plus semitrailer

4x2 artic plus tandem axle semitrailer

4x2 artic plus triaxle semitrailer

BRAKES

Trucks have the most complex braking systems found on any vehicles. Air brakes, or full-air, are the most common. The truck's engine drives an air compressor. High pressure air from the compressor is sent to a tank called a reservoir, where it is kept until needed. When the driver presses the brake pedal on the cab floor, valves open and allow the air to flow from the reservoir along pipes, or "air lines," to the wheels.

At each wheel, the high pressure air pushes against a flexible diaphragm. This moves a push-rod, which forces brake shoes against the brake drum. The brake drum revolves along with the wheel. When the brake shoes are forced against it, the wheel stops.

In the past, if a truck's air brakes lost air pressure for any reason, the brakes failed and the truck could not be stopped. Trucks now have secondary braking systems which prevent a total loss of brakes. They also have spring brakes where the vehicle's air system holds off the brake. In the event of a total loss of air the spring brake is released and the brakes come on.

Coiled air lines carry air from the cab to operate the trailer's air brakes.

In an ABS system, detectors on the wheels are used to indicate when the wheels have locked. The brakes are then automatically released, so that the wheels do not skid. The greatest deceleration is achieved when the wheels are turning, rather than skidding. Brake shoes are coated with a material that wears away very slowly. Every time the brakes are operated, a little more of the shoe's coating is rubbed away. The brakes must be examined from time to ensure that they still have a safe thickness of this coating.

A truck's disk brake.

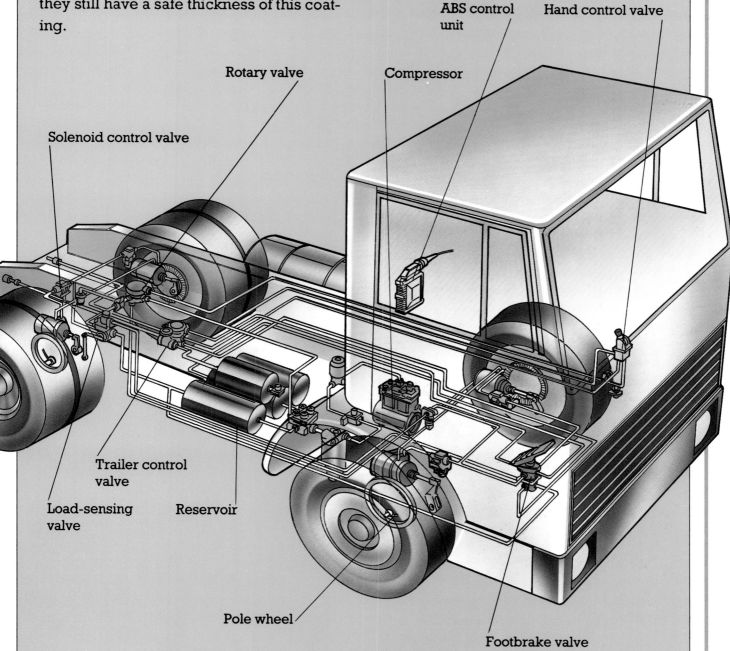

Solenoid control valve

Rotary valve

ABS control unit

Compressor

Hand control valve

Trailer control valve

Load-sensing valve

Reservoir

Pole wheel

Footbrake valve

THE DRIVER'S CABIN

The cabin, or cab, of a truck is the driver's workplace. It must be comfortable because the driver will be at the wheel for hours at a time. The position and height of the driver's seat must be adjustable to suit the individual shape and requirements of each driver. With a badly adjusted seat, the driver could get severe backache. A large windshield and the high-up position of the cabin give the driver an excellent view of the road ahead.

Long-distance drivers can be away from base with their trucks for weeks. A bed is usually built into the back of the cab so that the driver can sleep in the truck by the roadside. Some also have a television set for the driver's off-duty entertainment.

Many truck drivers now have a two-way radio in the cab. The Citizen's Band, or CB, Radio originated in the United States. It is used to contact other truck drivers or to call for assistance if there is a problem.

The tachograph

In the 1960s and 1970s there was increasing concern about the long hours that some truck drivers were working. They were becoming overtired, and this could be dangerous if they lost control of their vehicles.

Driving hours could be controlled only if there was some way of checking them. The answer was the tachograph, introduced at the end of the 1970s. It is a device that produces a trace on paper showing a driver's working hours and vehicle operations. It was an unwelcome device and was nicknamed "the spy in the cab."

A driver contacts fellow truckers by radio.

The speedometer in a driver's cab.

118

The cab of a modern truck is spacious and comfortable. The air temperature is controlled by a heating unit (10). All the controls (1-3) are situated within easy reach of the driver. All the dials and indicators (11-14) are positioned so that they can be seen clearly. Washers and wipers (7) keep the windshield clean. Mirrors (6,8) give the driver a clear view of the trailer, and of the road behind the truck. On many modern trucks there are computerized instrument systems that warn the driver of any vehicle faults, and monitor the efficiency of the engine. This helps to keep down the maintenance, servicing and repair costs.

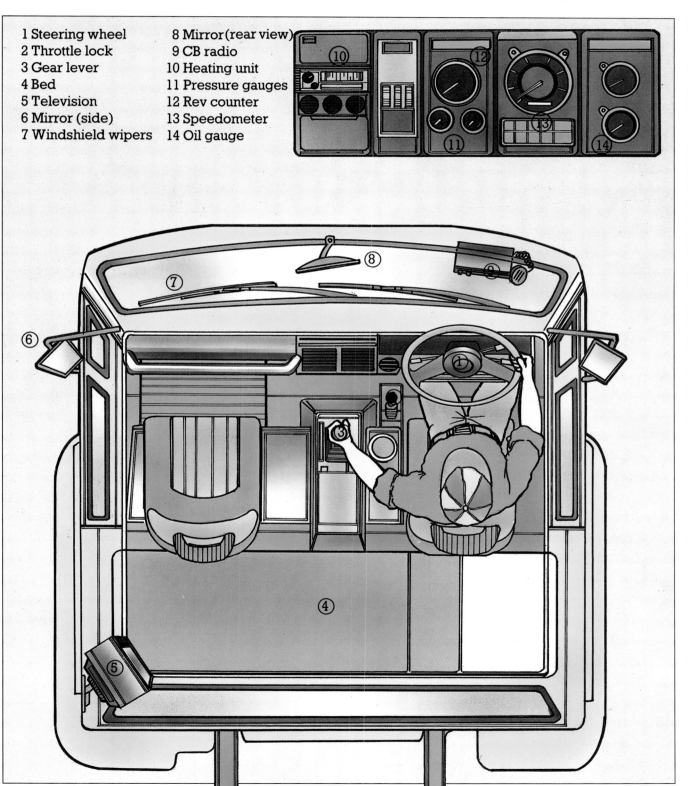

1 Steering wheel
2 Throttle lock
3 Gear lever
4 Bed
5 Television
6 Mirror (side)
7 Windshield wipers
8 Mirror (rear view)
9 CB radio
10 Heating unit
11 Pressure gauges
12 Rev counter
13 Speedometer
14 Oil gauge

VARIOUS LOADS

Trucks carry a wide variety of loads. A truck may pull a simple platform on which goods are stacked, but many trucks are specially designed for a particular type of load. Dump trucks are designed to carry loose materials such as gravel or rock. The trailers of some trucks are refrigerated so that foods such as raw meat or fish can be kept cold. Liquids ranging from gasoline to milk are transported in tankers, some of which are refrigerated.

The majority of trucks carry either solid goods or liquids, but not both. However, there are a few combination trucks that can carry all kinds of materials at the same time. They look like normal freight trucks. The difference is that they have "belly tanks" under the trailer floor that can be filled with a liquid load. They were first used in the 1950s, but were not successful because of their great weight. Now, lighter materials mean that these combination trucks can be built successfully

Some jobs cannot be done by a general-purpose transporter. A specially designed truck, for example a garbage lorry or tanker, is vital in a wide range of situations.

A garbage truck.

Freezer trucks enable frozen foods to be transported at sub-zero temperatures.

A "wrecker" recovers crashed or broken-down cars.

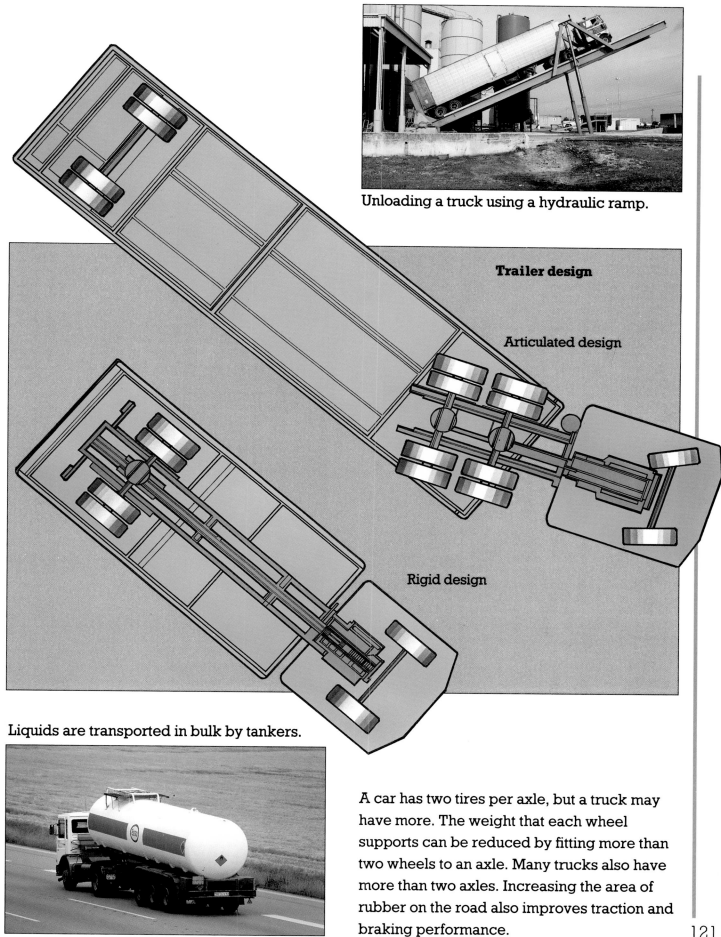

Unloading a truck using a hydraulic ramp.

Trailer design

Articulated design

Rigid design

Liquids are transported in bulk by tankers.

A car has two tires per axle, but a truck may have more. The weight that each wheel supports can be reduced by fitting more than two wheels to an axle. Many trucks also have more than two axles. Increasing the area of rubber on the road also improves traction and braking performance.

OFF-ROAD SPECIALS

The majority of trucks carry loads by road, but in some cases trucks must be able to travel where there are no roads. A truck specially designed for this is called an off-road vehicle. It may have all-wheel drive – that is, all the wheels are connected to the engine and are driven by it. There may also be a separate suspension system for each wheel, called independent suspension, because off-road vehicles may have to travel across very bumpy ground. Independent suspension gives a smoother ride than the suspension system fitted to road vehicles.

There are different types of off-road vehicles, each designed to do a particular job. The construction industry uses many of them. Small dump trucks transport rocks, gravel, sand or dirt around building sites. Giant dump trucks move hundreds of tons of rock and soil from earthworks in each load.

Military off-road vehicles are used to transport troops and equipment over rough or muddy ground. They also carry cranes, help build bridges, and rescue broken-down tanks and other vehicles. Some are amphibious – they can float and propel themselves through water, as well as ride over rough ground.

A military off-road vehicle.

A back-up truck used in the Paris-Dakar car rally.

The Terex Titan can transport loads weighing up to 550 tons.

Snow wheels

Even the special tires that off-road vehicles use have difficulty in gripping a surface covered with snow or ice. In countries where snow and icy conditions are common, trucks are frequently equipped with snow chains. These are designed to bite into the surface and improve grip.

Wide tyres are used in arctic conditions.

Chains in place on truck wheel give extra grip.

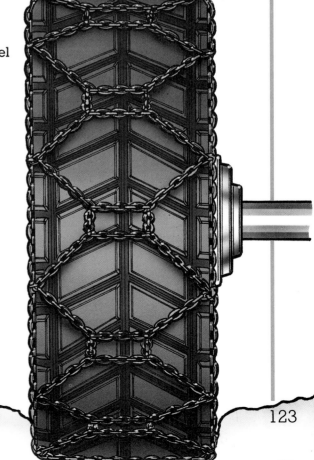

123

SPORTING TRUCKS

Custom trucks originated in the United States among drivers who owned their trucks. They tried to make their trucks look different from all the others on the road by painting them with startling designs and pictures. Customization may also include replacing some of the standard parts of a truck, such as the exhaust "stack" (a vertical exhaust pipe), and the fuel tank, with highly polished chromium plated parts. The demand for customized trucks is so great in the United States that many manufacturers now supply their trucks in a range of different color schemes. These serve as a starting point for the owner's unique "paint job."

Articulated truck tractors are mostly used to pull especially heavy loads along public highways at normal speeds, but the powerful tractors without their trailers are capable of traveling at very high speeds. Truck racing is one of the fastest growing motor sports in Europe.

Trucks have also taken part in ordinary car rallies including the annual Paris-Dakar race.

A truck "Superprix" race at the Brands Hatch circuit in England.

Truck racing using truck tractor units started in the United States, and then rapidly spread to Europe. There is now a European Truck Racing Championship. Every year, professional racing teams supported by many of the truck manufacturers compete for the title. The races test the trucks' top speeds and road-holding to the limit. The majority of the drivers still earn their living by driving ordinary trucks on the roads when they are not racing. Truck racing drivers do not yet receive the enormous amounts of money that Formula 1 racing drivers enjoy.

As with motor car racing, many of the improvements in ordinary truck design, engine efficiency and safety are made as a result of experimentation on the race-track.

A "funny car" with outsize wheels.

A Leyland Land train doing a "wheelie" at an exhibition event.

HISTORY OF TRUCKS

The first self-powered vehicles used to transport goods and freight in the 19th century were driven by steam engines. The steam engine was heavy and slow and steam-powered trucks were not very successful.

The gasoline-fueled internal combustion engine developed by the two German engineers Gottlieb Daimler and Karl Benz in 1887 provided a much cleaner and more compact source of power for all types of vehicles. Daimler built the first motor truck (1896).

A 1911 British Lacre 2-ton lorry.

Although horses were widely used to transport supplies during World War I (1914-1918), motor trucks were also used in large numbers. After the war, they began to take over from horses as a means of transporting goods. They were powered by gasoline engines and this remained the most common type of truck engine until the 1930s. During World War II (1939-1945), the heavy oil engine, invented by Rudolf Diesel in 1897, began to increase in popularity.

Soon after its invention, the heavy oil engine became known as the diesel engine. It became more popular because it was more economical than the gasoline engine.

The Chevrolet 1-tonner, 1926.

Diesel trucks developed more quickly in Europe than in the United States because the US had its own supplies of cheap gasoline. Gasoline engines remained popular there until the 1960s, when rising imports of more expensive oil made diesel trucks more attractive.

Throughout Europe, the majority of trucks have had diesel engines since World War II.

A 1931 Chevrolet pickup truck.

Until the 1950s, truck driving needed great physical strength. The steering wheel was hard to turn, especially when the truck was fully loaded, because of the great weight pressing the tires onto the road. Power-assisted steering made trucks easier to control. Bigger and heavier trucks, with two steering axles instead of one, could be built.

A modern articulated truck with freezer.

In the 1950s, Swedish manufacturers found that a turbocharger could boost a diesel engine's power output by up to 50 percent. Since the 1950s, articulated trucks have become very popular. Most are cab-over models, where the whole driver's cab tilts forward to reveal the engine for inspection and repairs.

In the late 1960s, truck designers tried a new type of engine, the gas turbine. It was unsuccessful because of high fuel costs. Freight transportation changed dramatically in the 1970s with the adoption of standard size containers. Trucks are now becoming more aerodynamic, using their shape to reduce air resistance and, therefore, fuel costs.

Facts and figures

The world's most powerful truck is a 1987 Ford LTL 9000. The truck, which weighs 4.4 tons, has reached a speed of more than 338 kph (210 mph) over a 400 meter (1,312 feet) track from a standing start.

The biggest transportation vehicles ever constructed are the two Marion crawler-transporters used to carry Apollo-Saturn 5 rockets, and now Space Shuttles, to their launch pad. Each crawler weighs 2,721 tons unloaded and 8,165 tons fully loaded with a Space Shuttle sitting on top on its mobile launcher platform. The crawler's maximum unloaded speed is 3.2 kph (2 mph). When loaded, it travels at 1.6 kph (1 mph).

The world's most powerful fire engine is the Oshkosh airport pumper. It weighs 60 tons and can spray 190,000 liters (over 40,000 gallons) of foam in 2½ minutes.

The world's largest tires are those used for for dump trucks. They each measure 3.65 meters (12 feet) in diameter and weigh 5.6 tons (12,500 pounds).

The largest dump truck in the world is the Titan 33-19, built by the Terex Division of General Motors. The giant vehicle stands 17 meters (56 feet) high when tipping and weighs 548.6 tons when fully loaded. It is so big that it cannot be driven on the roads. It is carried to its workplace in pieces and constructed there.

Chapter Seven

BATTLE
TANKS

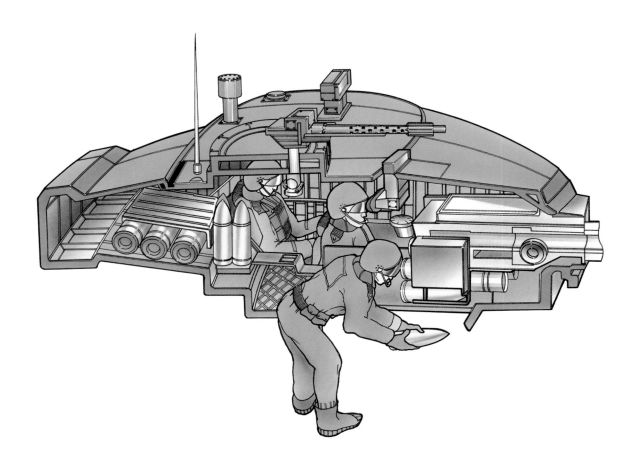

CONTENTS

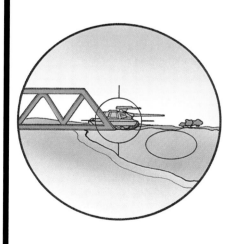

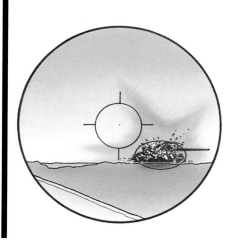

THE MAIN PARTS

The battle tank is the main weapon of modern land combat. Its job is to disable or destroy enemy tanks. Every tank is also therefore itself the target of another tank. It may also be attacked by a range of lethal weapons carried by soldiers and aircraft. To survive so that it can do the job it was designed for, it must be able to protect itself from these attacks.

The design of every tank is a combination of three important factors – mobility, protection and firepower. A powerful engine driving a pair of metal tracks gives it mobility. It is protected by

hull. The hull must be large enough to hold the engine, fuel, weapon systems, ammunition and the tank's electronic systems, with enough space left over for the tank's crew of three or four.

A tank's electronic systems include fire control and radio communications. Fire control is a computerized system that helps the gunner to aim the main gun accurately. The tank may also be equipped with specialized instruments

105mm low recoil gun

Wing mirror

Engine dials

Driver's controls

a thick covering of heavy armor plate. Firepower may be provided by any of a variety of weapons, but by far the most important is the tank's main gun. This is mounted in a rotating compartment called a turret.

Some tanks are designed for very high speed and mobility. To save weight, they may carry less armor. Others are designed for maximum firepower and protection. The extra weight they have to carry reduces their mobility. This is why tanks come in many different shapes and sizes. Tank designers balance the three basic requirements in different ways.

The structure of the tank has two main components, the turret and the body, or

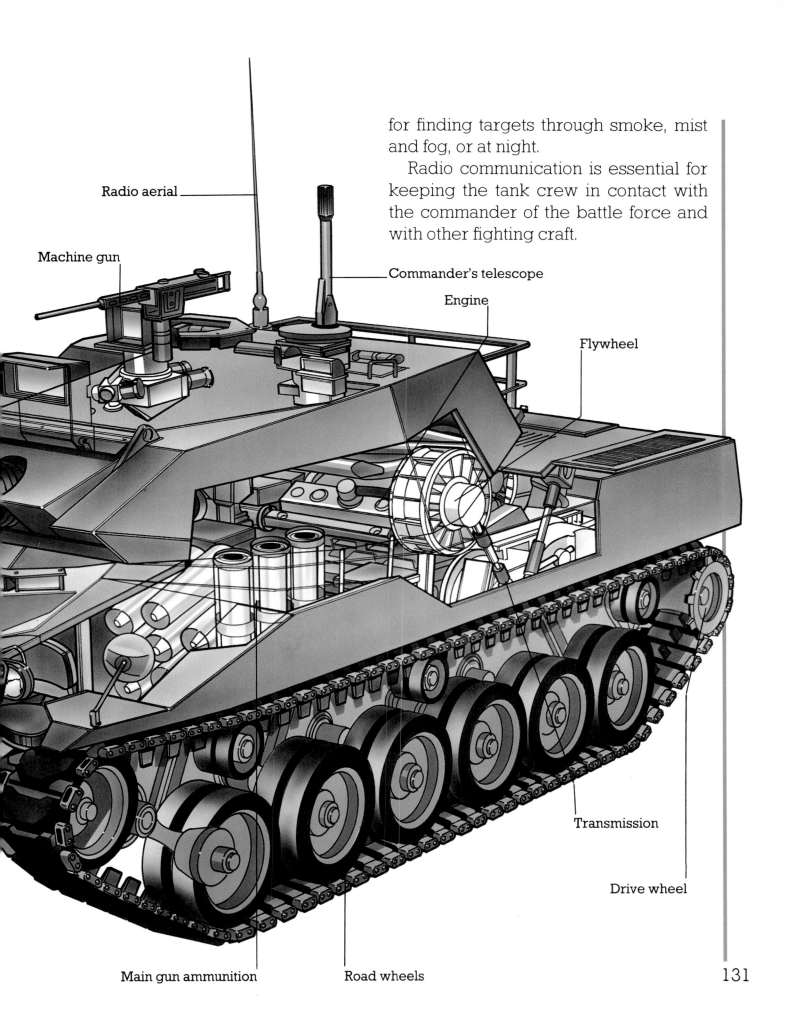

for finding targets through smoke, mist and fog, or at night.

Radio communication is essential for keeping the tank crew in contact with the commander of the battle force and with other fighting craft.

Radio aerial

Machine gun

Commander's telescope

Engine

Flywheel

Transmission

Drive wheel

Main gun ammunition

Road wheels

All main battle tanks have tracks.

The first successful suspension system developed for tanks was the Christie suspension (bottom right). It used large road wheels with solid rubber tires. The wheels moved up and down against the action of springs or shock absorbers.

The next system to be developed was torsion bar suspension (top right). This is still the most commonly used system. Each road wheel is linked to a steel rod extending across the bottom of the hull. If the wheel moves up or down, the rod twists. It acts like a spring.

The most recently developed system is hydropneumatic suspension (center right). This uses a cylinder of oil and gas as a spring. Vertical movements of the road wheels compress the gas in the cylinder and this has a "push-back" effect like the springiness in an air-cushion.

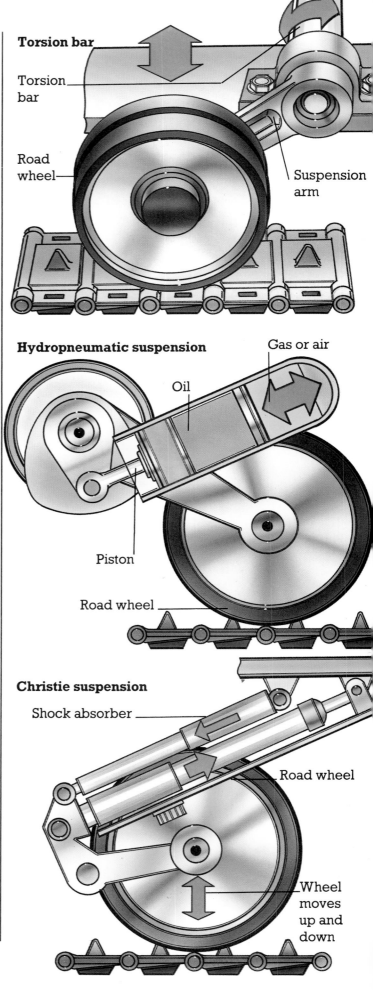

Torsion bar

Torsion bar

Road wheel

Suspension arm

Hydropneumatic suspension

Gas or air

Oil

Piston

Road wheel

Christie suspension

Shock absorber

Road wheel

Wheel moves up and down

TRACKS AND SUSPENSION

The most obvious difference between the main battle tank and most other military and civilian vehicles is that the tank's wheels are covered by flexible tracks. The tracks spread the great weight of the tank so that it does not sink into soft ground. They also help the tank to drive smoothly over bumps and holes in the ground. Tracks wear out and have to be replaced. The Leopard 2's tracks, for example, are replaced at least every 4,650 miles.

A tank's wheels are connected to the hull by springs and mechanical linkages called the suspension system. The suspension is very important because a tank's top speed is limited by the amount of hull vibration and bouncing the crew can tolerate.

There are several different types of suspension system, but they all try to do the same thing. They allow the tank's wheels to move up and down, following the shape of the ground, while the hull remains quite steady. This enables the tank to travel faster over rough ground.

The height of a battle tank fitted with hydropneumatic suspension can be varied by pumping up the system's gas cylinders. The Swedish S-tank uses this in a unique way to raise and lower its gun. Pumping up the front suspension raises the gun (top). Pumping up the rear lowers the gun (above). The suspension can also lift the tank to "see" over obstacles or lower it to hide it.

When the tank is driving across level ground, the suspension system holds it almost perfectly horizontal.

When the tank comes to uneven ground, the road wheels move one by one, while the hull and gun remain level.

Loading and firing

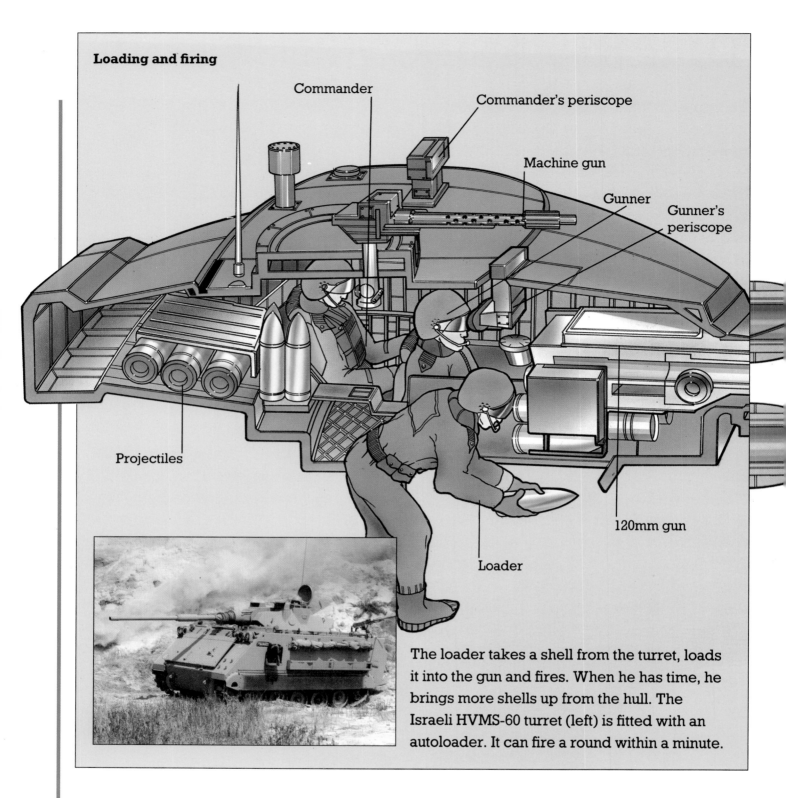

Commander

Commander's periscope

Machine gun

Gunner

Gunner's periscope

Projectiles

120mm gun

Loader

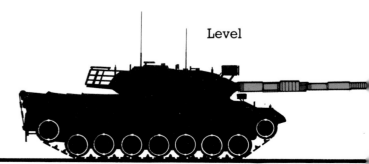

The loader takes a shell from the turret, loads it into the gun and fires. When he has time, he brings more shells up from the hull. The Israeli HVMS-60 turret (left) is fitted with an autoloader. It can fire a round within a minute.

The main gun can be raised (middle right) and lowered (far right). When the tank is moving, it is normally carried level (right) as this is the most stable position. The safest firing position is "hull down" with the tank on one side of a ridge, firing down on the target (far right) beyond the ridge. This exposes the least turret and hull area to an enemy.

Level

TURRETS AND GUNS

Most tank guns have a rifled barrel (below). Its spiral grooves make the shell spin as it is projected forward and keep it pointing at the target as it flies through the air.

Some guns have a smoothbore barrel (bottom) for firing armor-piercing projectiles which are stabilized by fins instead of spinning.

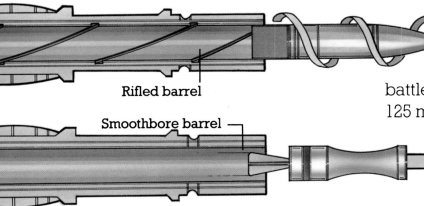

Rifled barrel

Smoothbore barrel

A battle tank in action.

The turret is the tank's fighting compartment. It carries the main gun and it is motorized so that it can be rotated quickly. The gun is aimed by rotating the turret and tilting the barrel up, which is called elevation, or down, called depression. The turret's shape and height limit how much the gun can be depressed. Its size is measured by the width of the hole through the barrel, known as its caliber. Main battle tanks are fitted with guns of 105 to 125 millimeters caliber.

The barrel is made as long as possible because this makes the gun more accurate. If it is too long, it can bend or vibrate due to its weight. Temperature differences along its length resulting from the firing of shells can also cause bending. This can be solved by covering the barrel with a sleeve to spread the heat more evenly. Vibration and bending can also be reduced by making the barrel stiffer. Some tanks are fitted with a system that detects barrel droop and corrects for it when aiming. In addition to the main gun, the turret may carry several machine guns mounted on top of the turret.

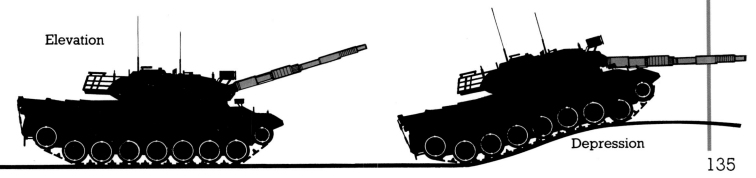

Elevation

Depression

Until the end of World War II, tank guns were made increasingly large to fire larger shells. The invention of subcaliber ammunition ended this trend. These shells are made long and thin to minimize air resistance. This ensures that they hit the target at the maximum speed. They must also be very hard to punch their way through tank armor. They are usually made from tungsten metal. Conventional shells are kept pointing at the target, or stabilized, while they are in flight by making them spin. Spin stabilization does not work with long, thin ammunition. Instead, they are stabilized by a set of tail fins. But all shells wobble slightly on leaving a gun before they fly through the air straight. As they reach the limit of the gun's range, they wobble again.

A battle tank hit on the turret.

The Armor-Piercing Fin Stabilized Discarding Sabot round has three parts. The long, thin penetrator (1) is encased in a collar called a sabot (2). In flight, it is stabilized by tail fins (3).

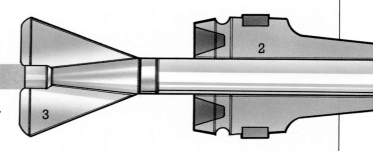

A High Explosive Squash Head (HESH) round is composed of a propellant (4), a fuse (5) and a charge of high explosives (6). The nose of the round is deliberately made soft to collapse on impact and detonate the explosives against the hull.

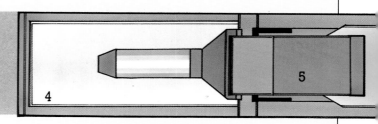

The warhead of a High Explosive Anti-Tank (HEAT) round (7) is specially shaped to concentrate its blast in a small area. In flight, like the APFSDS round, HEAT is stabilized by tail fins (8).

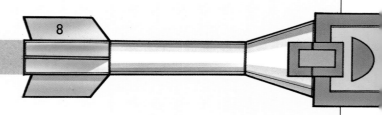

AMMUNITION

Three main types of armor-attack ammunition are in current use – High Explosive Anti-Tank (HEAT), High Explosive Squash Head (HESH) and subcaliber. They work in different ways. A HEAT round is detonated at a precise distance from the target's armor. A cone-shaped hollow in front of the explosives focuses the energy of the explosion onto a tiny spot, blasting a hole through the armor. HEAT is also called hollow-charge ammunition. A HESH round contains explosives packed inside a soft case. When it hits a tank, the case collapses and the explosives squash against the armor. When it explodes, pieces of metal called scabs are blown off the armor inside the tank.

Subcaliber ammunition uses a thin, sharp dart of very hard metal to punch a hole through armor. It is much thinner than the gun barrel caliber, hence the name subcaliber. To make it a tight fit inside the barrel, it is surrounded by a collar called a sabot, which drops away in flight. Subcaliber ammunition is also called Armor Piercing Discarding Sabot ammunition (APDS) or APFSDS if it uses fin stabilization (FS).

An antitank missile hits its target with devastating effect.

HITTING THE TARGET

If a tank's gun were pointed directly at a target and fired, the round would hit the ground before it reached the target. As the round flies through the air, it is pulled down by gravity. The gun must, therefore, be aimed higher than the target, at an angle called the elevation angle. It depends on the distance between tank and target, the range. As the range increases, so must the elevation.

The first tank gunners had to guess the range. As guns became more powerful and ranges increased, guess-work became quite useless. Optical rangefinders were developed, but were unpopular with many gunners, who preferred to use a ranging machine gun (RMG) mounted beside the main gun. Firing this gave the target's range, and the main gun could then be set accurately. The most modern tanks use laser rangefinders. A laser beam is fired at the target. The time taken for the reflected beam to return is used by a computer to calculate the range and set the main gun.

A tank crew locates a target moving from left to right. The gunner triggers his laser rangefinder.

The moving target option is selected and a grid appears in the gun sight. It is set to match the target speed.

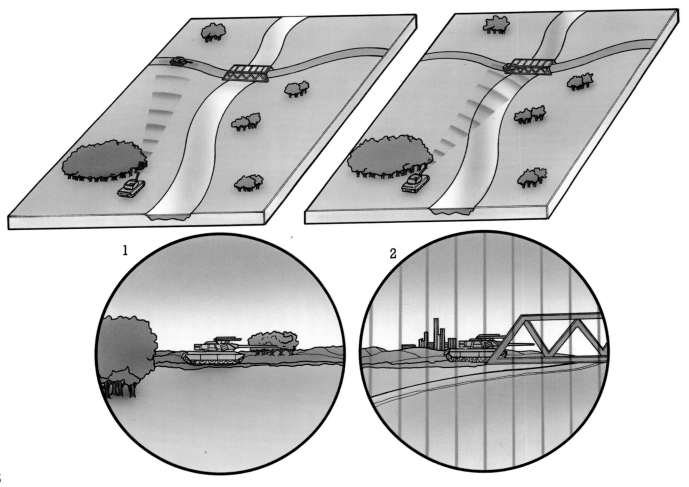

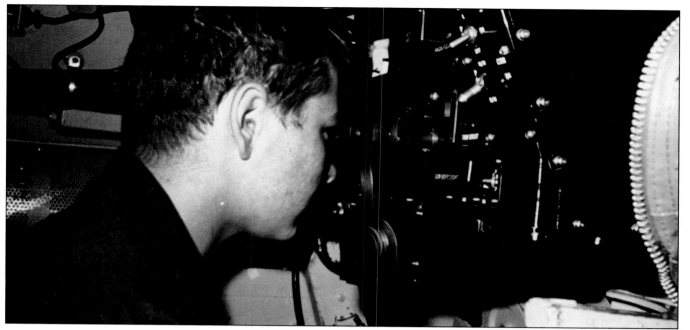

A gunner seated at his sight.

A computer calculates the range, speed and direction of the target and displays an aiming mark.

If the gunner now aims at this position and fires, the round should score a direct hit on the target.

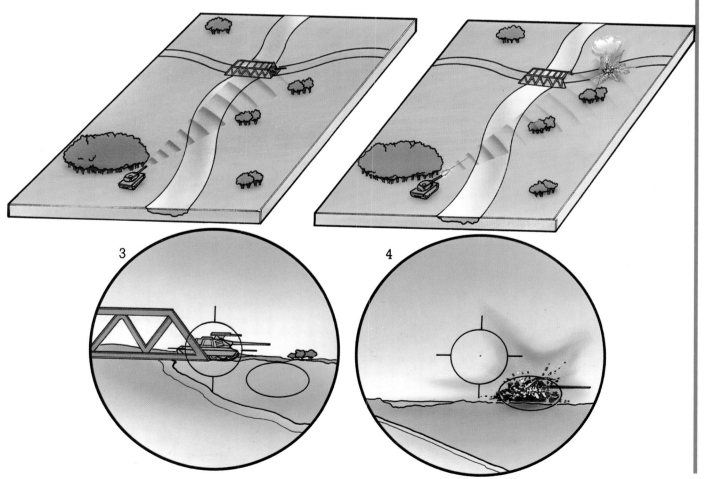

A tank crew has to work in very cramped and noisy conditions.

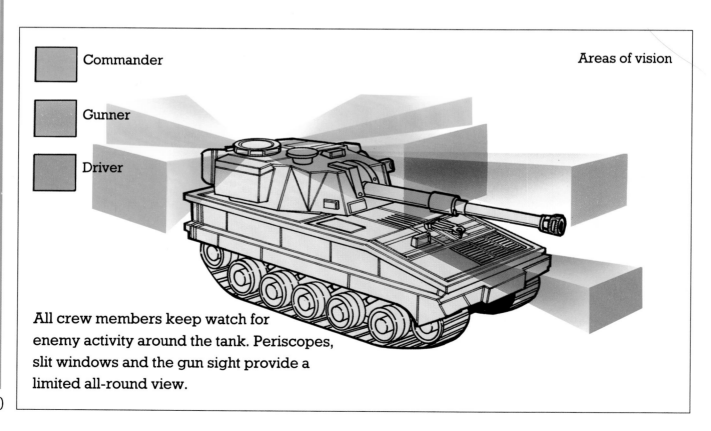

Commander

Gunner

Driver

Areas of vision

All crew members keep watch for
enemy activity around the tank. Periscopes,
slit windows and the gun sight provide a
limited all-round view.

THE CREW

Most modern tanks are designed to carry a crew of four – commander, loader, gunner and driver. Until World War II, a bow (front) gunner was also carried. As battle ranges increased, the bow gunner became unnecessary. The loader can be replaced by an automatic loading system, or autoloader, enabling the tank to operate with a crew of only three. The Swedish S-tank was the first to use an autoloader.

Each crew member has a particular job to do, but some jobs are shared. The commander decides what the tank will do, acting on orders from battle-control received by radio. The gunner operates the gunsight, rangefinder, fire control system and, of course, the main gun itself. The loader ensures that the main gun is always loaded and ready to fire. The driver controls the tank's engine and movements. All crew members use their various sights and periscopes to look for the enemy and report any sightings to the commander.

Most tanks are rear-engined and have a four-man crew, but there are other arrangements. The driver of a three- or four-man rear-engined tank sits at the front in the middle. If the tank is front-engined, the driver sits to one side, beside the engine. In a three-man front-engined tank, the driver can be moved back into the turret, allowing the height of the tank to be reduced. This makes the vehicle a smaller target to enemy tanks. The arrangement is based on the Soviet T-72. The tank's height could also be reduced if the driver worked lying face down, but this is still experimental.

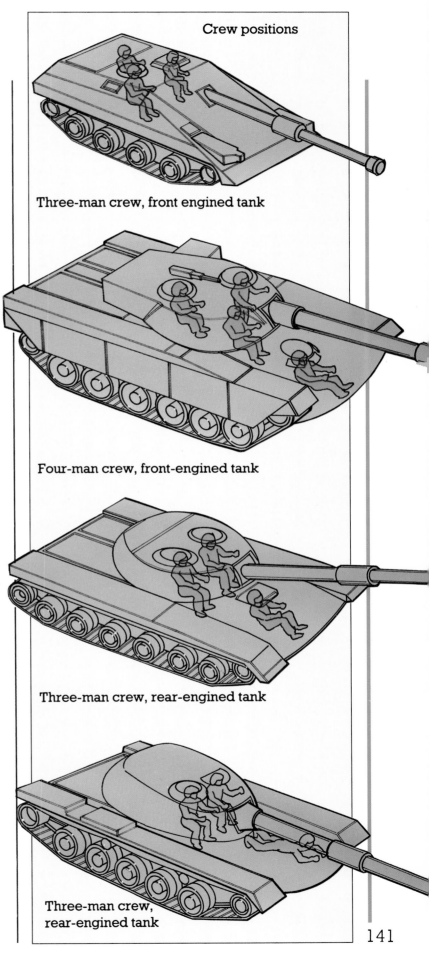

Crew positions

Three-man crew, front engined tank

Four-man crew, front-engined tank

Three-man crew, rear-engined tank

Three-man crew, rear-engined tank

141

DEFENSES

As each new type of weapon or ammunition is developed for attacking tanks, a new means of defense must also be developed. The tank's armor is an effective defense against all but the most specialized antiarmor weapons. Armor-piercing shot is most effective against vertical surfaces. It can be deflected by sloping the armor.

Sloping armor also presents a greater thickness to the shot, making it more difficult for armor-piercing shot to get through.

New types of armor have been developed to defeat antitank weapons by deflecting the shot or absorbing its energy. Chobham armor, named after the British research establishment where it was developed, is secret, but it is believed to be a "sandwich" of metal and plastic sheets.

The latest development is known as active or reactive armor. The tank is covered by panels that are designed to explode when struck. When any shot hits one of these panels, it explodes outward against the shot. Israeli tanks were the first to use active armor, which they call Blazer armor. Soviet tanks are now using it too.

Camouflage paint and netting breaks up a tank's outline and makes it more difficult to see.

Laminated armor is an effective defense against antitank shot. It is made from a "sandwich" of different materials. Most of the shot's energy is absorbed by the outer armor and a soft metal or plastic layer underneath. Rods of titanium metal between the plates are designed to deflect armor-piercing rounds. Sloping the armor also helps by increasing its horizontal thickness. Sometimes, sheets of steel are added to a tank's original armor plating to give it more protection. This outer layer absorbs much of a shell's energy.

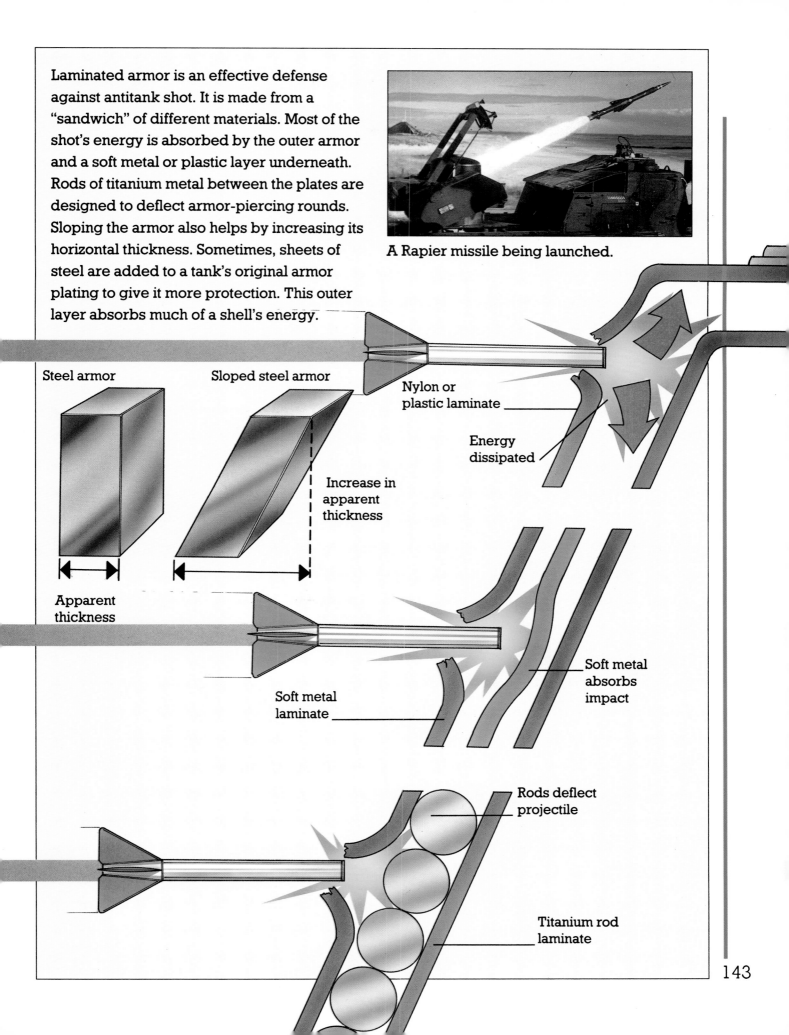

A Rapier missile being launched.

Steel armor

Sloped steel armor

Increase in apparent thickness

Apparent thickness

Nylon or plastic laminate

Energy dissipated

Soft metal laminate

Soft metal absorbs impact

Rods deflect projectile

Titanium rod laminate

143

THE FUTURE

Tank design is continually changing as engineers experiment with new materials, systems, and ways of using tanks. The Israeli Merkava tank, already in production, has many new features. With the engine at the front, it can have rear doors for crew escape and loading ammunition. Its turret is specially shaped to present a small target to the enemy. Future tanks may not have turrets. In the "gun-over-hull" design the gun is fixed to the top of the hull and operated remotely by the crew in the armored hull below.

Tanks need tracks to spread their weight over a large area, but tracks also limit a tank's maneuverability. The Swedish UDES XX-20 bends in the middle to combine a long track length with greatly improved maneuverability. Remotely controlled robot tanks are also being developed. They would be used to clear minefields and observe enemy positions by day or night, using video cameras and night vision systems.

Future tanks will be faster and more maneuverable. They will not rely on armor alone for protection. The Israeli Merkava tank already has an explosion and fire protection and suppression system. It extinguishes any fire in the crew compartment in a fraction of a second. The Swedish UDES XX-20 attempts to make a tank more agile by splitting it in two. US engineers have built an agile tank test vehicle to study the benefits of greater mobility. Another idea is to design a basic hull to which any one of various "pods" can be fitted – gun turret pod, crane pod and so on.

The US HIMAG experimental tank is tested.

The US HSTV.

The Israeli Merkava main battle tank incorporates many unique features.

HISTORY OF TANKS

The tank was developed during World War I. It was the result of the need for a new type of vehicle to cope with conditions on the battlefields. In 1916, the Mark 1 Tank was the first tank to enter service. The 28-ton British tank carried its four-man crew at a top speed of only 4mph. At this time, tanks were also being developed in France. The first, the St Chamond, went into action in 1917. It used a farm tractor's tracks.

The first tank, the British Mark I – "Mother."

Germany was slow to recognize the value of the tank, but finally began building tanks of its own.

The United States joined World War I in 1917 and US engineers began designing tanks. US inventor J Walter Christie introduced new ideas that were copied in later Soviet and British tanks. The Christie suspension system was very successful. It enabled Christie's M1919 tank to drive on wheels or tracks. The Christie M1928 had a top speed of 69.5mph on wheels and 42mph on tracks. The landing craft that took soldiers from ships on to beaches in World War II were quite like Christie amphibious vehicles.

The Christie M1931 tank.

After World War I, the major military powers began to develop more advanced tanks. The Soviet Union was particularly eager to develop very large armored units of heavy tanks. Germany favored lighter, faster tanks.

The standard German light tank was the Panzer Kampfwagen IID. Germany also developed new ways of using tanks. Britain and France used their tanks in groups and formations like fleets of ships. Their tanks were also often split up into small attack groups. German tanks were used in concentrated, unstoppable attacks. When they seized ground, they left its defense to artillery guns, freeing the tanks to attack elsewhere.

A WWII German Panzer Kampfwagen.

The German Panther D was one of the most successful tanks of World War II. It was designed to combat the Soviet T34. The most successful American tank of the war was the Medium M4 Sherman.

The British Centurion tank of the 1940s-1960s.

British tank design lagged behind other nations until the Centurion Mark 1 was developed in 1945, too late for war service. The Centurion Mark 3 had an electronically stabilized gun. The Centurion remained in service with the British Army until the 1960s.

The US M1 Abrams battle tank of the 1980s.

Centurion was replaced by Chieftain, which has now been replaced by Challenger. The Soviet Union's latest tank is the T-80, the first Soviet tank to have a gas turbine engine.

Facts and Figures

The first tank ever built was the British experimental No.1 Lincoln, which became known as Little Willie. It ran for the first time in September 1915.

Tanks were used in battle for the first time at the battle of Fleurs-Courcelette in France, in September 1916.

The first battle between tanks took place at the French village of Villers Bretonneux during World War I. On April 24, 1918, 14 German A7V tanks fought with three British Mark IV and seven Whippet tanks. The German tanks came out of the encounter best.

The heaviest tank ever built was the German Panzer Kampfwagen Maus II. It weighed over 190 tons. It was designed for use in World War II, but when production models were not ready by the time the war ended, the project was abandoned.

The heaviest tank to enter service was the French Char de Rupture 2C bis. Built in 1922, it weighed over 75 tons and needed a crew of 13.

The fastest tank in the world is the British Scorpion lightweight tank. The Scorpion can reach a speed of over 50mph. To save weight, its hull is made from welded aluminum instead of steel plate. It is also amphibious.

Chapter Eight
SUBMARINES

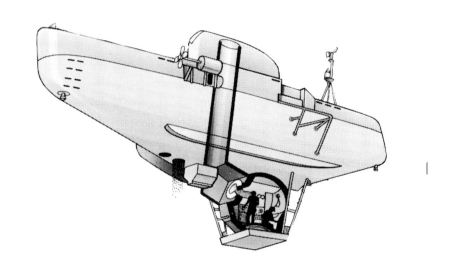

CONTENTS

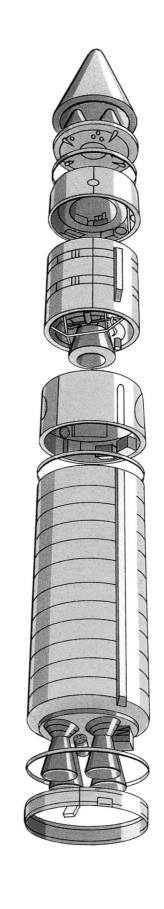

TYPES OF SUBMARINES

Most of the world's submarines are warships. They are designed to carry and fire torpedoes and missiles, or to lay mines, to destroy enemy vessels. Only the smallest submarines, called submersibles, are used for non-military, or civilian, work. Submersibles are built for repairing oil rigs, laying pipes on the seabed, and to study the underwater world.

There are two main types of submarine. The most common is the diesel-electric. This is powered by a diesel engine when on the surface of the water and by an electric motor when submerged. The second type is the nuclear submarine. This is powered at all times by a nuclear reactor. Diesel-electric submarines are the easiest and cheapest to build.

Military submarines are given code letters that describe their engines or the weapons they carry. For example, diesel electric attack subs are coded SS, and nuclear powered ones SSN. Attack subs are designed to find and destroy enemy warships. Submarines that carry missiles which can be guided to a ship or target on land are coded SSG or, if nuclear powered, SSGN.

The nuclear powered hunter-killer submarine is fast and well-armed.

A submersible – for underwater research.

A nuclear missile-carrying submarine.

Submarines range in size from submersibles less than 6m (20ft) long to the 170m (558ft) Soviet Typhoon class submarine. This is nuclear powered and carries "ballistic" missiles (SSBN class).

A diesel-electric submarine.

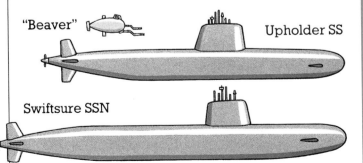

"Beaver"

Upholder SS

Swiftsure SSN

Typhoon SSBN

This submarine is blowing air out of its ballast tanks in order to dive.

Diving and surfacing

A submarine dives by taking in seawater to make it heavier. When the seawater is forced out again by compressed air, the submarine floats up to the surface.

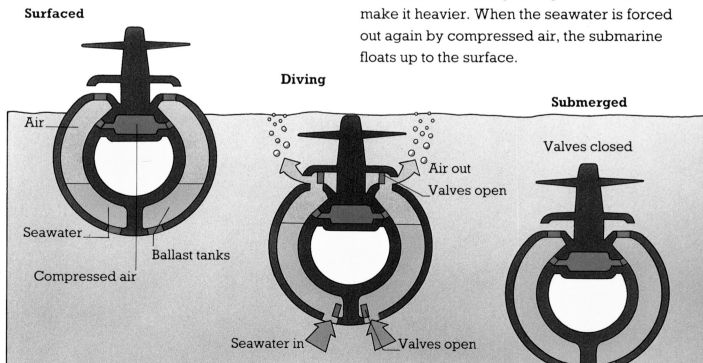

Surfaced

Air

Seawater

Ballast tanks

Compressed air

Diving

Air out

Valves open

Seawater in — Valves open

Submerged

Valves closed

SINKING AND RISING

A submarine floats on the surface of the sea like a ship. To make it sink underwater, it must be made heavier than the water around it. This is done by opening valves to allow seawater to flood into tanks, called ballast tanks, located between the inner hull and the outer hull.

As the seawater rushes in through valves at the bottom of the ballast tanks, it pushes air out through valves at the top of the tanks. The seawater is heavier than the air it replaces and makes the submarine sink. By controlling the amount of water that flows into the ballast tanks, a submarine can be lowered to any depth and kept there.

Air can be pumped into the ballast tanks to force the water out again. The submarine, now lighter than the surrounding water, rises back to the surface. Water pressure on the submarine increases as it sinks. If a submarine continued to dive deeper and deeper, it would eventually be crushed by the water surrounding it.

Submarine tilted down and front heavy

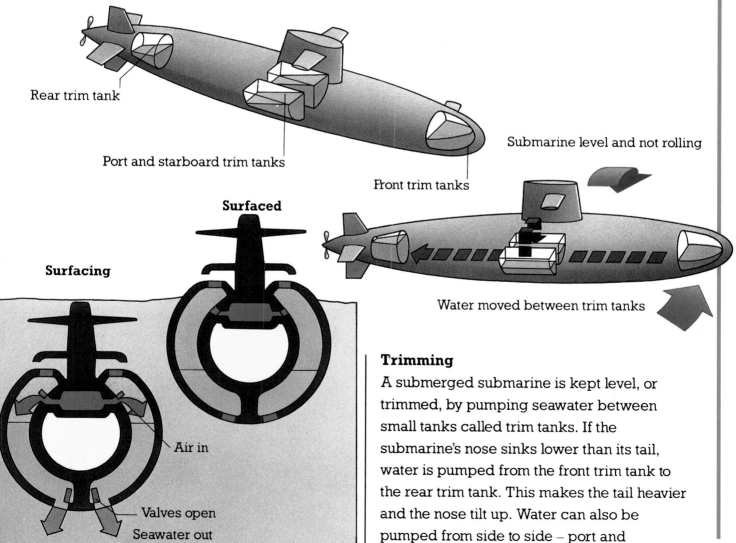

Rear trim tank

Port and starboard trim tanks

Front trim tanks

Surfaced

Surfacing

Air in

Valves open

Seawater out

Submarine level and not rolling

Water moved between trim tanks

Trimming

A submerged submarine is kept level, or trimmed, by pumping seawater between small tanks called trim tanks. If the submarine's nose sinks lower than its tail, water is pumped from the front trim tank to the rear trim tank. This makes the tail heavier and the nose tilt up. Water can also be pumped from side to side – port and starboard – to prevent rolling.

153

STEERING

A submarine is steered to the left and right by turning rudders on its tail, just as a surface ship is steered. But unlike a surface ship, a submarine also needs to maneuver up and down when it is underwater. Flooding and emptying its ballast tanks produces large changes in depth for diving and surfacing. But once a submarine has dived, hydroplanes are used to control its depth.

A hydroplane looks like a small aircraft wing. There are two pairs of hydroplanes – one pair at the front and the other at the back. When the hydroplanes are tilted up or down, the pressure of water against them as the submarine powers its way through the water forces the front or back of the vessel up or down. Because the action of hydroplanes depends on the force of water flowing across them, they only work when the submarine is moving.

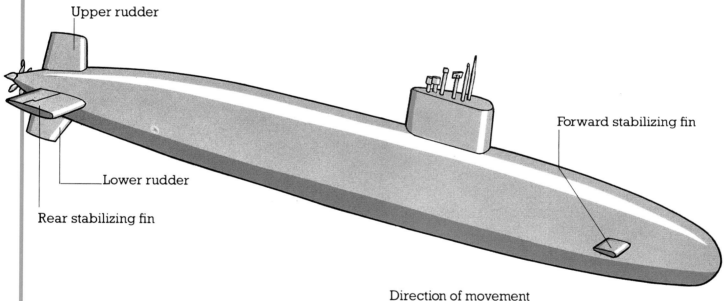

Upper rudder

Lower rudder

Rear stabilizing fin

Forward stabilizing fin

Steering underwater

If a submarine's front hydroplanes are tilted down and its back hydroplanes are tilted up, the whole submarine tilts nose-down. At this angle, its forward motion drives it deeper underwater.

If the front hydroplanes are tilted up and the back hydroplanes are tilted down, the nose comes up, the tail is forced down and the submarine rises again. The rudders are used to alter course to the left or right.

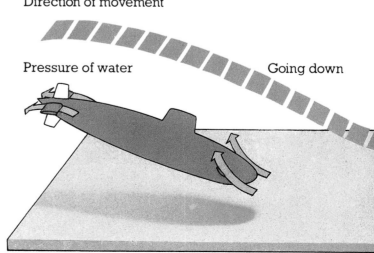

Direction of movement

Pressure of water

Going down

154

The submarine is steered by helmsmen who check the vessel's course on screens.

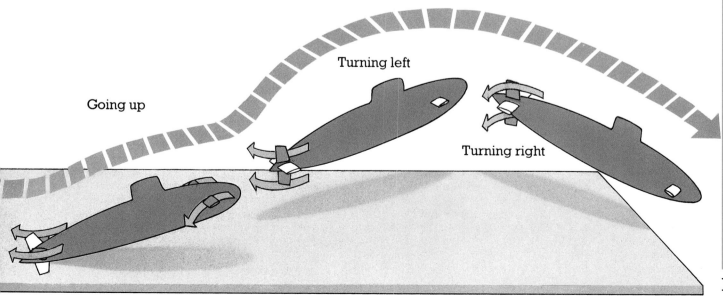

Going up

Turning left

Turning right

LOOKING AND LISTENING

Without specially developed looking and listening equipment, a submerged submarine would be unable to detect other vessels and obstacles in the sea around it. It could not be navigated safely through the seaways or detect an enemy nearby.

Near the surface, a periscope is used to give a view of the surrounding sea as far as the horizon. Radar is also used to scan the sea surface and the sky for ships and aircraft. Deeper underwater, below about 18m (59ft), neither the periscope nor radar can be used. Instead, a submarine uses sonar.

Like radar, sonar works by sending out signals and detecting their echoes. Radar uses radio signals, but sonar uses short bursts, or pulses, of sound. Underwater microphones, called hydrophones, attached to the sub's hull, pick up sound reflections from the seabed, ships, and other objects like icebergs.

Most of a submarine's sonar sensors are placed around the front of the hull to give early warning of obstacles in the sub's path.

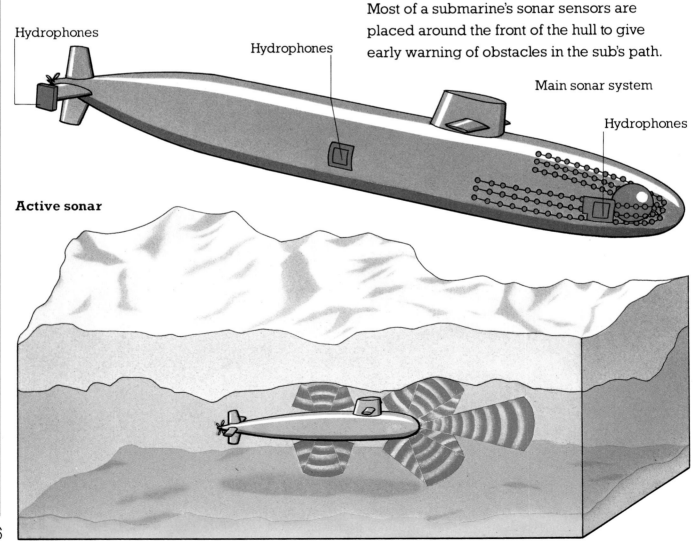

Hydrophones

Hydrophones

Main sonar system

Hydrophones

Active sonar

Up periscope! There is usually a choice of lenses to give wide angle and close-up views.

Sonar can be used in one of two ways. Pulses of sound sent out from "transducers" on the hull bounce off anything solid near the submarine. Hydrophones pick up the echoes. This is active sonar (below left).

Enemy submarines can detect active sonar. One answer is to switch off the sound transmitters and use the hydrophones to pick up engine and other sounds from enemy vessels. This is passive sonar (below).

Passive sonar

A U.S. Navy helicopter lowers a submarine-detecting sonar buoy toward the water below.

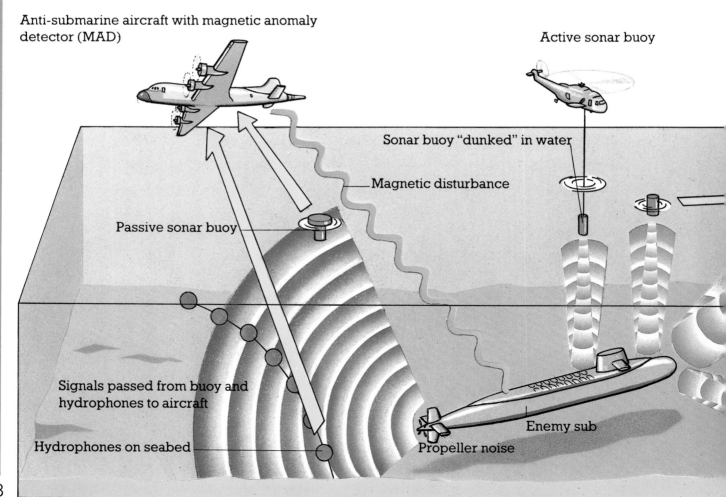

Anti-submarine aircraft with magnetic anomaly detector (MAD)

Active sonar buoy

Sonar buoy "dunked" in water

Magnetic disturbance

Passive sonar buoy

Signals passed from buoy and hydrophones to aircraft

Hydrophones on seabed

Propeller noise

Enemy sub

SUBMARINE DETECTION

Submarines are a serious threat in wartime. Not only can they attack and destroy other submarines and surface vessels, they can also inflict serious damage to military and civilian targets on land. It is important to be able to find enemy subs so that they can be dealt with swiftly and effectively.

All submarines make noises that can be picked up by sonar systems. For this reason, submarine designers are always trying to make the vessels work more quietly. Even if noises from inside the submarine – the whirring of motors and pumps – are cut down, propeller noise is difficult to eliminate. As the propeller spins around, it churns up the water and makes noise. As the sub travels through the water, any roughness on the hull, such as the edge of a hatch, stirs up the water and causes noises that a sonar system can detect. Sonar operators are trained to recognize the difference between echoes from shoals of fish and those from surface ships and submarines. Submarines also produce magnetic effects that can be detected by sensors in aircraft.

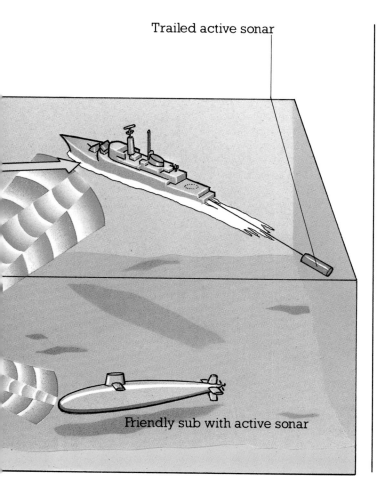

Trailed active sonar

Friendly sub with active sonar

An Anti-Submarine Warfare (ASW) group at work. Helicopters hover over the sea and dip sonar buoys into the water, a technique called dunking. Hydrophones planted on the seabed or dropped into the sea by helicopters listen for sounds from enemy submarines.

Friendly submarines use active sonar to detect hostile craft underwater. (During wartime, submarines do not use their radar navigation systems as the radar signals can be easily detected by enemy vessels and aircraft.) On the surface, a ship uses a sonar buoy, trailed through the water behind it (to reduce noise from the ship itself).

A submarine is such a large metal structure that it disturbs the Earth's magnetic field as it moves along. An aircraft circling overhead carries a Magnetic Anomaly Detector (MAD), which detects this effect to locate subs.

Together, an ASW group is likely to locate an enemy sub within a few minutes.

An Ikara radio-controlled aircraft with homing torpedo is being prepared for launch.

An enemy submarine has been detected. Destroyer ships, helicopters and a hunter-killer sub move in to attack it.

The hunter-killer may fire a "homing" torpedo, which uses its own sonar to follow and hit the target submarine. It might also fire Subroc (short for submarine-launched rocket), a nuclear weapon with a range of 56km (35 miles). Subroc leaves the water and flies fast towards its target before diving into the sea and exploding at a set depth.

Destroyers on the surface drop depth charges, which also explode at a set depth. Or they launch radio-controlled aircraft that fly over the target and drop a homing torpedo into the water. Homing torpedoes can also be dropped from helicopters.

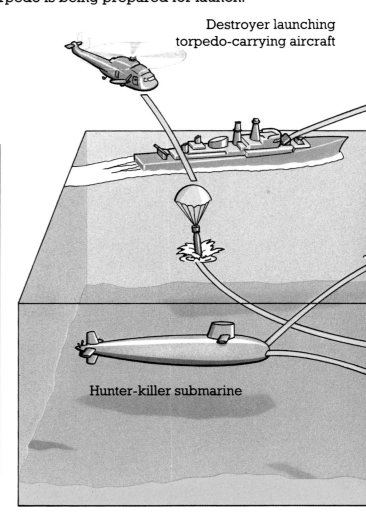

Destroyer launching torpedo-carrying aircraft

Hunter-killer submarine

HUNTER-KILLER SUBMARINES

One type of submarine, called an attack sub or "hunter-killer," is used to seek out and destroy enemy submarines and surface ships. It can also be used to protect friendly ships from attack.

In wartime, large amounts of supplies for armies and civilians are transported by sea. One of the hunter-killer submarine's most important wartime jobs is to stop enemy supplies getting through while protecting friendly supply ships.

The world's first nuclear hunter-killer submarine (code SSN) was the USS *Tullibee*, built in 1960. Some of the *Tullibee's* design features are still used today in the most modern nuclear powered hunter-killer subs, such as the United States' *Los Angeles*. Built in 1976, the *Los Angeles* weighs 6,000 tons and carries a crew of 127. When an enemy submarine or ship is detected, the hunter-killer sub can use a range of weapons against it.

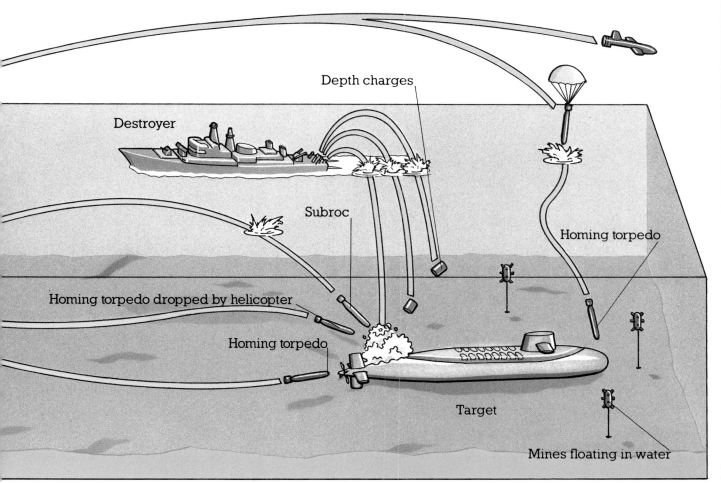

Depth charges

Destroyer

Subroc

Homing torpedo

Homing torpedo dropped by helicopter

Homing torpedo

Target

Mines floating in water

STRATEGIC WEAPONS

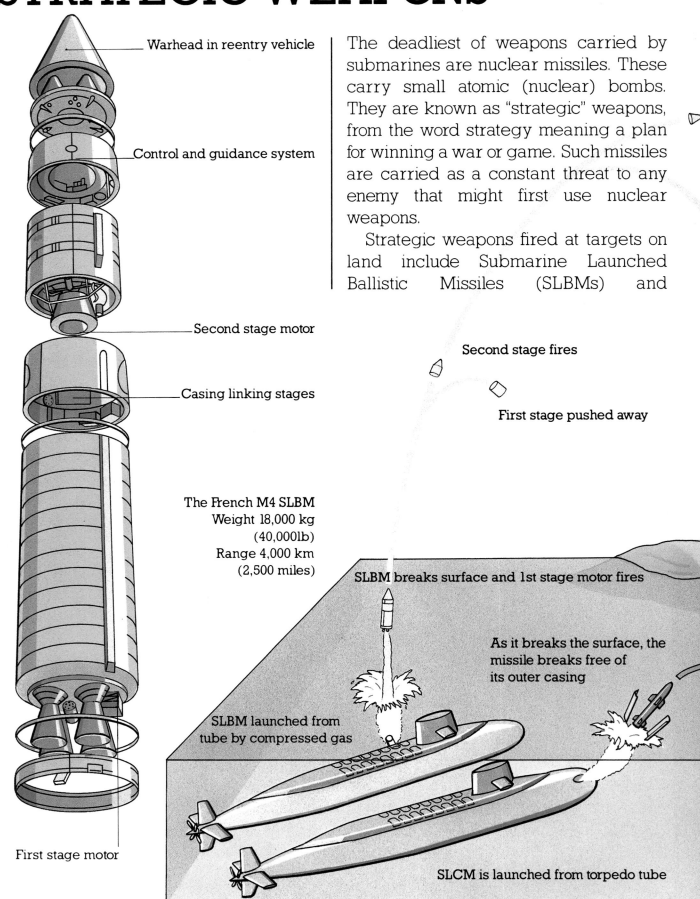

Warhead in reentry vehicle

Control and guidance system

Second stage motor

Casing linking stages

The French M4 SLBM
Weight 18,000 kg
(40,000lb)
Range 4,000 km
(2,500 miles)

First stage motor

The deadliest of weapons carried by submarines are nuclear missiles. These carry small atomic (nuclear) bombs. They are known as "strategic" weapons, from the word strategy meaning a plan for winning a war or game. Such missiles are carried as a constant threat to any enemy that might first use nuclear weapons.

Strategic weapons fired at targets on land include Submarine Launched Ballistic Missiles (SLBMs) and

Second stage fires

First stage pushed away

SLBM breaks surface and 1st stage motor fires

As it breaks the surface, the missile breaks free of its outer casing

SLBM launched from tube by compressed gas

SLCM is launched from torpedo tube

Submarine Launched Cruise Missiles (SLCMs). An SLBM has several stages. When the fuel in one stage is used up, the fuel tank and its rocket motors drop away and the next stage takes over. An SLBM flies high above the Earth's atmosphere. When it reenters the atmosphere, it releases many separate warheads, each aimed at a different target. SLCMs fly low, following the shape of the ground to avoid detection by enemy radar.

Missile unit releases warheads on to targets

**Second stage
pushed away**

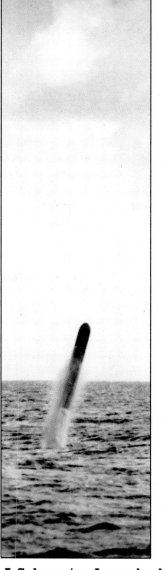

A Submarine Launched Cruise Missile (SLCM)

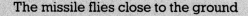

The missile flies close to the ground

SLBMs can strike targets 7,000km (4,300 miles) away. SLCMs have a range of about 2,500km (1,500 miles). "Ballistic" missiles fall under gravity (the Earth's pull) once their fuel is used up. "Cruise" missiles swerve like an aircraft.

TACTICAL WEAPONS

Weapons used by one vessel against another are called tactical weapons. They are smaller and have a shorter range than strategic weapons. They include torpedoes, antisubmarine missiles and anti-ship cruise missiles.

The torpedo shown below has a sonar system for finding and following its target. Alternately, information about the target's position can be sent from the submarine to its torpedo along a wire connecting the two. "Smart" torpedoes can detect when they have missed their target, then double back to try to hit it again. Simpler torpedoes similar to those used in World War II are still in use today. Once fired, they continue in a straight line at the same depth.

The fastest nuclear sub can travel faster than a torpedo, and so missiles such as Subroc must be used to destroy them. Submarines can also use missiles to attack ships. "Harpoon" is a cruise missile that flies just above the waves for up to 110km (68 miles).

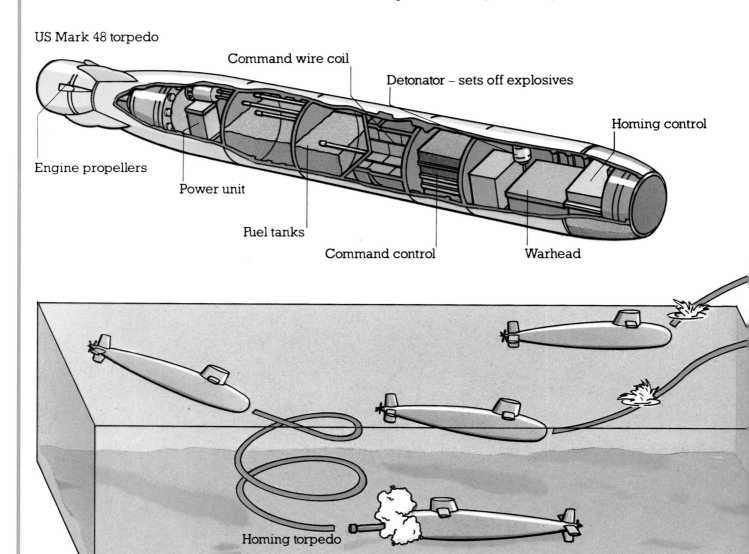

US Mark 48 torpedo

Command wire coil

Detonator – sets off explosives

Homing control

Engine propellers

Power unit

Fuel tanks

Command control

Warhead

Homing torpedo

In the torpedo room, the crew get ready to fire the sub's underwater weapons.

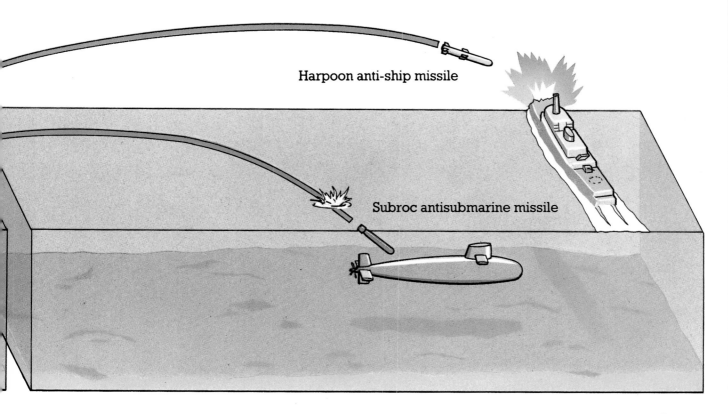

Harpoon anti-ship missile

Subroc antisubmarine missile

SPECIAL SUBMARINES

Some submarines are specially designed to do a particular job. Small submarines, or submersibles, are used to inspect underwater pipelines and telephone cables. They may be fitted with robot arms to enable the crew to pick things up and bring them back to the surface. Other craft, known as Deep Submergence Rescue Vehicles (DSRVs), are designed to connect to a submarine's escape hatch so that the crew of a damaged submarine can be rescued.

Submersibles also help scientists to investigate the deepest parts of the world's oceans. Deep underwater it is very dark and the water is at great pressure. Deep-diving craft must carry their own lights and must be strengthened to resist the crushing water pressure. The submersible *Alvin* was used to photograph the wreck of the passenger ship *Titanic*. The *Titanic* sank after hitting an iceberg on its first voyage across the Atlantic in 1912. *Alvin's* titanium (an especially strong metal) hull enabled it to dive to 4,000m (14,000ft) just enough to reach the floor of the Atlantic Ocean where the *Titanic* lay. A French craft, *Trieste*, has made the deepest dive 11,000m (38,500ft) to the bottom of the Pacific Ocean.

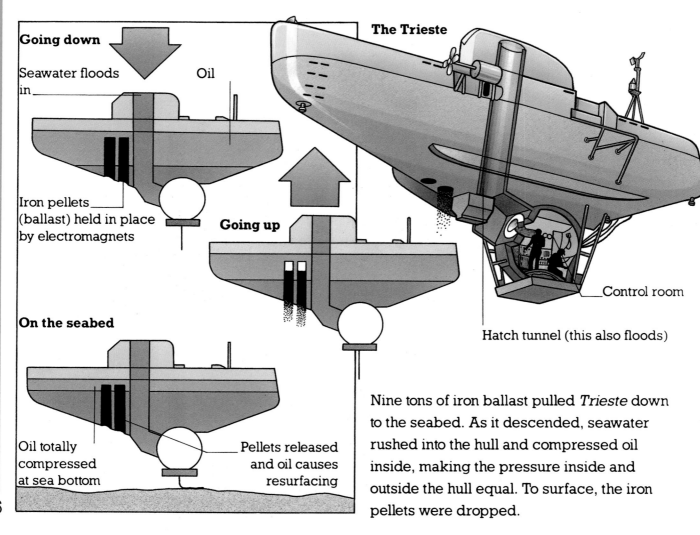

Going down

Seawater floods in

Oil

Iron pellets (ballast) held in place by electromagnets

Going up

On the seabed

Oil totally compressed at sea bottom

Pellets released and oil causes resurfacing

The Trieste

Control room

Hatch tunnel (this also floods)

Nine tons of iron ballast pulled *Trieste* down to the seabed. As it descended, seawater rushed into the hull and compressed oil inside, making the pressure inside and outside the hull equal. To surface, the iron pellets were dropped.

A deep sea submersible explores the seabed using lights and cameras.

Inside the control unit of a submersible.

HISTORY OF SUBMARINES

Early days

The first military submarine was designed in the 1770s by an American David Bushnell. It was built to attack British ships during the Revolutionary War. It was to be steered beneath a ship and an explosive charge attached to the ship's hull. The attempt failed, however.

The Turtle – the first sub used in war.

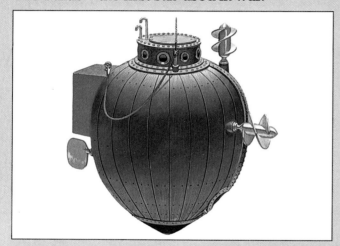

In the 1800s, there were two important advances in submarine technology. The *Nautilus*, designed by another American, Robert Fulton, in 1800, was the first submarine to have a metal hull. Then in the 1890s the Irish-American, John P. Holland, built a submarine powered by an internal combustion engine (an automobile engine) when on the surface and by an electric motor when submerged. This efficient combination produced the first successful long-distance submarine.

1900-1950

Submarines were first used in large numbers during World War I (1914-1918). There were about 400 submarines in service with the world's navies. By then, the gasoline-fueled engines used by earlier submarines had

A U-boat and crew return to port.

been replaced by engines using safer diesel oil. Submarines such as the successful German Unterseeboote, or U-boats, could attack ships with torpedoes.

During World War II (1939-1945) submarines were again very successful in sinking supply ships. Electronic aids such as active sonar, developed during the war, made it easier to detect enemy submarines. Work on nuclear weapons during the war led to the development

Nautilus – the first nuclear submarine.

of nuclear reactors instead of diesel engines for generating power.

1950-present-day

In 1954, the first submarine to use a nuclear power plant, the USS *Nautilus*, was launched. Unlike diesel-electric submarines, which have to return to the surface regularly to charge their batteries, nuclear submarines can remain submerged for thousands of miles.

The only nuclear submarine that has ever carried out an attack is Britain's HMS *Conqueror*, which in 1982 sank the Argentinian battleship *General Belgrano* during the Falklands War.

A Soviet Typhoon class SSBN

In the future, designers will attempt to make submarines even quieter than they are now in order to avoid detection. The greatest advances are likely to be made in electronic warfare, with new ways of escaping the submarine hunters. From the 1990s onward, new classes of submarines will be able to dive deeper and faster.

FACTS AND FIGURES

Biggest
The world's biggest submarines are Soviet Typhoon Class vessels. They weigh 30,000 tons and are 558ft long.

Fastest
Submarine speeds are secret, but the fastest are believed to be Soviet Alfa Class submarines (over 42 knots or 48 miles per hour) and American Los Angeles Class submarines (over 30 knots or 34 miles per hour).

First
The first practical submarine was the wooden-hulled *Turtle* built in the United States in the 1770s.

Smallest
The smallest manned submarines are submersibles such as *Alvin* or the *Beaver IV*. They have enough space for a crew of two or three people.

Deepest
In 1960, the *Trieste II* submarine descended 38,500 feet into the Pacific Ocean.

Largest submarine fleets
The three "superpowers" have by far the largest numbers of submarines, with fleets of at least 400 (USSR), 150 (USA) and 110 (China) craft.

Longest underwater
Nuclear subs could stay underwater for up to 3 years, but most dive for a week at a time.

Chapter Nine
HELICOPTERS

CONTENTS

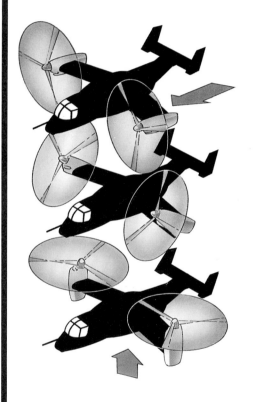

THE WORKING PARTS

A helicopter is an aircraft that can fly in any direction and hover in mid-air. Instead of fixed wings, it has a moving wing called a rotor that acts as a wing and a propeller.

The main working part of a helicopter is the rotor head. This is a complicated set of metal rods, hinges and plates that connects the engines and the pilot's controls to the rotor blades. The rotor head is spun at high speed by the engines. As the blades attached to it cut through the air, they behave like long thin wings. This produces a force called

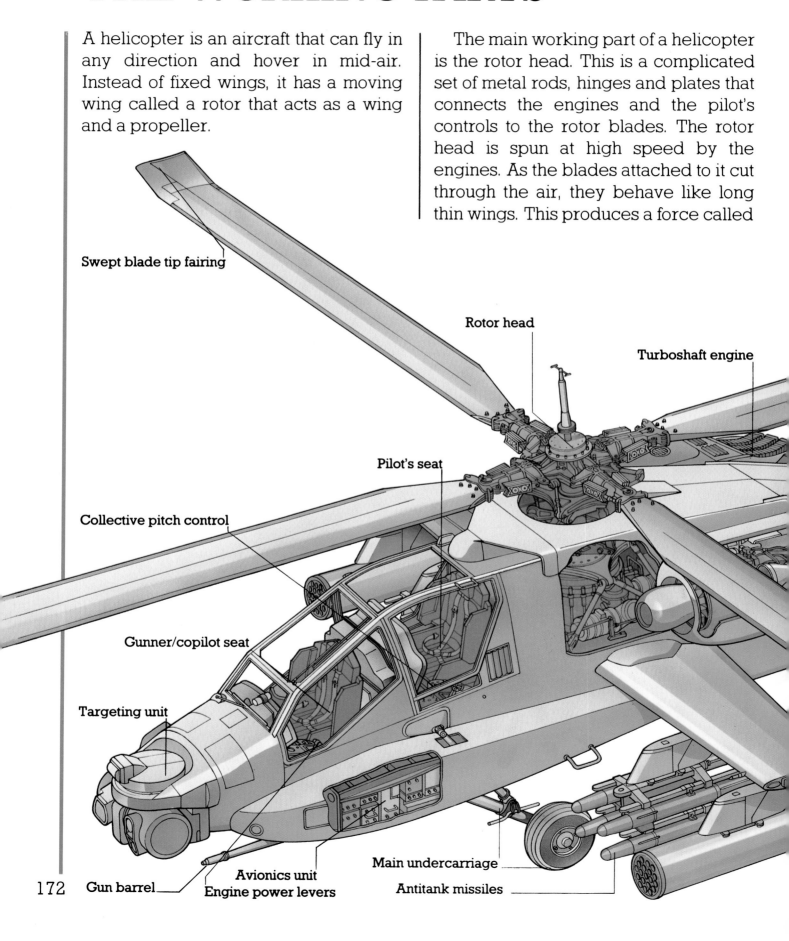

Swept blade tip fairing

Rotor head

Turboshaft engine

Pilot's seat

Collective pitch control

Gunner/copilot seat

Targeting unit

Main undercarriage

Antitank missiles

172   Gun barrel   Avionics unit
Engine power levers

lift that raises the helicopter straight up into the air. A second, smaller rotor on the tail stops the helicopter itself from spinning. The pilot can move the helicopter in different directions by pushing on a control stick in the cockpit. This changes the tilt, or angle, of the rotor head or blades.

The cockpit of each helicopter is positioned in front of the engines. It has large windows to give the pilot a clear view ahead and around the aircraft. The main engine drive-rod, or shaft, runs along the body, or fuselage of the helicopter to the tail section.

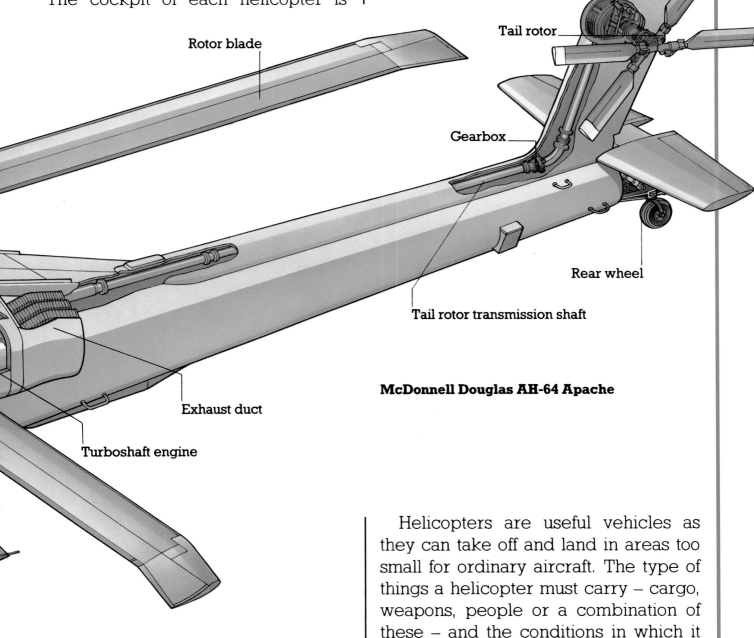

Rotor blade

Tailplane

Tail rotor

Gearbox

Rear wheel

Tail rotor transmission shaft

McDonnell Douglas AH-64 Apache

Exhaust duct

Turboshaft engine

Helicopters are useful vehicles as they can take off and land in areas too small for ordinary aircraft. The type of things a helicopter must carry – cargo, weapons, people or a combination of these – and the conditions in which it has to work determine its size, shape and rotor design.

173

Bell 47G helicopter with a piston engine.

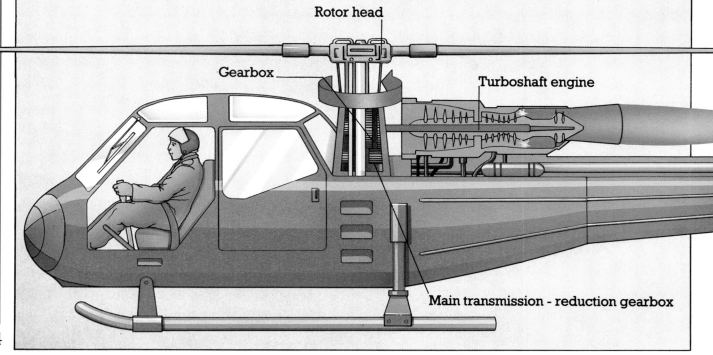

Rotor head

Gearbox

Turboshaft engine

Main transmission - reduction gearbox

CREATING THE POWER

The earliest helicopters, built in the 1930s and 1940s, were powered by gasoline-fueled engines similar to car engines. In the 1950s, a new type of engine called a turboshaft was developed for helicopters. It produced more power than a gas engine of the same size, and used kerosene fuel, which is less expensive and less flammable than gasoline. The Alouette, made in France in 1955, was one of the first helicopters to use such an engine.

Today, helicopters still use turboshaft engines. All but the smallest helicopters are fitted with two engines. This is for two important reasons. Firstly, two small engines can create more power than a single large engine. Secondly, two engines are safer than one in the event of a failure. If one engine fails and loses power, the remaining engine enables the pilot to make a controlled landing.

Turboshaft engine

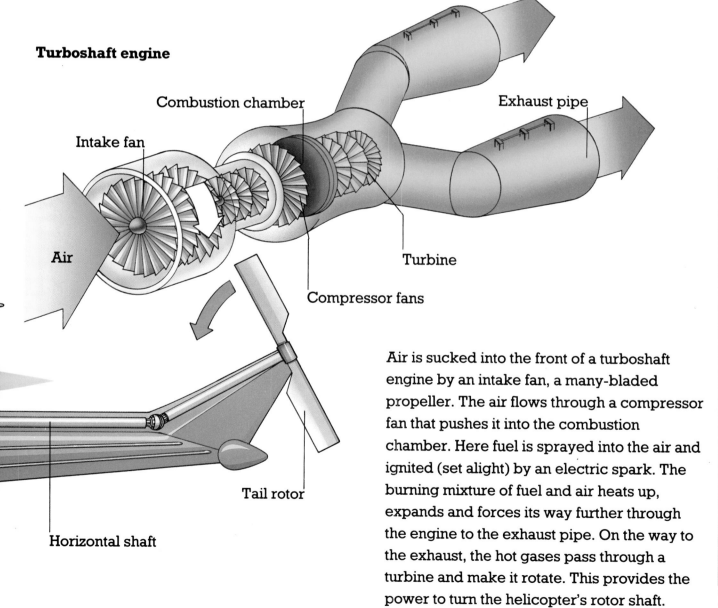

Combustion chamber

Exhaust pipe

Intake fan

Air

Turbine

Compressor fans

Tail rotor

Horizontal shaft

Air is sucked into the front of a turboshaft engine by an intake fan, a many-bladed propeller. The air flows through a compressor fan that pushes it into the combustion chamber. Here fuel is sprayed into the air and ignited (set alight) by an electric spark. The burning mixture of fuel and air heats up, expands and forces its way further through the engine to the exhaust pipe. On the way to the exhaust, the hot gases pass through a turbine and make it rotate. This provides the power to turn the helicopter's rotor shaft.

HOVERING

One of the major advantages that helicopters have over all fixed-wing aircraft is that they can hang motionless in the air. This is called hovering.

Airplane wings can only produce enough lift to support the aircraft's weight when the craft is traveling forward at great speed. A helicopter's rotor blades can produce lift even when the helicopter is stationary. This is because the blades themselves are driven around very rapidly.

To hover, the pilot holds the cyclic control stick in a central position to keep the rotor disc level. Any forces from crosswinds that try to push the helicopter sideways can be overcome by tilting the rotor disc to produce a force in the opposite direction.

Hovering is useful for several jobs that helicopters do. An air-sea rescue helicopter can hover over a ship in difficulty while the crew is lifted off the deck one or two people at at time. A mountain rescue helicopter can hover just above rough ground that no other vehicle could reach while an injured mountaineer is placed on board.

The force that spins a helicopter's blades in one direction could also spin the rest of the helicopter in the opposite direction.

A small rotor at the end of the helicopter's tail provides a sideways force to prevent the helicopter itself from spinning.

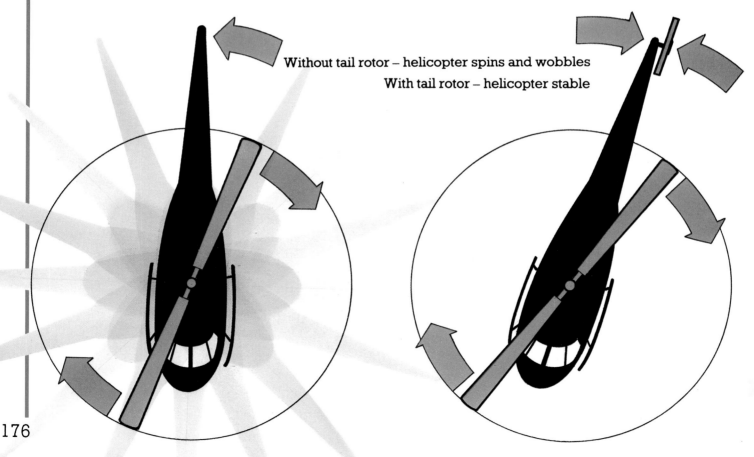

Without tail rotor – helicopter spins and wobbles

With tail rotor – helicopter stable

A Sea King hovers over the sea and dips a submarine sensor under the water.

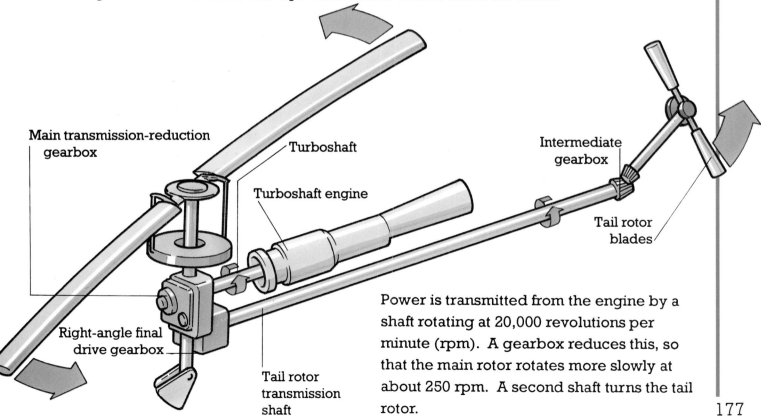

Main transmission-reduction gearbox

Turboshaft

Turboshaft engine

Intermediate gearbox

Tail rotor blades

Right-angle final drive gearbox

Tail rotor transmission shaft

Power is transmitted from the engine by a shaft rotating at 20,000 revolutions per minute (rpm). A gearbox reduces this, so that the main rotor rotates more slowly at about 250 rpm. A second shaft turns the tail rotor.

MANEUVERS

A helicopter is a very agile aircraft. The ability to tilt its rotor disc means that the power of its engines can be applied in any direction. The helicopter can therefore fly up or down, sideways, forwards, even backwards, in a very controlled way. This ability is used for hovering and for maneuvering on to landing areas in difficult locations such as a clearing in a forest, a mountain top or the deck of a ship at sea.

Small combat, scout, and observation helicopters, for example the Hughes 500-MD, are highly maneuverable. They can fly fast and very low, hugging the ground contours, which makes them difficult to locate and attack. For these reasons, the helicopter has become important in modern warfare. It can observe the enemy and guide other aircraft in for an attack. In future, the fastest and most agile helicopters may be used to hunt and attack the enemy's helicopter forces.

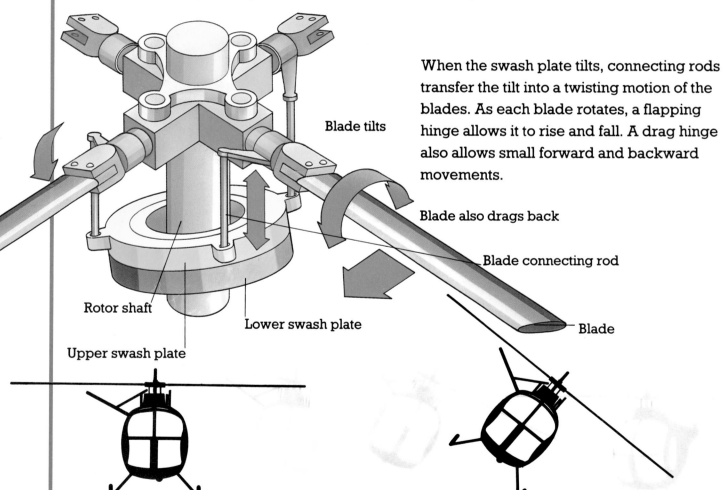

Blade tilts

When the swash plate tilts, connecting rods transfer the tilt into a twisting motion of the blades. As each blade rotates, a flapping hinge allows it to rise and fall. A drag hinge also allows small forward and backward movements.

Blade also drags back

Blade connecting rod

Rotor shaft

Lower swash plate

Blade

Upper swash plate

Maneuvering a helicopter involves tilting the rotor disc to point the downdraft of air from the rotors in different directions.

To fly to one side, the pilot pushes the cyclic control stick to that side. The swash plate is tilted slightly to create the desired flight.

Some helicopters have rotor blades without hinges. Instead, each blade has a flexible section where it joins the rotor hub. It twists like a hinged blade but in a much more controllable way. This allows helicopters like the Lynx and Apache to fly in ways that other helicopters cannot. They can roll, loop-the-loop or fly upside down. If a helicopter with normal blades tried such maneuvers, the force of the air against the rotor unit would snap the blades or cause the connecting rods to fracture.

Flexible and elastic damper and beam section

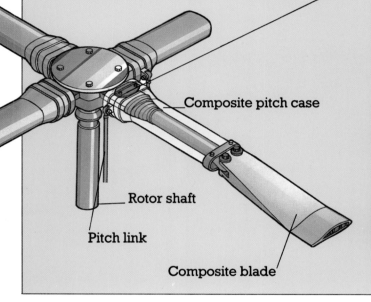

Composite pitch case

Rotor shaft

Pitch link

Composite blade

A Lynx helicopter makes a nose-dive

To fly backward, the pilot pulls back the cyclic control stick. This makes the rotor disc tilt backward. The helicopter's tail drops and its nose comes up. The downdraft from the blades is now directed forward and the lift rearward.

LANDING

Although helicopters can be made to hover and to move up and down in the air while staying level, they are rarely landed vertically. A pilot bringing his or her helicopter straight down to the ground cannot see directly underneath the craft. So unless the helicopter is continually rotated on the way down, the pilot cannot ensure that its tail will not be struck by an object. Closer to the ground, the effect of the helicopter's downdraft rocks the aircraft about.

To overcome these flight problems helicopters are usually made to descend at an angle called the glide-slope. If the helicopter is to land at an airport, the pilot may use an Instrument Landing System (ILS). Radio beams transmitted from the ground are received by the helicopter and are used to show the helicopter's position relative to the glide-slope on an ILS instrument in front of the pilot. To make the helicopter lose height, the pilot lowers the collective pitch lever to lower the angle of the rotor blades.

Decreasing height at a 40°-60° angle

Decreasing height on its own slipstream

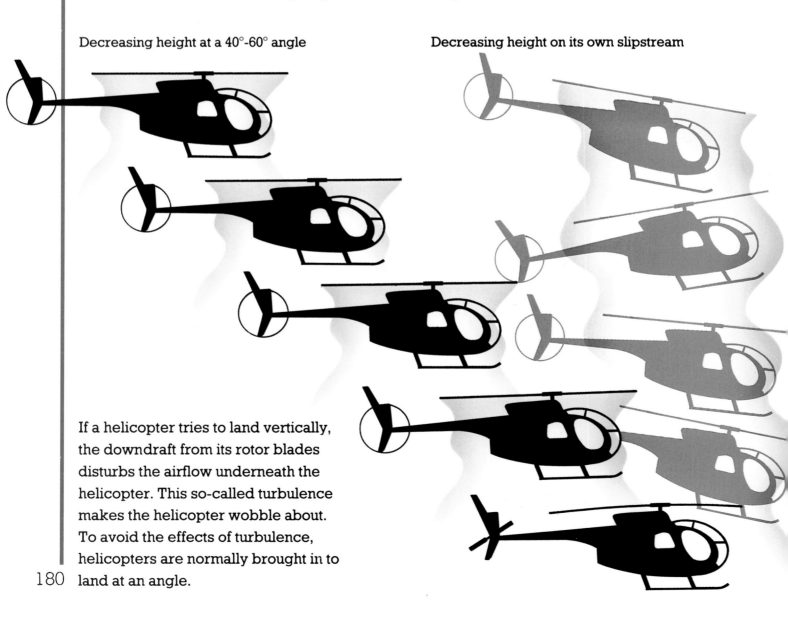

If a helicopter tries to land vertically, the downdraft from its rotor blades disturbs the airflow underneath the helicopter. This so-called turbulence makes the helicopter wobble about. To avoid the effects of turbulence, helicopters are normally brought in to land at an angle.

Helicopters can carry passengers into city centers where other aircraft cannot operate.

Helicopters are used to ferry oil workers between offshore oil rigs and land bases.

CONTROLS

A helicopter is not an easy aircraft to fly. The pilot needs to use both hands and both feet to operate the flight controls. Tiny adjustments must be made to the controls all the time to keep the helicopter stable and flying in the desired way. In addition, the pilot must operate navigation and communications equipment and, in a military helicopter, weapons systems too.

When any one of the controls is operated, its effect on the helicopter is shown on an array of instruments on a panel in front of the pilot. The pilot has to watch these instruments as well as look out through the windshield. In a helicopter with a crew of two, some of the instruments are fitted to both sides of the panel so that the pilot and the copilot can each check the craft's workings. Control levers and pedals may also be fitted to both sides of the cockpit, so that the copilot can take over flight control in an emergency.

The control panel of a Dauphin II

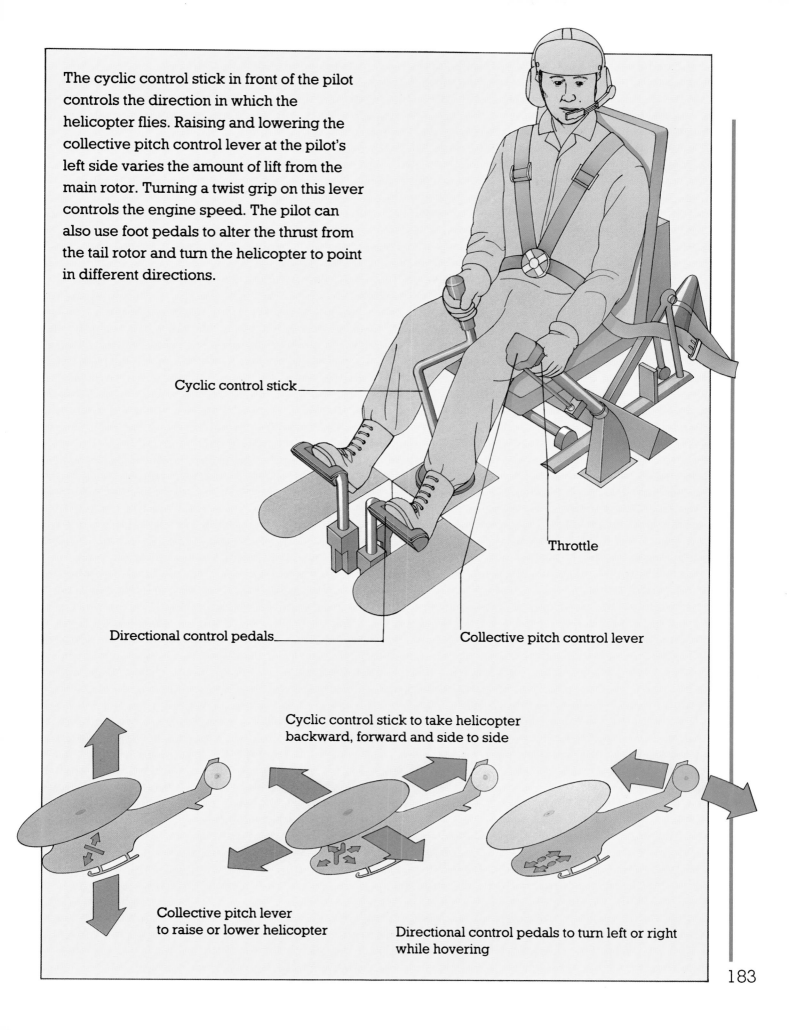

The cyclic control stick in front of the pilot controls the direction in which the helicopter flies. Raising and lowering the collective pitch control lever at the pilot's left side varies the amount of lift from the main rotor. Turning a twist grip on this lever controls the engine speed. The pilot can also use foot pedals to alter the thrust from the tail rotor and turn the helicopter to point in different directions.

Cyclic control stick

Throttle

Directional control pedals

Collective pitch control lever

Cyclic control stick to take helicopter backward, forward and side to side

Collective pitch lever to raise or lower helicopter

Directional control pedals to turn left or right while hovering

EMERGENCY

If a helicopter has an engine failure or any other fault that cuts off power to the main rotor, it does not simply fall out of the sky. The unpowered rotor slows down and loses lift. As the helicopter begins to lose height, the direction of the air flowing through the main rotor is reversed, from downward to upward. This creates some lift.

The pilot must always keep the freewheeling rotor spinning as its wing-like effect will be needed later if power cannot be restored. This is done by changing the pitch (angle) of the blades. If engine power is lost while the helicopter is flying slowly or hovering, the pilot may deliberately tip the helicopter's nose downward in order to increase its airspeed and keep the rotor turning as fast as possible.

As the helicopter rushes down toward the ground, the blade angle is altered once more to provide enough lift to soften the landing. All except the smallest helicopters, and especially those that are intended to operate over the sea, have two engines to provide an extra margin of safety.

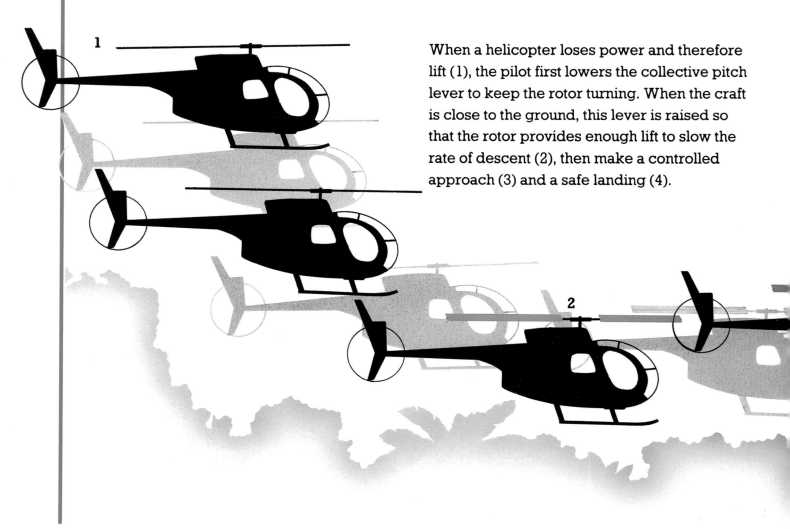

When a helicopter loses power and therefore lift (1), the pilot first lowers the collective pitch lever to keep the rotor turning. When the craft is close to the ground, this lever is raised so that the rotor provides enough lift to slow the rate of descent (2), then make a controlled approach (3) and a safe landing (4).

A helicopter ditches into the sea in an emergency.

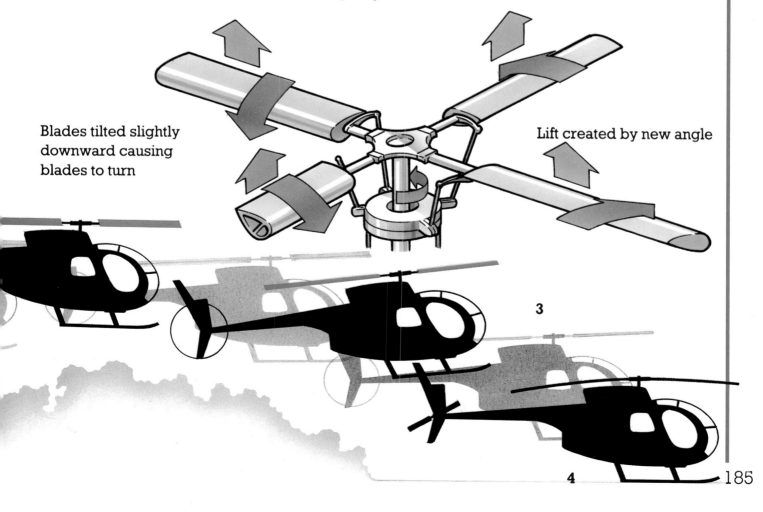

Blades tilted slightly downward causing blades to turn

Lift created by new angle

3

4

SPECIAL HELICOPTERS

New kinds of aircraft are being developed all the time as designers search for ways of combining the best features of helicopters and airplanes. Helicopters can take off vertically, but they cannot fly faster than 400 km/h (240 mph). Fixed-wing aircraft can fly at over 2,000 km/h (1,200 mph) but, apart from the Harrier "Jump-jet," they cannot take off vertically.

The tilt-rotor combines the two by having engines that rotate from horizontal to vertical. The first tilt-rotor aircraft will enter service with the U.S. military in the 1990s. It will be able to take off vertically and fly at up to 560 km/h (335 mph). An X-Wing looks like a helicopter, but its four broad, stiff rotors behave more like wings. The X-Wing will take longer to develop.

The X-Wing is an advanced aircraft being developed by Sikorsky in the U.S.A.

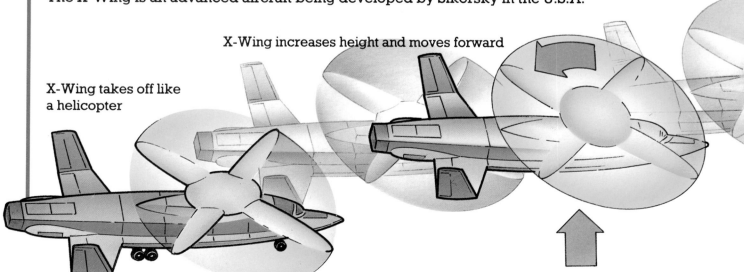

X-Wing increases height and moves forward

X-Wing takes off like a helicopter

The V-22 Osprey tilt-rotor aircraft

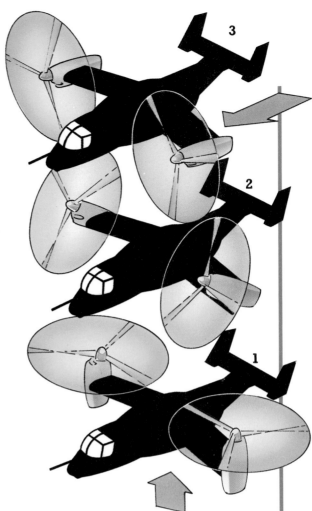

The Osprey tilt-rotor craft takes off vertically by using its two rotors (1). The blades can be twisted to vary the amount of lift they produce. When the Osprey is airborne, its engines are tilted forward slowly (2) until all their thrust is directed backward (3). The Osprey then flies forward like an airplane, with its wings providing all the necessary lift. To land, the Osprey's engines and their rotors tilt back to the vertical.

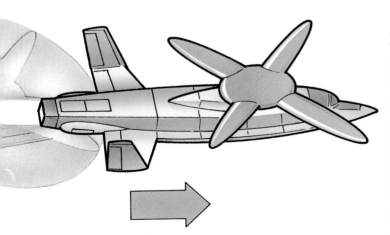

When X-Wing reaches speed, the rotor is turned off

X-Wing is a new type of aircraft that is neither a helicopter nor an airplane. It takes off like a helicopter by rotating its four wings. The wings cannot be twisted like helicopter rotors, and as the rotor disc cannot be tilted, the X-Wing must use the thrust of a jet or propeller for forward flight. When the flying speed is high enough, the wings stop spinning. From then on they behave like fixed wings, and the aircraft can increase speed up to about 850 km/h (510 mph).

187

HISTORY OF HELICOPTERS

Detailed drawings of a helicopter-like flying machine were made as long ago as the 15th century by the Italian painter and engineer Leonardo da Vinci. Leonardo's design used a device called an airscrew to provide lift instead of the rotor blades that modern helicopters use. It is not known if Leonardo's helicopter was ever built, but it would not have lifted far off the ground.

Leonardo's drawing for a helicopter

The first helicopters were built in the early years of the 20th century. In 1907, four years after the Wright brothers made the first flight in a heavier-than-air machine, a man was lifted into the air by the first helicopter. It was the Breguet-Richet Gyroplane No. 1. It was very unstable and had to be kept steady by four people holding onto ropes.

The modern helicopter took shape in the 1930s. The Breguet-Dorand 314 (1936) was the first helicopter to use collective and cyclic pitch control. In 1939, the Ukranian-born American, Igor Sikorsky, demonstrated a helicopter with a single main rotor and a smaller tail rotor, the arrangement still used by most helicopters today.

Early Sikorsky V3-300 (1939)

Few helicopters were built or used during World War II. The development of a new type of engine, called a turboshaft, enabled extremely rapid advancements to be made in all helicopters in the 1950s. During the Korean War (1950-53) helicopters were used to pick up wounded soldiers and aircrew trapped in enemy-held land. During the Vietnam War in the 1960s and 1970s helicopters were used extensively for this and other jobs. Bell "Huey" and Chinook helicopters ferried troops into and out of battle, and the world's first attack helicopter, the Huey Cobra "gunship," went into service. The Huey's nickname came from its original 1955 model name, the HU-1A.

A Bell Huey in use in Vietnam

During the Vietnam War the helicopter was used to attack tanks for the first time and it is now a very effective antitank weapon. Its success led to the design of other fast, very maneuverable combat helicopters, like the Hughes AH-64 Apache and the Soviet Mil MI-24 "Hind."

The importance of the submarine in modern warfare has also led to the development of anti-sub helicopters, for example the Sea King. These are equipped with sonar detectors.

A Hughes AH-64 Apache

Helicopters have become such effective combat machines that it will be important to destroy them in future wars. The best weapon to use against a helicopter is another helicopter, a small, fast and very agile anti-helicopter helicopter.

Passenger-carrying helicopters will continue to serve on the shorter air routes, especially to small city center landing pads, called heliports, that airplanes cannot use. Civilian tilt-rotor craft will also begin to operate during the 1990s, probably first in air-sea rescue and coastguard duties, then with passenger services.

FACTS AND FIGURES

The heaviest load ever lifted by a helicopter was carried by a Soviet Mil MI-26 "Halo" in 1982. Its eight-bladed main rotor powered by two 11,000 horse power engines enabled it to lift a total of 56.77 metric tonnes to a height of 2,000 m (6,600 ft).

The world's largest helicopter is a Soviet Mil MI-12 "Homer," also known as a V-12. It has a span across its two rotors of 67 m (220 ft), it is 37 m (121 ft) in length and weighs 114 tons.

The world helicopter speed record is held by a modified Westland Lynx. Its specially shaped rotor blades enabled it to achieve a speed of 400.87 km/h (248.5 mph) in August 1986.

The highest a helicopter has ever flown is 12.44 km (7.69 mi). An SA-315B Lama built by the French company Aérospatiale achieved this record over France in 1972.

The first helicopter pilot's license was issued to British Wing Commander Reginald Brie, the former chief test pilot of the Cierva Autogiro Company in 1947.

The world's first heliport opened at Pier 41 in New York City on May 23, 1949.

The first successful autogyro flight was made by the Spanish engineer Juan de la Cierva, on January 9, 1923, with his model C.4 craft. This consisted of a rotor mounted on the fuselage of a single-engine aircraft.

Chapter Ten

COMBAT AIRCRAFT

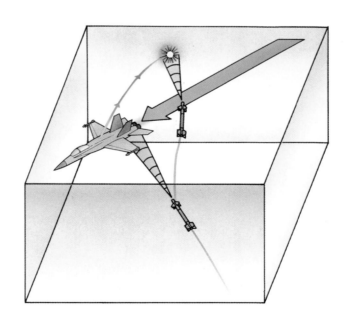

CONTENTS

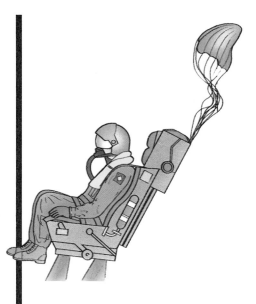

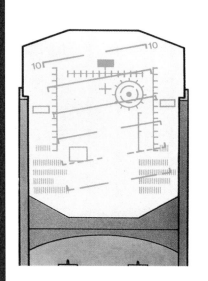

WORKING PARTS

A combat aircraft is a flying weapons machine. The McDonnell Douglas F-18 Hornet shown here is 18.6 yards long, 13 yards across its wing-tips and, with a full fuel and weapons load, weighs 21 tons. It is powered by two turbofan engines, each producing almost 16,500 lbs of pushing force, or thrust.

In flight, the aircraft is controlled by three major structures. Ailerons in the trailing edges of the wings hinge, one up and the other down, to make the craft roll to one side or the other. In the tailplane, elevators move up or down together to lower or raise the tail.

Rudders in the tail fins hinge to the left or right and push the tail in the opposite direction to help turn the craft.

Apart from these basic "control surfaces," which most aircraft have, combat aircraft have a number of extra

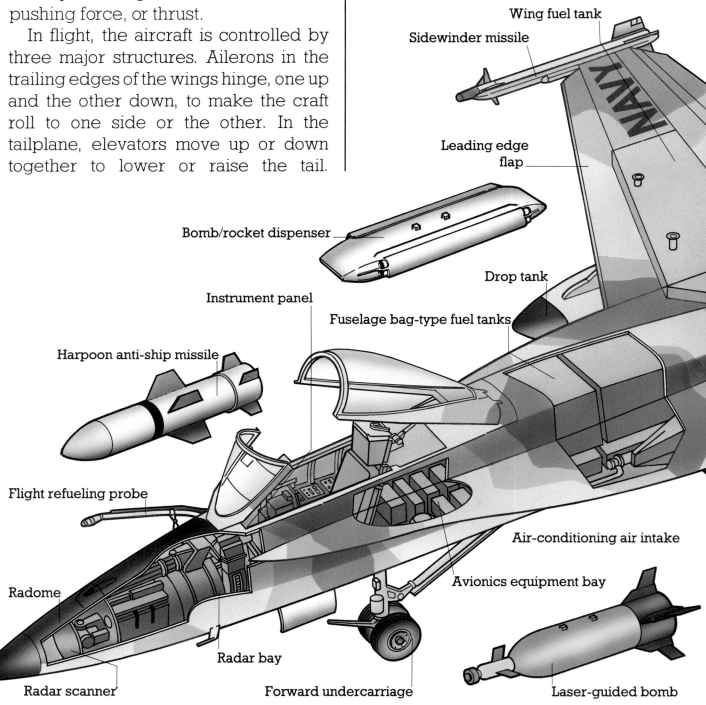

Wing fuel tank

Sidewinder missile

Leading edge flap

Bomb/rocket dispenser

Drop tank

Instrument panel

Fuselage bag-type fuel tanks

Harpoon anti-ship missile

Flight refueling probe

Air-conditioning air intake

Radome

Avionics equipment bay

Radar bay

Radar scanner

Forward undercarriage

Laser-guided bomb

features. A panel in the tail section, called an airbrake, can be raised to slow the aircraft down. The F-18 has wings with both leading and trailing edge flaps to improve its performance at a range of speeds and in tight combat maneuvers. Attachment points called pylons enable bombs, rockets and missiles to be hung underneath the aircraft. Finally, the F-18 is packed with electronic systems including a sensitive radar scanner inside its nose-cone.

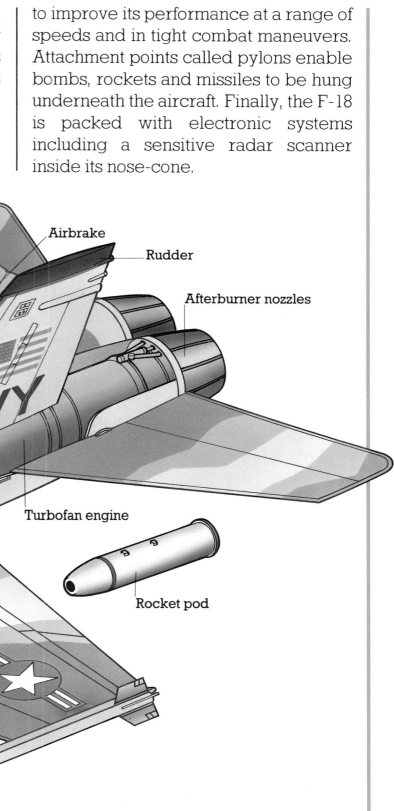

Tailplane

Single slotted flap

Airbrake

Rudder

Afterburner nozzles

NAVY

Turbofan engine

Rocket pod

Aft (rear) undercarriage

THE JET ENGINE

Modern combat aircraft are powered by one or more jet engines. In a jet engine, air is heated and so expands, creating thrust. With the gas turbine – the power unit that is commonly called a jet engine – cold air is sucked in at the front and then heated. The air expands and forces its way out fast through the engine's exhaust pipe. It is this "jet" of hot exhaust gases that gives the engine its popular name.

The first jet engines were designed and built by Sir Frank Whittle in Britain in 1930. They enabled aircraft to fly much faster than was possible with the piston engines used at the time. These were similar to car engines.

There are different types of jet engine. The most common is the turbofan. A large, many-bladed fan at the front of the engine draws in air. Only part of the air is sucked into the engine and heated; the rest just flows around it. This type of engine is quieter than the simplest type of jet engine, called a turbojet. A gas turbine can also be used to spin a propeller. In this case, the engine is known as a turboprop.

Air sucked into an engine by a turbofan passes through a compressor. This device "squeezes" the air, thereby increasing the air pressure inside the engine. The air is then forced into a combustion chamber. Fuel is sprayed into this and the air-fuel mixture is burned. The hot, expanding gases that are produced rush out of the engine through a

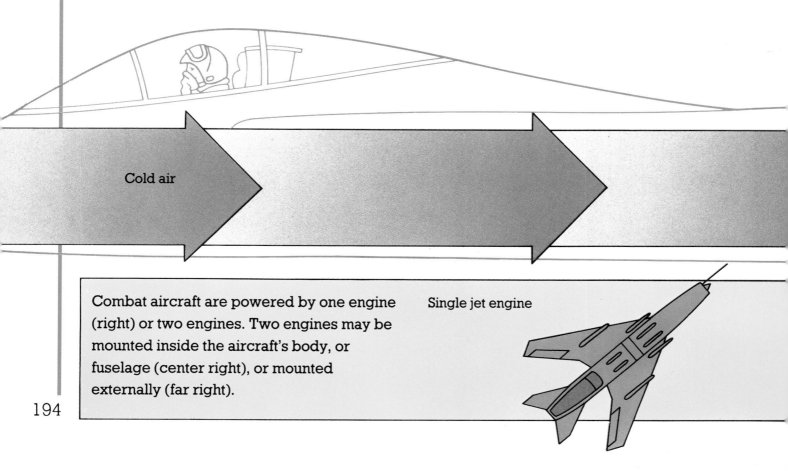

Cold air

Combat aircraft are powered by one engine (right) or two engines. Two engines may be mounted inside the aircraft's body, or fuselage (center right), or mounted externally (far right).

Single jet engine

Military aircraft use their afterburners in short bursts.

turbine, which drives the compressor. Engine power can be boosted by burning more fuel in the exhaust. This process is often called afterburning or reheat.

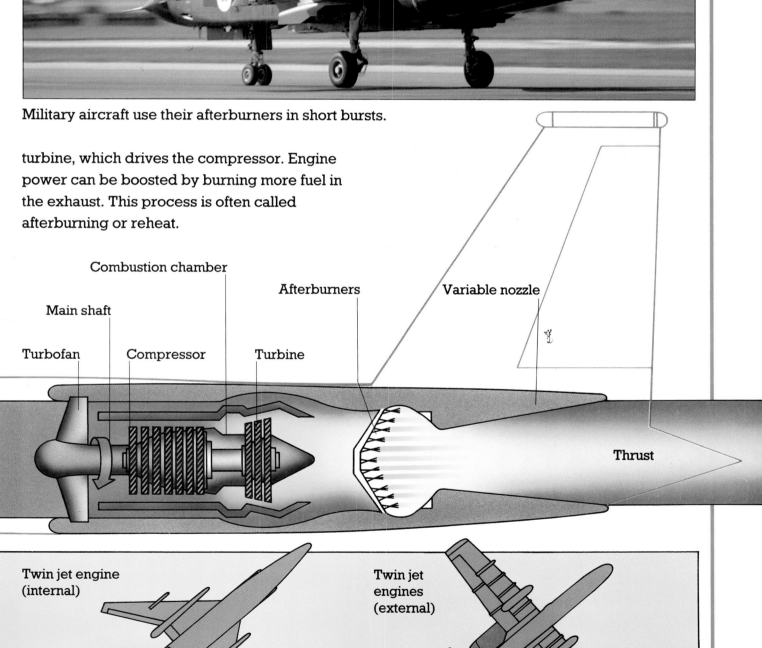

Combustion chamber

Main shaft

Afterburners

Variable nozzle

Turbofan   Compressor   Turbine

Thrust

Twin jet engine (internal)

Twin jet engines (external)

THE WINGS

All combat aircraft are heavier than air. In order to fly, they must create an upward force, called lift, to overcome their weight. This is done by the wings.

As an aircraft travels forward on the ground, its wings divide the air streaming past the craft into two flows. Some air is deflected over the top of each wing and the rest flows underneath it. The wing is shaped so that air has to travel farther over the curved top surface than the flatter lower surface. This makes the air above the wing flow faster than the air underneath it. This produces a difference in air pressure above and below the wing, and it is this pressure difference that produces the upward force of lift.

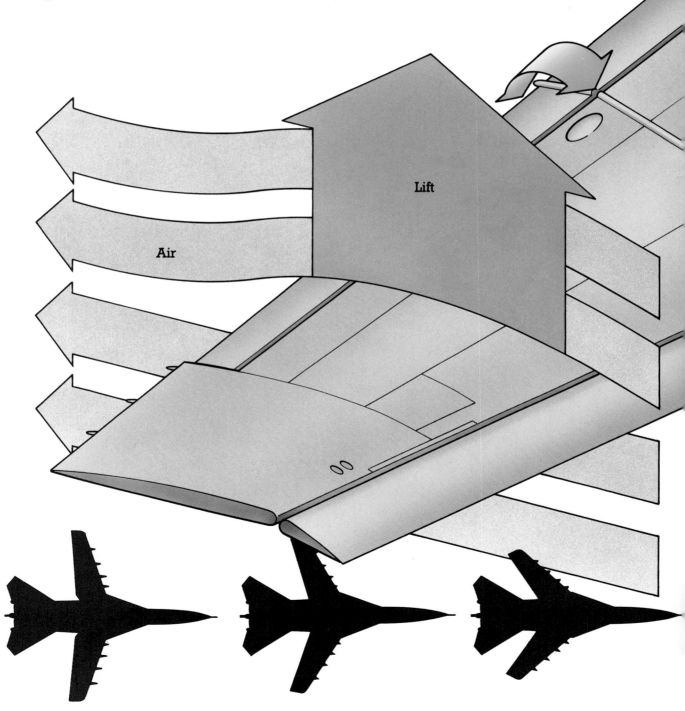

Air

Lift

If an aircraft's speed increases, the difference in air pressure produced by the wings increases and so the amount of lift produced also increases. When the lift becomes greater than the aircraft's weight, the aircraft begins to rise into the air. Equally, as an aircraft slows, the amount of lift decreases and the craft begins to descend.

At very low air-speeds, the air flow around the wings may break up. If so, the wings lose all lift, which is called stalling. Movable extensions along the edge of the wings, called leading edge slats, help stop the air flow from breaking up and maintain lift.

In swing-wing aircraft, the wings are spread wide for slow flight and to carry heavy loads. With fully swept-back wings, drag is reduced and highspeed flight is possible.

An aircraft's wings are shaped according to its speed and agility. The A-10 Thunderbolt's broad straight wings are best for slow flight and tight turns. Swept-back wings are better for high-speed flight. The delta is the most efficient shape for supersonic (faster than sound) flight. Small wings called canards on the aircraft's nose increase lift during take off and landing. Extending flaps along the trailing edge of wings helps to stop the aircraft losing lift.

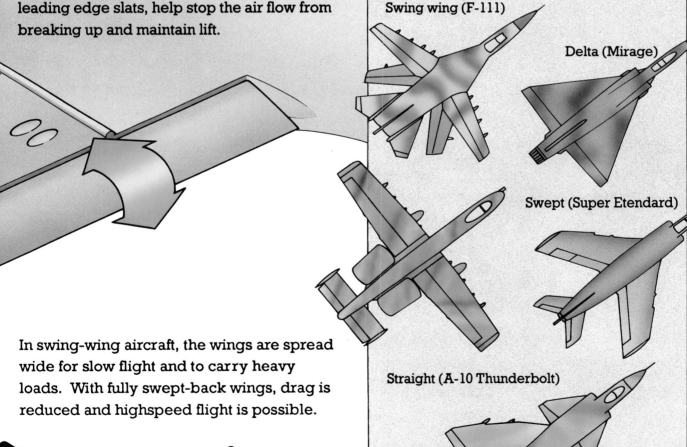

Swing wing (F-111)

Delta (Mirage)

Swept (Super Etendard)

Straight (A-10 Thunderbolt)

Canard foreplanes (Saab Viggen)

197

FLYING THE AIRCRAFT

If the pilot of a passenger aircraft were to let go of the controls, the plane would continue to fly straight and level. However, some combat aircrafts would fly all over the place because they are not designed for stability, but agility. This makes them more nimble in the air, but also more difficult to fly. Only computers work fast enough to make tiny adjustments to the control surfaces - perhaps 100 times every second - to keep the aircraft under control.

As the pilot of a combat aircraft moves the flight controls, their movements are turned into electrical signals. These pass along wires to computers, where they are interpreted and processed in order to operate the plane's control surfaces. The system is known as fly-by-wire. Other systems, like navigation and terrain following radar, also send data to the flight computers.

Important data is projected onto a glass screen in front of the pilot. All the data on this Head-Up Display (HUD) can be seen without having to look down into the cockpit.

If a combat aircraft's Terrain Following Radar (TFR) detects dangerously high ground ahead, it can automatically pull the aircraft up to clear the obstacle safely. The radar operates continuously during flights.

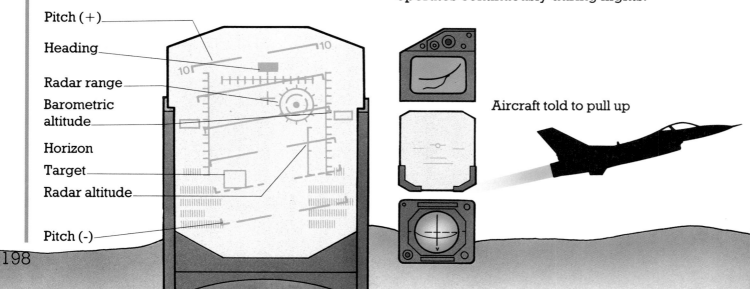

Pitch (+)
Heading
Radar range
Barometric altitude
Horizon
Target
Radar altitude
Pitch (-)

Aircraft told to pull up

The F-16's fly-by-wire (FBW) computers combine the pilot's control movements with data from motion sensors to set the plane's control surface (aileron, elevator and rudder) positions.

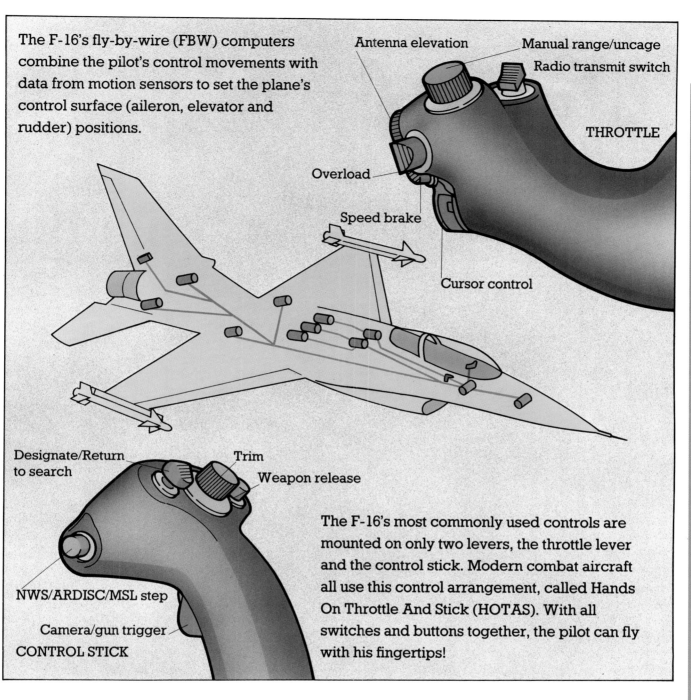

Antenna elevation

Manual range/uncage

Radio transmit switch

THROTTLE

Overload

Speed brake

Cursor control

Designate/Return to search

Trim

Weapon release

NWS/ARDISC/MSL step

Camera/gun trigger

CONTROL STICK

The F-16's most commonly used controls are mounted on only two levers, the throttle lever and the control stick. Modern combat aircraft all use this control arrangement, called Hands On Throttle And Stick (HOTAS). With all switches and buttons together, the pilot can fly with his fingertips!

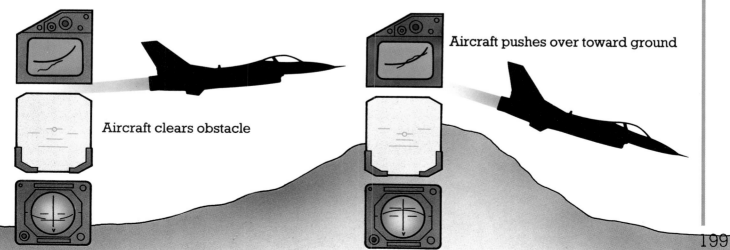

Aircraft clears obstacle

Aircraft pushes over toward ground

Electronic displays in the cockpit give the pilot vital information.

An incoming fighter uses its radar to show the position and range of any other aircraft nearby. But using the radar also gives away its presence to intercepting aircraft.

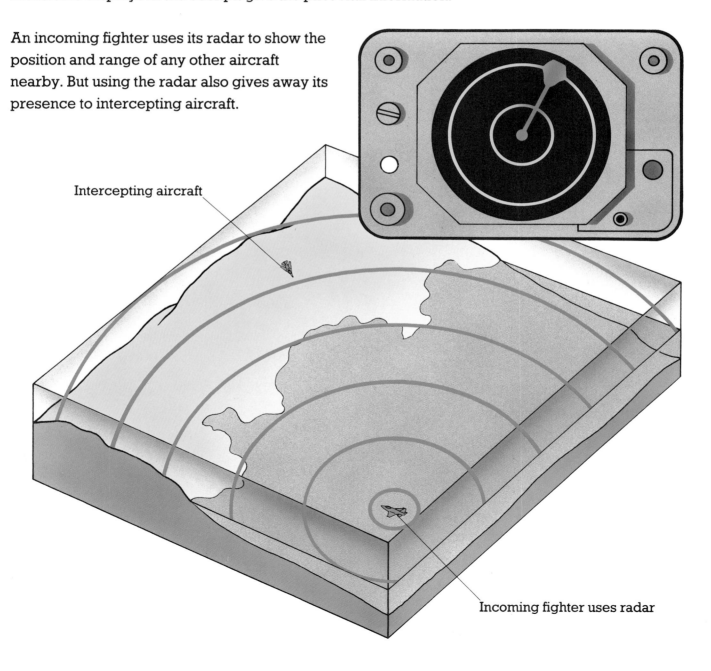

Intercepting aircraft

Incoming fighter uses radar

NAVIGATION AND RADAR

To detect the approach of enemy aircraft long before they can be seen, a combat aircraft pilot uses radar. This works by transmitting radio waves and detecting any reflections that bounce back from solid objects like aircraft. The reflections (echoes) are presented as bright dots on a television screen, showing where the objects are and their distance from the transmitter.

When a radar system based on land or on a ship at sea detects approaching enemy aircraft, messages are sent to combat pilots to fly their aircraft on a course that will intercept them. The outgoing aircraft navigate (follow the correct flightpath) using a system that senses the planes' movements, and calculates how far they have moved from their start-point and in which direction. The system can be checked and altered by signals from navigational satellites or from radio beacons in known positions on the ground.

This F-16B Fighting Falcon carries a crew of two.

ATTACK!

Fighter pilots try whenever possible to take their airborne targets by surprise. They may do this in one of two ways.

Firstly, the attacking fighters may fly at very low level underneath enemy radar to avoid detection and only come up to attack height at the last moment. The best position for the attacking aircraft is directly behind the targets. This is because the target aircraft can only attack from the front, and their engine exhausts are in full view of the attacker's heat-seeking missiles.

Secondly, the attack force may present targets with a decoy. A pair of fighters approach the target aircraft head-on as if they are to attack. They pull away, though, without firing. While the targets are giving all their attention to the decoys, the real attack pair have flown around behind the targets.

The Thunderbolt can destroy light tanks with its gun

A surprise attack from the rear is not always possible. In the example shown, a pair of fighters have detected a pair of enemy aircraft flying directly towards them (1). The enemy craft are approaching at high speed, so the attackers act fast. The two fighters fly several miles to one side of the targets' flight line and approach the enemy craft from the side. One fighter's attack radar locks on to the first target (2). When one attacker (the "eyeball") comes within visual range of the first target, the second attacker (the "shooter") is instructed to fire a missile at the second target (3). If the missile is successful, the second target can be fought at visual range by both attackers using guns and missiles. All of this action takes place within less than a minute.

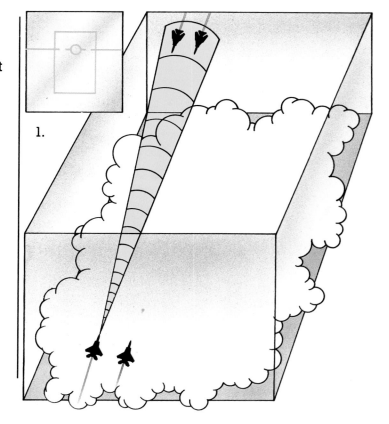

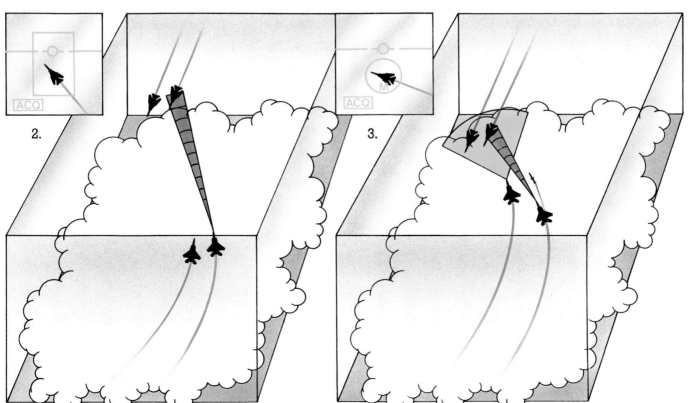

2.

3.

DEFENSE

An aircraft can be defended from a missile attack in several ways. Missiles guided by radar lock on to the largest radar reflection. A cloud of metal fibers called chaff can be blown into the air to form a larger target than the aircraft. Alternatively, a transmitter known as a jammer can send out radio signals to confuse a radar-guided missile.

Infrared homing missiles can easily be confused by the firing of burning flares out of the aircraft under attack. The missiles follow the flares instead of the aircraft.

A missile's rocket motor fires for a very short time. After that, the missile is gliding. If it has to turn in the air, it slows more rapidly than in straight flight. By twisting and turning, an aircraft may be able to outrun the slowing missile.

A Surface-to-Air Missile (SAM).

If a pilot fears an attack from heat-seeking missiles, one defense against them is to eject flares whose heat may divert the missiles.

Radar-guided missiles home in on the largest radar reflection, whether this is an aircraft or a cloud of hair-like metal fibers or chaff.

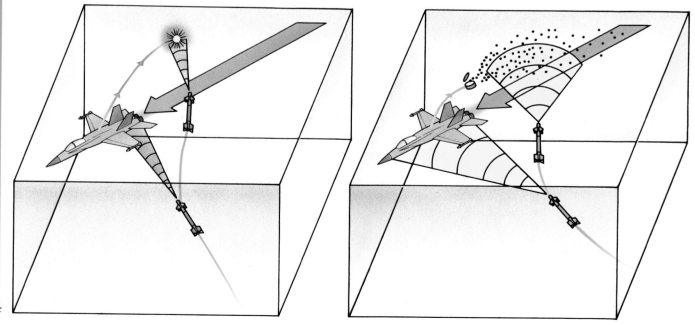

When flying in formation, fighters form a large target and are especially vulnerable.

A missile's radar guidance system can be jammed by transmitting misleading radio signals into the missile's flight path.

A missile's motor burns out soon after launch. If the target aircraft maneuvers as the missile slows down, it may be able to outrun it.

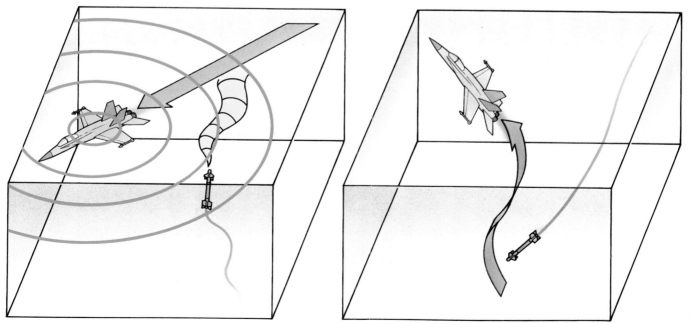

DOGFIGHT

In combat between two aircraft, the attacking pilot tries to place his aircraft in the best position to fire at the other aircraft. The defender rolls and turns his aircraft to avoid the attacker's guns. The fast moving series of attack and defense maneuvers is called a dogfight.

Every fighter pilot is trained in the maneuvers that can be flown in a dogfight to gain the advantage against an enemy. Each attack maneuver has a defensive countermove. Even with electronic aids, one pilot on his own cannot constantly watch the whole sky for enemy fighters.

Because of this, fighter aircraft normally hunt for their enemies in pairs. Two aircraft flying side by side some 2 miles apart in "combat spread formation" are better able to protect each other. Each pilot watches the other's tail, as this is the most likely direction of an attack.

If an aircraft is in danger of crashing, the pilot can save himself by using his ejector seat. First the canopy over his head is blown off. Then rockets under the seat fire and force it out of the cockpit. The pilot and the seat descend to the ground slowly and safely by parachute.

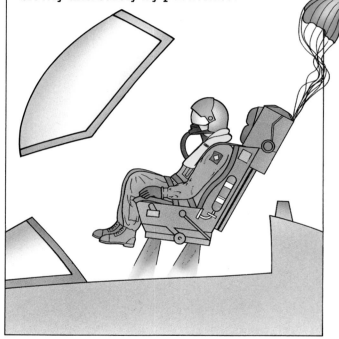

An F-16 fires a missile at high speed.

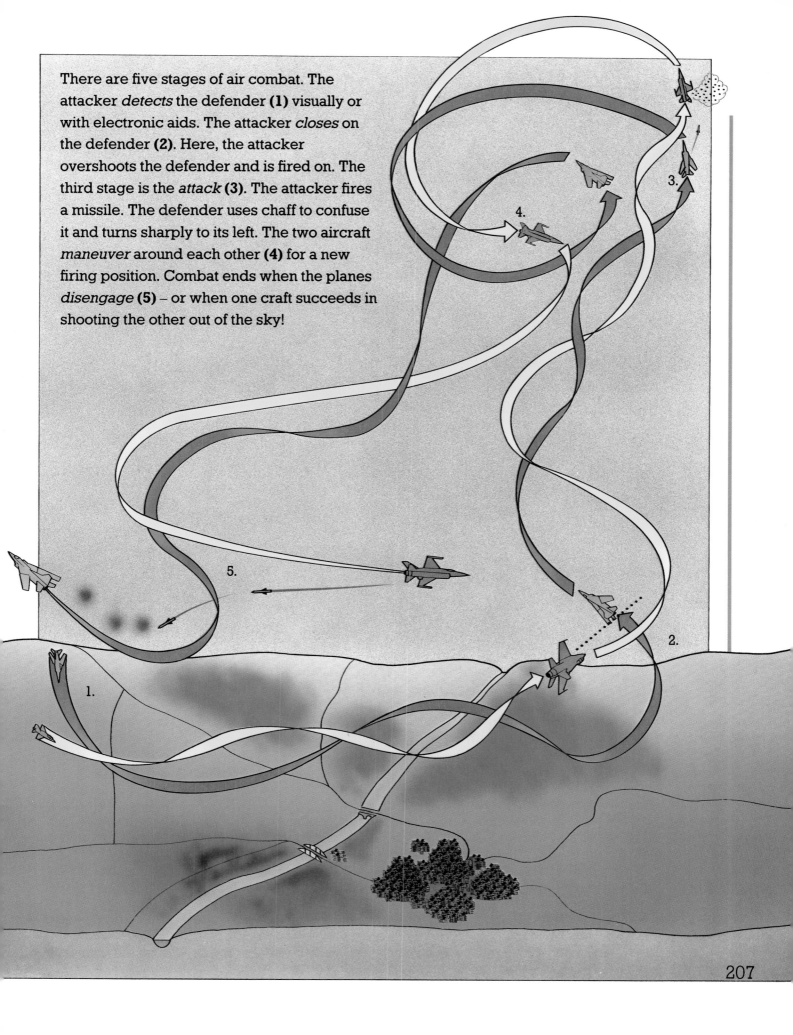

There are five stages of air combat. The attacker *detects* the defender **(1)** visually or with electronic aids. The attacker *closes* on the defender **(2)**. Here, the attacker overshoots the defender and is fired on. The third stage is the *attack* **(3)**. The attacker fires a missile. The defender uses chaff to confuse it and turns sharply to its left. The two aircraft *maneuver* around each other **(4)** for a new firing position. Combat ends when the planes *disengage* **(5)** – or when one craft succeeds in shooting the other out of the sky!

THE FUTURE

Today's research will, in the next 10 to 20 years, produce combat aircraft that look and behave quite differently from existing aircraft. They will make more use of stealth technology and electronic defense systems to avoid detection by radar. Stealth requirements will result in aircraft with a more rounded shape. The use of new construction materials will enable wings to be made thinner and to be swept far forward instead of backward. The Forward Swept Wing (FSW) fighters can be made smaller, lighter and more maneuverable than any of today's ordinary fighters.

As the number and complexity of electronic aids fitted inside aircraft increase, pilots will need more help from computers to reduce the amount of information they have to take in, think about and act upon.

Almost all existing fighters and attack aircraft depend on long concrete runways for take off and landing. The ease with which runways can be bombed may result in more Short Take Off and Vertical Landing (STOVL) combat aircraft like the Harrier.

The Grumman X-29 Forward Swept Wing fighter.

The first Forward Swept Wing aircraft, code named the X-29, was designed and built by the American company Grumman. Its computers carry out 80 control actions each second. It is a test-bed for the technology that fighters of the next century will use.

The Lockheed F-117A "stealth" fighter.

Stealth fighters have fewer flat or vertical surfaces or sharp edges than other fighters. Instead, they have smooth joints, rounded edges and angled fins to reduce the strength of the radar beam reflected back to the enemy. This makes the aircraft more difficult to detect. To date, almost all stealth technology has been developed in the United States.

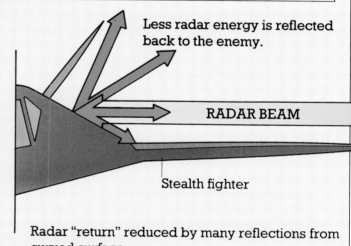

Less radar energy is reflected back to the enemy.

RADAR BEAM

Stealth fighter

Radar "return" reduced by many reflections from curved surface.

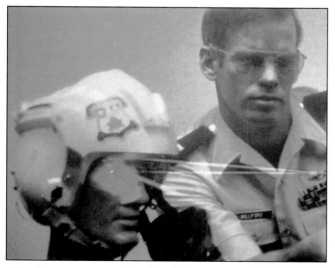

Aiming weapons by looking at a target.

Fighter-systems designers are experimenting with new ways of selecting, aiming and firing weapons. The Helmet Pointing System (HPS), for example, enables pilots to aim a gun or a missile at a target simply by looking at the target. Sensors in the helmet follow, or track, the pilot's eye movements and feed this information, via the aircraft's computers, to the weapons. The positions of several targets can be stored and tracked simultaneously by advanced versions of the system. The pilot then judges which target is the best, easiest or least dangerous to attack.

HISTORY OF COMBAT AIRCRAFT

The history of combat aircraft is almost as old as powered flight. The first controlled flight of a powered aircraft was made by the Wright brothers in 1903. Eleven years later, World War I began. Unlike today's single-wing (one per side) aircraft, many of the early fighters used in the war had two wings. They were called biplanes. Some, like the Fokker Dr. I Triplane, had three. The craft were powered by piston engines driving propellers. They were made from wooden frames covered by stretched canvas, and they carried machine guns. The propellers were linked to the gun's firing mechanism so that the guns fired only when the propeller blades were not in front of them. The pilots navigated by following landmarks such as railway lines.

The World War I Fokker Dr. I Triplane.

After World War I, fighter development continued. The monoplane (single wing) with a tail plane and fin at the rear became the standard aircraft design. Metal replaced wood as the material for the aircraft frame, but this remained covered by canvas until metal "skins" were introduced in the 1930s.

The Supermarine Spitfire.

World War I fighters had to hunt for the enemy by sight. In World War II, enemy aircraft could be detected by radar. Fighters were instructed to "scramble" (take off) and were guided to the enemy by radio messages. The most successful fighters of the war included the British Spitfire, the American Mustang, Germany's Focke-Wulf 190 and Japan's Zero. All were fast, agile, single-engine aircraft. In 1944, the first jet fighters, the British Gloster Meteor and the German Messerschmitt 262, entered service. By the 1950s, fighters could fly faster than sound (760 mph, or Mach 1). The F-100 Super Sabre was the first such "supersonic" fighter.

The supersonic F-100 Super Sabre.

Guided missiles enabled aircraft to attack from beyond visual range for the first time. This led to new electronic detection systems. In the late 1970s, "variable geometry," or swing wing, aircraft like the F-14 combined supersonic speeds with excellent low-speed performance. The Harrier first showed the value of Short Take Off and Vertical Landing (STOVL) fighters that do not need runways. To counter the Soviet MiG-25, the United States developed the F-15 Eagle, and the F-16 used fly-by-wire technology.

The General Dynamics F-16.

Combat aircraft are so expensive that each must be able to carry out more than one type of mission. The F-18 Hornet and the Panavia Tornado were developed as "multi-role" aircraft. In the 1980s, stealth technology has begun to influence fighter design, to minimize their radar reflections.

FACTS AND FIGURES

The gas turbine (or jet) engine was invented in 1930 by the British engineer Sir Frank Whittle.

The world's first jet-powered aircraft, the Heinkel 178, flew for the first time in Germany in 1939.

The first jet fighter to enter service was the Messerschmitt 262 in 1944.

The first and only rocket-powered fighter was the Messerschmitt 163 "Komet" (1944).

The most powerful gun carried by a combat aircraft is the Fairchild A-10 Thunderbolt's GAU-8/A Avenger. It can fire up to 4,200 rounds a minute.

The world's fastest combat aircraft is the Soviet MiG-25 interceptor, with a top speed of 2,108 mph.

A bomb was dropped from an aircraft for the first time in 1910, when the U.S. Army Signal Corps dropped a homemade bomb from an aircraft in San Francisco.

The earliest recorded ground attack was in November 1911, when Italian airmen dropped bombs on Turkish troops.

The first recorded episode of air combat took place on October 5, 1914. A French airman shot down a German Aviatik B1 aircraft with his machine gun.

Chapter Eleven
SPACE
SHUTTLES

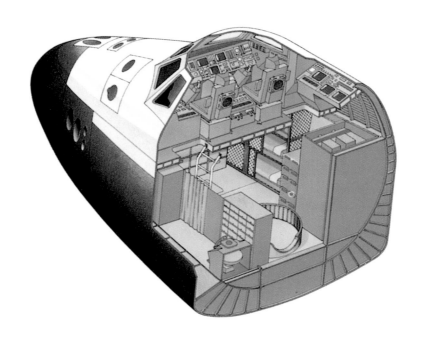

CONTENTS

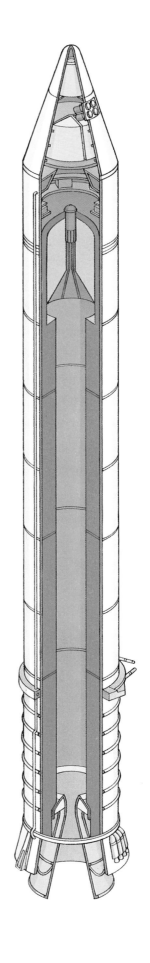

THE WORKING PARTS

A Space Shuttle is a rocket-powered craft used to transport people, satellites and scientific experiments between the Earth and space. To do this, it must be able to fly in the Earth's atmosphere and in space. Unlike most rockets, which are used only once, a Space Shuttle is reusable. It can be used for many missions.

Shown here is the aircraft-like Orbiter, part of the United States' Space Shuttle. It has a large storage area, the payload bay, measuring 18 m (60 ft) long by 4.5 m (14 ft) wide for carrying cargo.

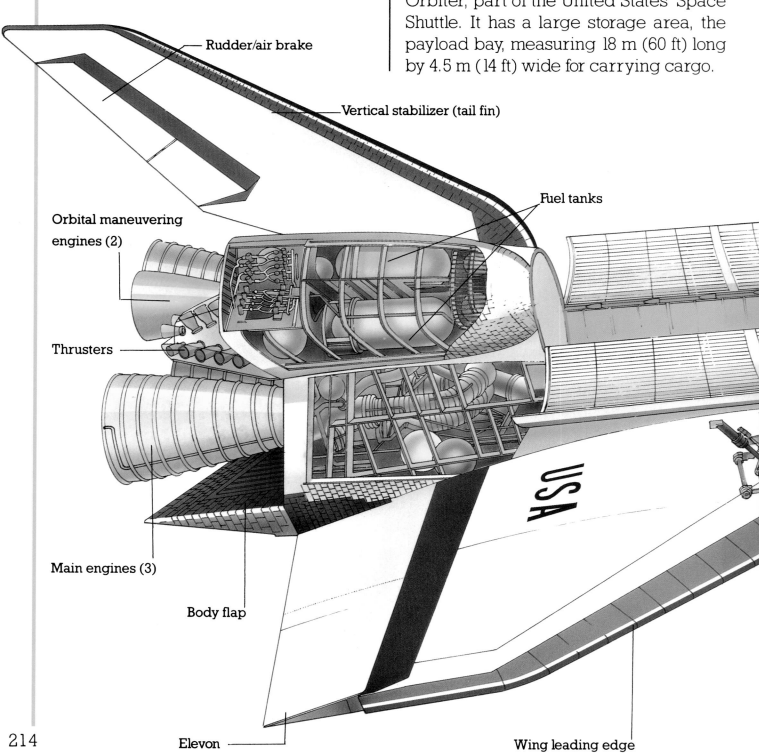

Rudder/air brake

Vertical stabilizer (tail fin)

Fuel tanks

Orbital maneuvering engines (2)

Thrusters

Main engines (3)

Body flap

Elevon

Wing leading edge

When the payload bay doors are opened, radiators inside them help to cool the Orbiter by allowing heat to flow from them into space. A robot arm is used to move objects into or out of the payload bay.

In front of this bay is the crew compartment, where the astronauts live and work. The tail of the Orbiter houses five rocket engines. Three of them, called Space Shuttle Main Engines (SSMEs), are the most advanced liquid-fueled rocket engines ever built. Their nozzles can be turned to steer the craft and their power can be varied to control the Orbiter's speed. The SSMEs

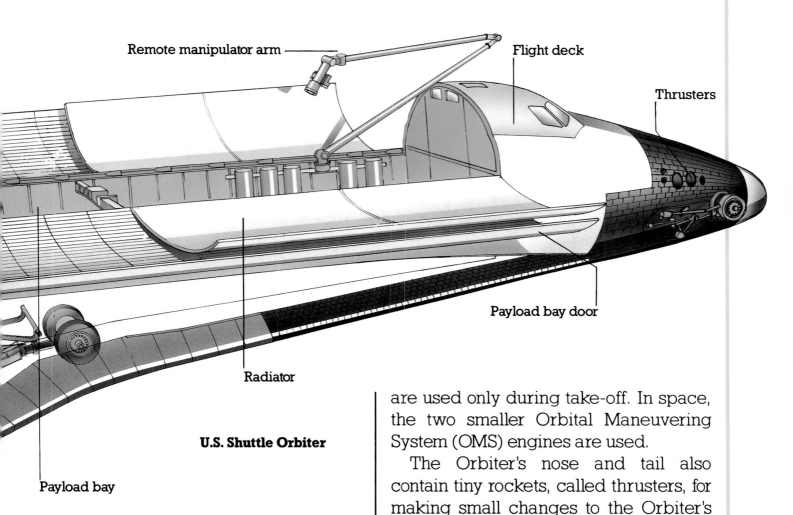

Remote manipulator arm

Flight deck

Thrusters

Payload bay door

Radiator

U.S. Shuttle Orbiter

Payload bay

are used only during take-off. In space, the two smaller Orbital Maneuvering System (OMS) engines are used.

The Orbiter's nose and tail also contain tiny rockets, called thrusters, for making small changes to the Orbiter's position. The Orbiter's wings have movable flaps called elevons. These, together with the body flap beneath the engines and the rudder, enable the Orbiter to maneuver when it re-enters the atmosphere before landing.

The U.S. Shuttle is carried to its launch site. The used SRBs fall away from the craft.

The outline of a typical Space Shuttle flight is shown below. On average, a flight lasts for about 7 days, although flights of up to 30 days are possible.

The external tank is discarded when it is almost empty

The Orbiter is propelled into orbit by its orbital maneuvering engines

Orbital operations (such as launching a satellite) take place

The solid rocket boosters are discarded at a height of about 45 kilometres

The tank breaks up in the atmosphere and falls into the ocean

The Space Shuttle is launched with three main engines and two rocket boosters

The boosters parachute down to the sea and are picked up by ship

THE REUSABLE CRAFT

Before the U.S. Space Shuttle came into service in 1981, astronauts and satellites were launched by rockets that were used only once and then scrapped. A different type of launcher was needed for a new Space Transportation System (STS). It would be a mixture of aircraft and spacecraft that could be used many times. The result is the Space Shuttle.

The Shuttle has three parts - the Orbiter, the Solid Rocket Boosters (SRBs) and the external fuel tank. After its work in space, the Orbiter returns to Earth and is used again. The two SRBs are also used again. When their job is finished, they parachute into the sea where they are collected by ship and used on a future flight.

The external fuel tank is not reusable. It is destroyed when it is dropped into the atmosphere during take-off to burn up or fall into the ocean.

Each Space Shuttle Orbiter should be capable of flying on 100 missions. The SRBs are designed to last for about 20 flights each. The precise lifetime and the number of flights an Orbiter or SRB is used for depends on the results of tests carried out after each flight.

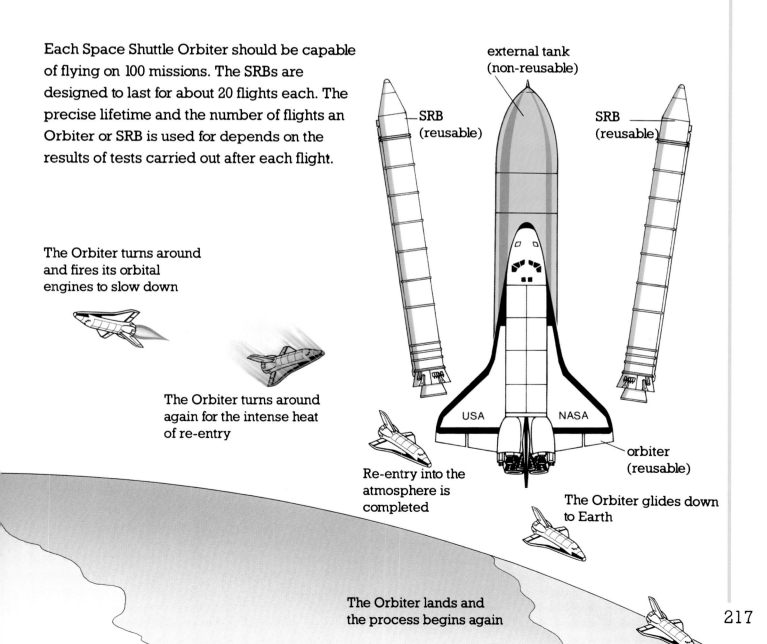

The Orbiter turns around and fires its orbital engines to slow down

The Orbiter turns around again for the intense heat of re-entry

Re-entry into the atmosphere is completed

external tank (non-reusable)

SRB (reusable)

SRB (reusable)

orbiter (reusable)

The Orbiter glides down to Earth

USA   NASA

The Orbiter lands and the process begins again

TAKE-OFF

The events leading up to a Space Shuttle launch happen according to a timetable called the countdown. The final part of the countdown begins 5 hours before take-off, or at T minus (T−)5:00:00, when technicians go onboard the Orbiter and make sure that all its hundreds of switches are set correctly. At T−4:30:00, filling of the external fuel tank with hydrogen and oxygen begins.

The crew enters the Orbiter at T−1:50:00 and checks its systems, such as communications and guidance. The countdown clock is stopped several times before take-off for a few minutes (longer if necessary), to allow for any unexpected problems to be dealt with. These stops are called "holds." The final planned hold, of 10 minutes, starts at 19 minutes before take-off.

Three seconds before take-off (T−0:00:03), the three main engines are ignited. If the Orbiter's computers detect any faults, the engines can be shut down. If all is well, the two SRBs are fired. Once the SRBs fire, the Shuttle must take off. Clamps holding the craft down and keeping it steady are released and it lifts off the launchpad with tremendous force and noise.

A U.S. Space Shuttle launch (left) is controlled by the Kennedy Space Center at Cape Canaveral, Florida. When the Shuttle rises above the launch tower, less than 7 seconds after lift-off, "Mission Control" at the Johnson Space Center in Texas (above) takes over. It keeps constant links with the astronauts.

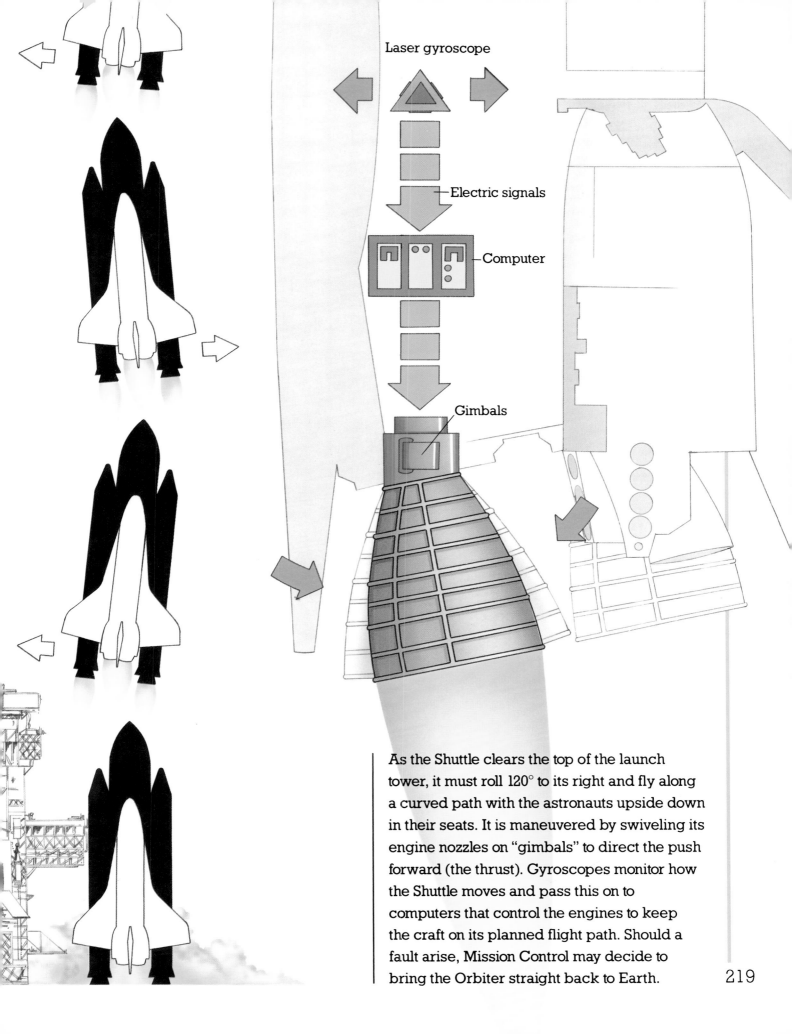

Laser gyroscope

Electric signals

Computer

Gimbals

As the Shuttle clears the top of the launch tower, it must roll 120° to its right and fly along a curved path with the astronauts upside down in their seats. It is maneuvered by swiveling its engine nozzles on "gimbals" to direct the push forward (the thrust). Gyroscopes monitor how the Shuttle moves and pass this on to computers that control the engines to keep the craft on its planned flight path. Should a fault arise, Mission Control may decide to bring the Orbiter straight back to Earth.

219

Liquid hydrogen and oxygen are pumped into the main engine and heated to 760°C by pre-burners. The hot gases are then mixed and burned in a combustion chamber at 3,300°C. Some cold fuel is pumped into tubes around the nozzle to cool it. Each engine is designed for 7.5 hours use before needing to be serviced. At 8 minutes use per flight, it should last for 55 flights.

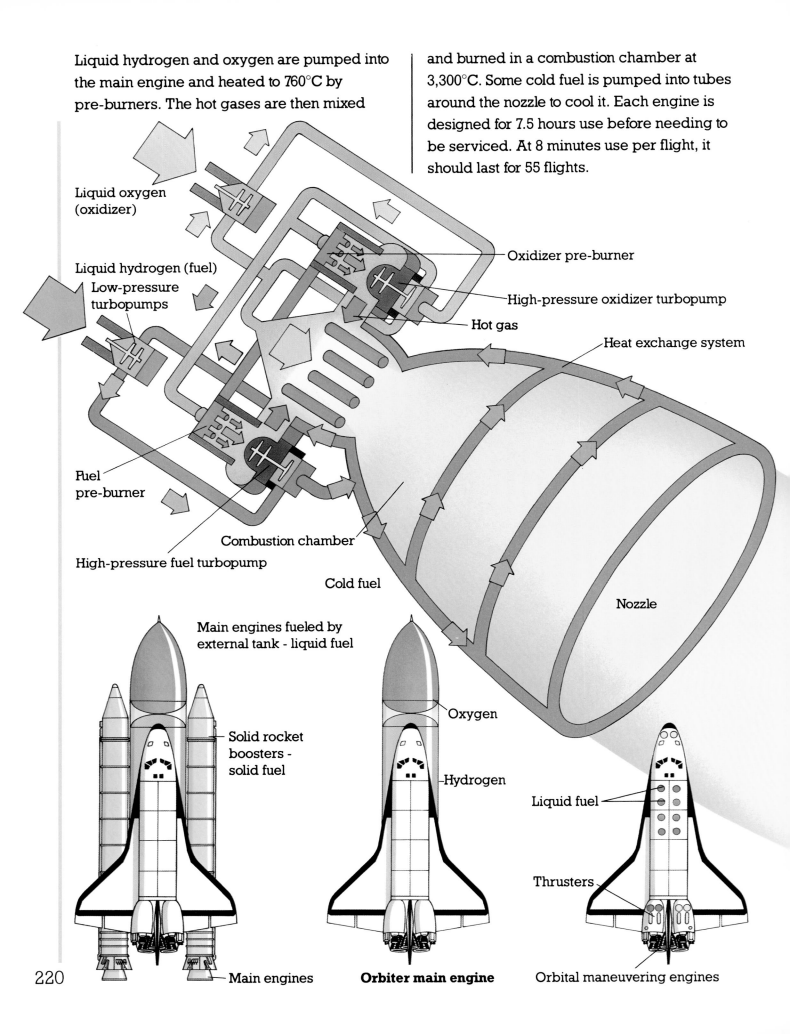

Liquid oxygen (oxidizer)

Liquid hydrogen (fuel)
Low-pressure turbopumps

Oxidizer pre-burner

High-pressure oxidizer turbopump

Hot gas

Heat exchange system

Fuel pre-burner

High-pressure fuel turbopump

Combustion chamber

Cold fuel

Nozzle

Main engines fueled by external tank - liquid fuel

Solid rocket boosters - solid fuel

Oxygen

Hydrogen

Liquid fuel

Thrusters

220

Main engines

Orbiter main engine

Orbital maneuvering engines

CREATING THE POWER

The Space Shuttle's engines work by burning a fuel mixed with an oxidizer. The oxidizer provides oxygen which is essential for burning. (The oxidizer may be oxygen itself.) The fuel and oxidizer mixture is known as the propellant.

The Orbiter's main engines burn hydrogen fuel and oxygen pumped from containers in the external tank at over 300,000 liters per minute. The hot gases produced by burning the propellant rush out of the engines nozzles, which can be swiveled to help steer the Shuttle. The engine power can be varied to control the Shuttle's speed. Each engine produces thrust capable of lifting a 170,000 kg (370,000lb) weight.

Each of the two booster rockets is a 45 m (148 ft) long tube packed with solid propellant, mainly a mixture of aluminum powder fuel and an oxidizer, ammonium perchlorate. Once each booster is ignited, it cannot be turned off. It burns until its fuel is used up. It produces 1.4 million kilograms of thrust.

In only two minutes, each solid fuel rocket booster consumes all of its 1,350,000lbs of propellant to help the shuttle take off. When the Orbiter is in space, it uses two liquid fueled engines, the orbital manoevering engines, to change its orbit and forty-four tiny rocket motors, the thrusters (left), to to make fine adjustments to its position. The thrusters are arranged in three groups - on the Orbiter's nose and on either side of its tail. When switched on, the orbital manoeuvering engine, releases a volatile liquid, which has been turned into gas.

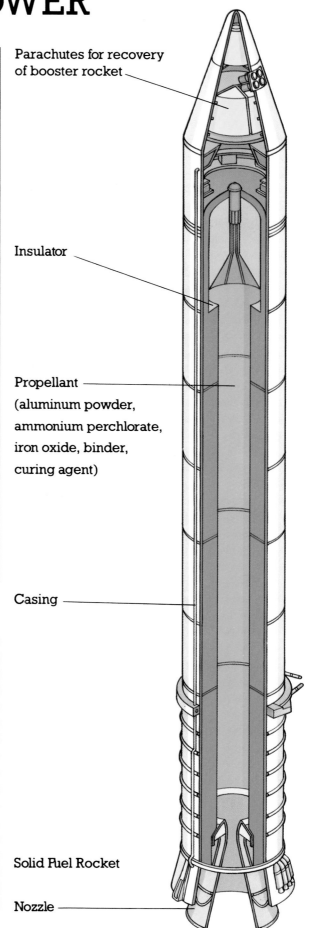

Parachutes for recovery of booster rocket

Insulator

Propellant (aluminum powder, ammonium perchlorate, iron oxide, binder, curing agent)

Casing

Solid Fuel Rocket

Nozzle

IN ORBIT

While the Shuttle is in orbit, it provides an Earth-like atmosphere for the crew members. They do not need to wear spacesuits. Instead they wear a loose-fitting jacket, shirt and pants.

The Orbiter has a small galley with an oven for preparing food. The astronauts sleep inside bags called sleep restraints to stop them from floating weightlessly around the shuttle. The Orbiter has four beds, or sleep stations. Three are horizontal and one is vertical, but as the astronauts are weightless, they are not aware of their orientation. Only four beds are needed because not all of the crew (of up to seven) will rest at the same time. Of course the Orbiter has a toilet. Unlike a toilet on Earth, the Orbiter's has handles and foot straps to keep an astronaut from floating off it!

Electrical power for the Orbiter is made by combining oxygen and hydrogen in fuel cells. A byproduct of this chemical reaction is water. This is used for drinking, washing, preparing food and cooling the cabin. About 3 kg (7lb) of water is produced every hour; up to 150 kg (330lb) can be stored in tanks. Excess water is dumped in space via outlet valves.

Secure in a sleep station on board the Orbiter

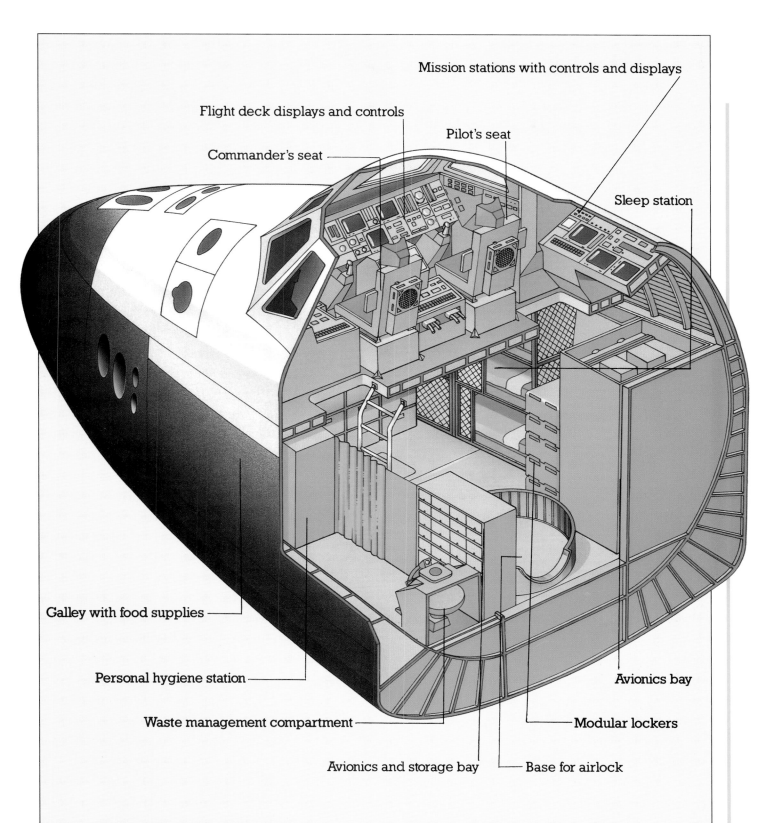

Mission stations with controls and displays

Flight deck displays and controls

Pilot's seat

Commander's seat

Sleep station

Galley with food supplies

Personal hygiene station

Waste management compartment

Avionics bay

Modular lockers

Avionics and storage bay

Base for airlock

The Orbiter has three decks, built one above the other. The commander and pilot control the Orbiter from the top level. This is called the flight deck, and here each of these two crew members has an instrument panel and controls so that either can fly the craft. The mid deck contains the galley, sleep restraints and supplies. The lower deck contains equipment that controls and cleans the air supply to the Orbiter. Food prepared and eaten on the Orbiter is similar to that served on passenger airlines.

AT WORK IN SPACE

Astronauts may have to work outside the Orbiter. To do this, they must put on a protective spacesuit and backpack. The backpack contains enough oxygen to breathe for 6 hours in space. Before putting the suit on, the astronaut breathes through a face-mask for a time to change gradually from the Orbiter's oxygen-nitrogen atmosphere to the suit's pure oxygen supply. Water pumped through tubes woven into an undergarment keeps the astronaut cool. With the spacesuit on, the astronaut can move around inside the Orbiter's payload bay.

A Manned Maneuvering Unit (MMU) stored in the payload bay enables astronauts to move away from the Orbiter. The astronaut flies the MMU by firing its nitrogen gas-jets. An automatic control system, the autopilot, helps to keep the MMU in position. This saves the astronaut from having to make continual corrections with the gas-jets.

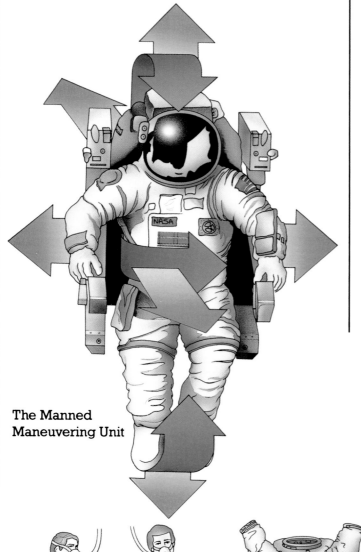

The Manned Maneuvering Unit

The Manned Maneuvering Unit was designed for NASA by the American aerospace company Martin Marietta. Two MMUs were built and they were used for the first time on Space Shuttle flight 41-B in February 1984.

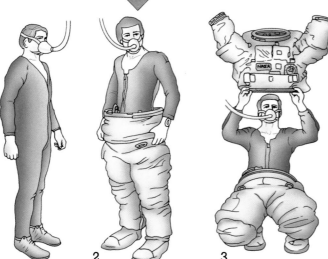

1   2   3   4   5

An astronaut uses the MMU to work in space away from the Orbiter

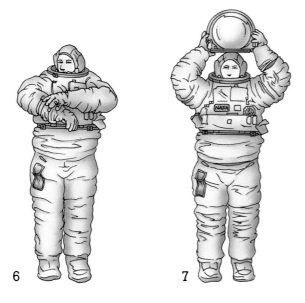

6   7

To put on a spacesuit an astronaut wearing an undergarment (1) pulls on the spacesuit legs first (2). Then the rigid aluminum body section is put on (3) and the two halves of the suit are connected (4). Next comes a headset, known as a "Snoopy Cap" (5). It contains headphones and a microphone for communications. Finally, gloves (6) and a helmet (7) are added. It takes 5 minutes to put on the spacesuit, which is reusable for up to 15 years. In space, the suit allows the astronaut to travel backward, forward, sideways, up and down, and to tilt and roll around.

RE-ENTRY

To begin the Shuttle Obiter's return to Earth, the thrusters are fired to turn the craft around to fly tail first. Then its manouvering engines are fired to slow it down and bring it out of orbit. The craft curves gently downward.

Flying nose-first again, the Orbiter enters the thinnest layers of air 140 km (87 mi) above the Earth. At a height of 130 km (81 mi), the air is thick enough to begin to slow the Orbiter and heat its outer surface. The craft is covered with tiles to protect it from the intense heat. At a height of 70 km (44 mi) the Orbiter is so hot that the air around it becomes disturbed. Radio waves cannot get through this layer of hot air, making all radio communications with the Orbiter impossible for 12 minutes until it slows to about 13,300 km/h (8,200 mph) at a height of 55 km (34 mi).

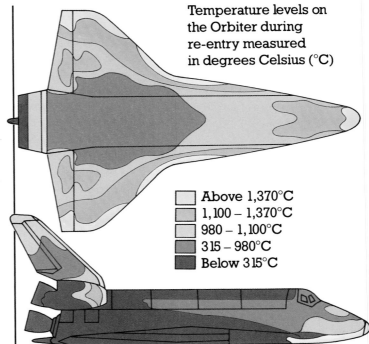

Temperature levels on the Orbiter during re-entry measured in degrees Celsius (°C)

- Above 1,370°C
- 1,100 – 1,370°C
- 980 – 1,100°C
- 315 – 980°C
- Below 315°C

During re-entry, the hottest parts of the Orbiter reach more than 1,500°C. By comparison, water boils at 100°C and aluminum metal melts at 662°C.

(1) Facing backward, the Orbiter uses its rocket engines to slow down for re-entry

(2) The Orbiter starts to flip over to assume the correct angle

Some 32,000 protective tiles being glued and stuck on to the Orbiter

(3) Once it is flying at the correct angle, it continues to fall toward the atmosphere

As the Orbiter begins to descend through the Earth's atmosphere, the crew-members, who were weightless in orbit, begin to feel the effects of gravity pulling them down again. In space there is no air to carry sounds. There is silence outside the spacecraft. On re-entry, the first sound the crew hears from outside the Orbiter is the roar of air rushing past.

(4) The Orbiter's tiles absorb the heat as it passes through the critical stage of re-entry

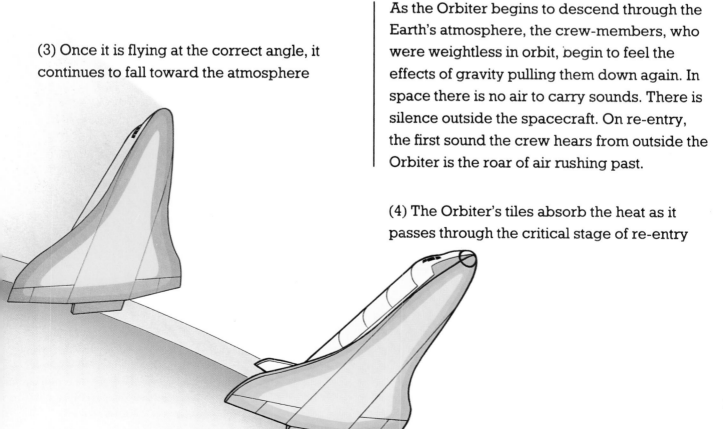

LANDING

After re-entry, air resistance continues to slow the Orbiter. Its rocket engines have run out of fuel and so the craft can only glide down to a landing. It must approach the runway correctly the first time because it has no power to fly around and try again.

Below about 90 km (56 mi) above the Earth, the air becomes thick enough to allow the Orbiter to maneuver by using its rudder and elevons like an airplane. The Orbiter descends along a flight path, the glideslope, which is very steep. A passenger airliner comes in to land on a glideslope with an angle of 2 to 3° (degrees). The Orbiter glides down at 22°. At 500 m (1,600 ft) above the ground and 3 km (2 mi) from the runway, the Orbiter's glideslope is reduced to only 1.5° by a maneuver called flaring.

The Orbiter lands at a speed of 350km/h (210 mph). The main (rear) wheels touch the ground first and then the nose is gently lowered until the nose wheel also touches the ground. Brakes then bring the Orbiter to rest within about 2.5 km (1.5 mi). The specially built Space Shuttle runway at the Kennedy Space Center is 4.5 km (2.7 mi) long.

(1) The Orbiter comes out of re-entry and begins to slow down

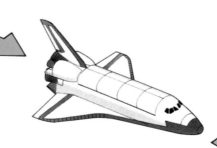

(2) It glides down as it has no fuel left in its engines

(6) When the Orbiter comes to a halt, the crew cannot leave for several minutes because of the heat and the danger from any poisonous or explosive fuel that may be left in the engines

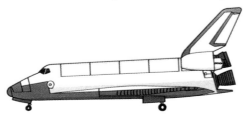

(5) The Orbiter uses its split rudder air-brake to help it slow down

The Shuttle lands safely on an airbase runway

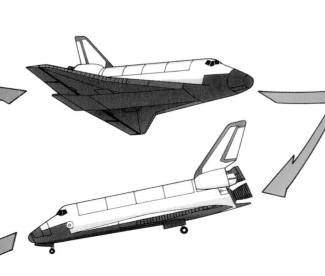

(3) The Orbiter may have to maneuver to land at certain runways

(4) A few feet from the ground the undercarriage is lowered

As the Orbiter has no engine power after re-entry, the place where it is to land must be decided even before it fires its engines to leave orbit. From that moment on, the Shuttle cannot change to another landing site. Below about 4km (2.5 mi), a radio system known as a microwave scanning beam landing system guides the Orbiter down to a safe landing.

229

HISTORY OF THE SHUTTLE

Engineers began to think about reusable space shuttles in the 1950s. Many of their early designs were for a two-part craft. The first part was a rocket-powered booster. This provided most of the thrust for take-off. The second part, the Orbiter, was attached to its back. When the booster lifted the Orbiter high enough and fast enough, the Orbiter would separate from it and carry on into orbit. The Bomi, from Bell Aircraft of the United States, was typical of this two-part design. However, none of these craft were built because of the cost and engineering problems.

During the late 1950s and 1960s, the United States built and tested a series of experimental aircraft. Their test flights provided valuable information about flying rockets with wings in the upper layers of the atmosphere. But these craft could not re-enter the atmosphere from space because they would become too hot and burn up. Another type of test craft called a lifting body was developed to research this problem.

An early design for the U.S. Shuttle

The X-15 winged rocket in flight

A series of triangular (delta) shaped lifting bodies were tested. They were launched by being dropped from beneath the wing of a bomber aircraft. The results of these test flights showed that the re-entry problems could be solved.

In 1970 the National Aeronautics and Space Administration (NASA) began a study of the engineering problems of building a reusable Space Shuttle. Different types of craft were studied, ranging from a fully reusable manned booster and Orbiter to a manned Orbiter with add-on booster rockets. The project proved to be very costly. To save money, the Orbiter was made smaller by taking out its main fuel tanks and mounting them separately. The manned booster was replaced by two solid-fueled booster rockets attached to the fuel tank. Studies showed that the Orbiter could glide down to a landing on its own, so the jet engines it was to use for this were taken out. Finally, in 1972, President Richard Nixon announced that NASA was to go ahead and build the Space Shuttle.

The first U.S. Orbiter, Enterprise

Five Orbiters were built. They were Enterprise, Columbia, Challenger, Discovery and Atlantis. Enterprise was only intended for test flights within the atmosphere. It has never flown in space. Columbia was the first to fly in space, in April 1981. Challenger was destroyed in an accident in 1986, killing its crew of seven. Following this, the whole Space Shuttle design was examined and many improvements were made. Shuttle missions resumed with the successful flight of Discovery in September 1988.

The U.S. Challenger explodes in mid-air

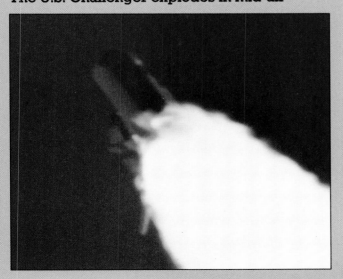

FACTS AND FIGURES

The world's most powerful rocket is the Energia launcher used by the Soviet Union to lift heavy loads such as its Space Shuttle. It measures 60 m (197 ft) in height, has a maximum diameter of 16 m (52 ft), weighs 2,000 tons and produces a thrust of 4,000 tonnes. It can place a satellite of 130 tons in Earth orbit. Energia was launched first in May 1987.

The largest crew carried on a single space mission was the crew of eight carried in the Challenger Orbiter of Shuttle flight 61-A, the 22nd Shuttle flight, on October 30th 1985. The mission was commanded by Frank Hartsfield and lasted for 7 days.

Of more than 200 people who have traveled in space, the oldest was Karl Henize who was a mission specialist on Shuttle flight 51-F in July 1985. He was then 58 years old.

The worst accident during a spaceflight was the destruction of the U.S. Challenger Orbiter by an explosion 73 seconds after take-off in January 1986. The seven crew members were all killed instantly.

Shuttle astronaut John Young has made more spaceflights than anyone else. At the end of the ninth Shuttle flight in 1983, he had made six flights and spent a total of 34 days 42 minutes and 13 seconds in space.

Chapter Twelve
MOTORCYCLES

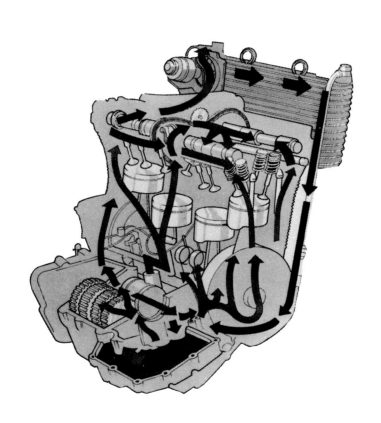

CONTENTS

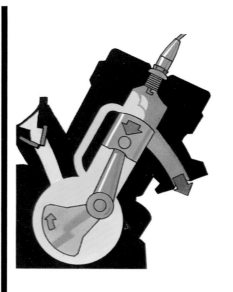

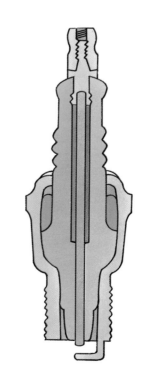

WORKING PARTS

Hundreds of different bits and pieces, large and small, are used to make a motorcycle, or motorbike. Each plays a part in making the bike run smoothly and safely.

Groups of parts work together in systems to carry out various jobs. For example, the fuel (or gas) tank and carburetor form part of the fuel system. This supplies fuel (gasoline) to the engine. The battery supplies electricity to the ignition system. This produces the

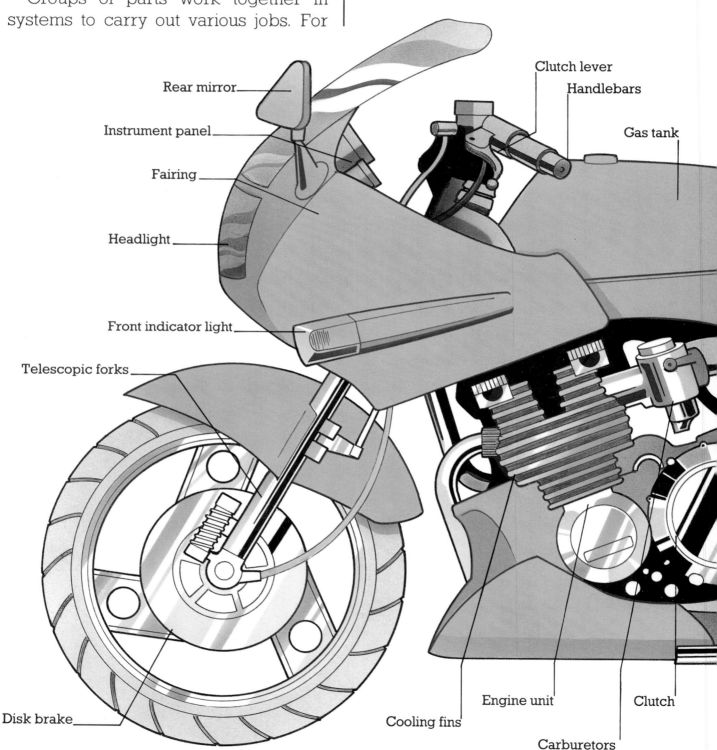

Rear mirror

Instrument panel

Fairing

Headlight

Front indicator light

Telescopic forks

Disk brake

Clutch lever

Handlebars

Gas tank

Engine unit

Cooling fins

Carburetors

Clutch

sparks to ignite the fuel. The battery also supplies power to the lights and instruments.

On this bike, fins around the engine form the cooling system for the engine. Oil travels to all the moving parts through the lubrication system.

The clutch, gear lever and drive chain are part of the transmission system. This sends turning power from the engine to the rear wheel. The brake calipers and disks are part of the braking system. This slows down the bike. Telescopic front forks and the rear suspension unit make up the suspension system. This helps give the rider a smooth ride over bumpy roads.

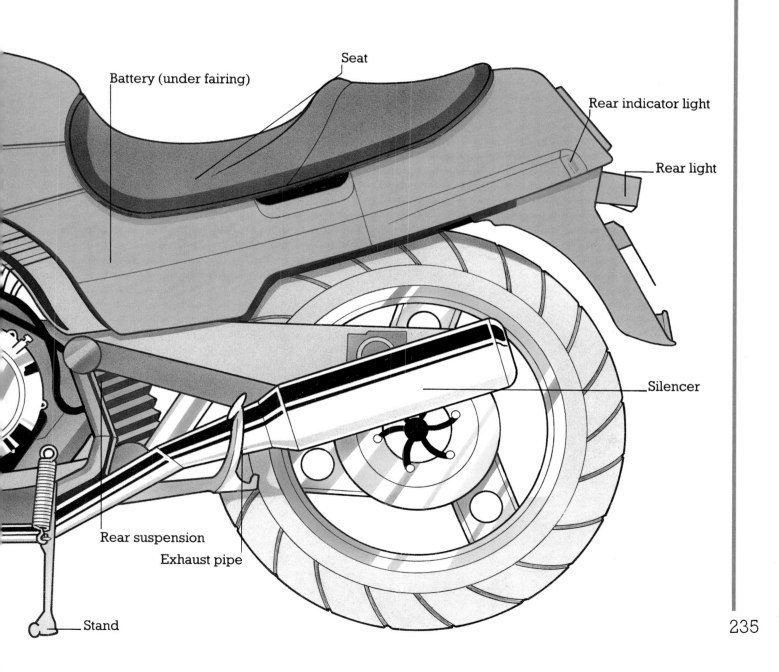

Seat

Battery (under fairing)

Rear indicator light

Rear light

Silencer

Rear suspension

Exhaust pipe

Stand

TWO-STROKE ENGINES

Motorcycle engines are mostly piston engines. They have a piston – a hollow pipe-shaped piece of metal – moving up and down in each cylinder. Power is produced in a cylinder when burning fuel forces the piston down. The movement of the piston turns the main shaft, the crankshaft.

For the engine to continue working, four things have to happen over and over again. (1) Fuel mixture must be drawn into the cylinders. (2) The mixture must be compressed, or squeezed. (3) The mixture must be ignited by a spark. (4) The burned gases must be removed from the cylinders.

In the simplest kind of motorbike engine these four things happen as each piston makes two strokes – one up, one down. We call this kind of engine a two-stroke engine.

Two-stroke engines are smaller and easier to look after than four-strokes (see page 10). But they use more fuel and make more smoke, or exhaust fumes.

In a two-stroke engine the fuel mixture enters through the intake opening, or port. It travels to the space above the piston through the transfer port.

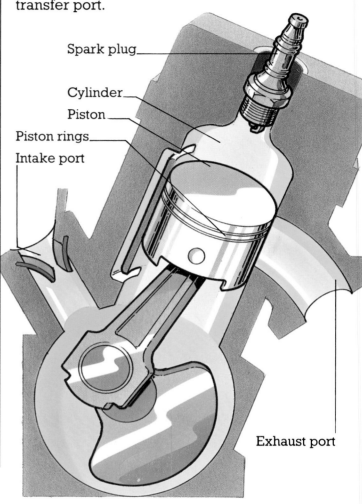

Spark plug

Cylinder

Piston

Piston rings

Intake port

Exhaust port

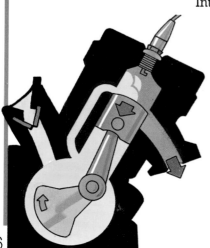
Piston moves down.

Piston ends downstroke.
Intake of fresh fuel.

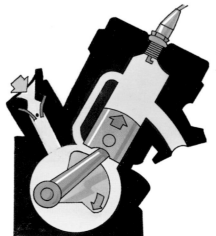
Upstroke begins.
Old fuel transfers.

A Japanese bike with a water-cooled, square-four, two-stroke engine

Fresh fuel mixture enters the engine as the piston finishes its downstroke (1). Old fuel mixture moves into the top of the cylinder through the transfer port. Then the piston starts to move up (2). Still moving upwards (3,4), it compresses the old fuel mixture. A spark from the spark plug explodes the mixture (5). This forces the piston down and produces power. The burned gases escape through the exhaust port (6).

Fuel is compressed.
Upstroke ends.

Mixture is burned.

Burned gases escape

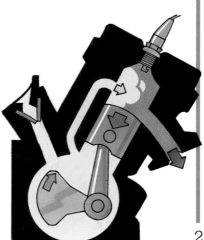

FOUR-STROKE ENGINES

Fast motorcycles, and indeed most bikes with engines of 250cc or more, are four-strokes. This means that the pistons have to move up and down four times to produce power.

Four-stroke engines are usually more powerful than two-strokes. But they are also more complicated and have more moving parts. They have valves, not ports (openings), to let gases in and out of the cylinders. Fuel mixture comes in through one set of valves (intake). Burned gases go out through another set of valves (exhaust).

The valves are opened by a rotating shaft. On the shaft are raised pieces called lobes. As this so-called camshaft rotates, the lobes in turn press down, then release plug-like stems to open and close the valves.

In a two-stroke machine, the engine is lubricated (oiled) by putting oil in with the fuel. The four-stroke engine has a separate lubrication system to keep the engine oiled.

This four-stroke engine has two camshafts, one for each valve. The camshafts are driven by a chain from a toothed-wheel, or sprocket, on the engine crankshaft.

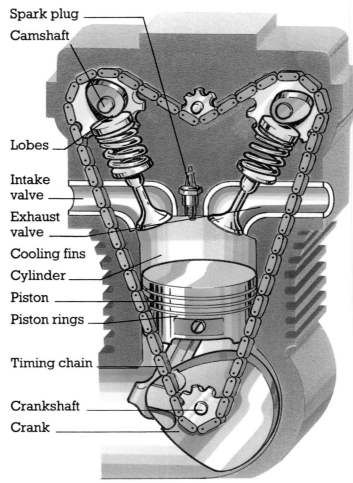

Spark plug
Camshaft
Lobes
Intake valve
Exhaust valve
Cooling fins
Cylinder
Piston
Piston rings
Timing chain
Crankshaft
Crank

FOUR-STROKE ENGINE CYCLE

Downstroke begins, intake valve opens

Downstroke continues, fuel mixture is drawn in

Upstroke begins, intake valve closes

Upstroke continues, mixture is compressed

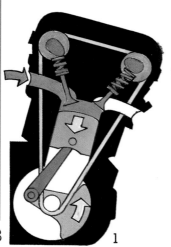

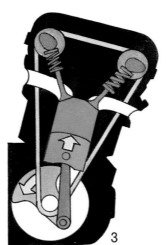

1

2

3

4

The top of an engine with four sets of cylinder valves and camshafts with toothed wheels

The four-stroke engine produces power once in every four strokes of the piston. On the first stroke (down), fuel mixture is drawn through the open inlet valve into the top of the cylinder (1,2). On the second stroke (up), the mixture is compressed (3,4,5).

The third stroke (down) occurs when the mixture explodes and pushes against the piston (6,7). On the fourth stroke (up), the piston pushes the burnt gases out of the exhaust valve (7,8). The engine is now ready to begin another set, or cycle, of four strokes.

Spark plug fires, igniting the mixture

Downstroke occurs as gases push down piston

Upstroke begins, exhaust valve opens

Upstroke continues, burned gases forced out

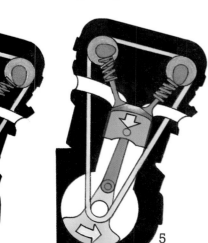

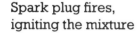

5

6

7

8

FUEL SYSTEM

Gasoline is stored in the fuel tank, and flows from there via a needle-and-seat into the carburetor. The carburetor is a small pot-like unit in which the fuel is mixed with air being sucked into the engine. The fuel mixture then goes past a flap-shaped valve, the throttle, into the engine cylinders, where it is ignited.

The rider opens and closes the throttle from the twist grip on the right handlebar, allowing the engine to work faster or slower.

A few bikes have a fuel injection system instead of a carburetor. Some have a turbocharger which is a pump that forces extra fuel mixture into the cylinders to create extra power.

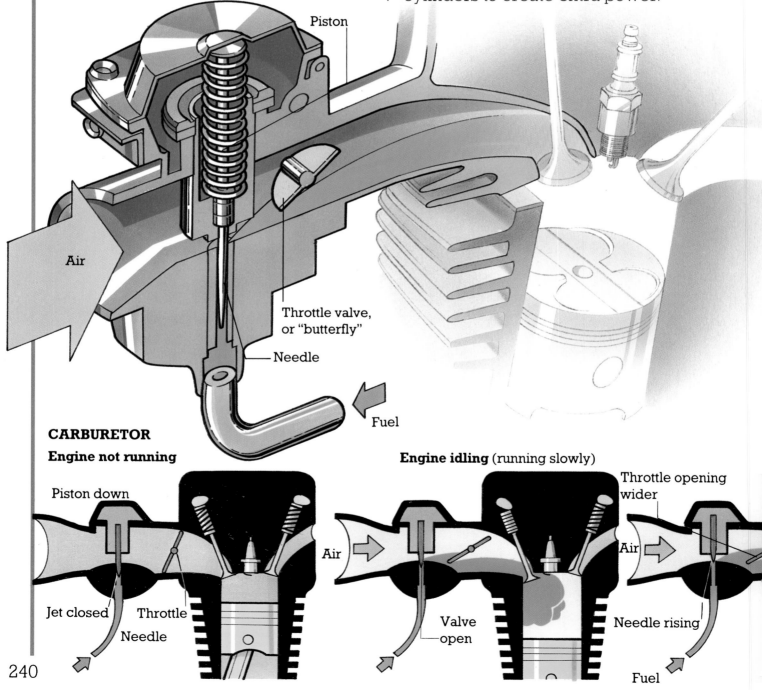

Piston

Air

Throttle valve, or "butterfly"

Needle

Fuel

CARBURETOR

Engine not running

Piston down

Jet closed   Throttle

Needle

Engine idling (running slowly)

Throttle opening wider

Air

Air

Valve open

Needle rising

Fuel

240

Powerful road and racing bikes like this one are often fitted with a turbocharger

In a carburetor, the piston lifts the needle out of the fuel intake, or jet, as the engine speeds up. Air flows over the jet and sucks up fuel. Then the fuel and air mixture enters the engine cylinder through the intake valve.

In an engine with a fuel injector instead of a carburetor, the gas is squirted into the air just before it goes into the cylinder. A tiny computer controls the fuel injector. A fuel injector can squirt many times a second.

Engine speeding up **Engine running fast** **Fuel injection**

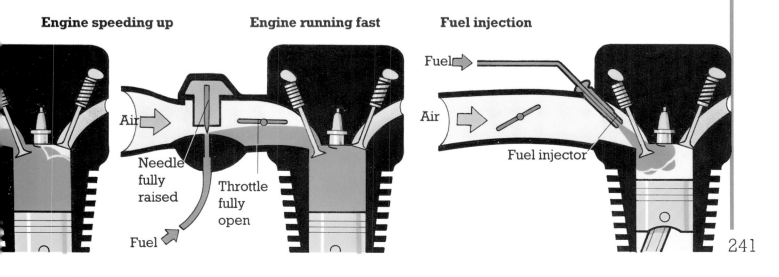

Air

Needle
fully
raised

Throttle
fully
open

Fuel

Fuel

Air

Fuel injector

BRAKES

Motorcycles today can accelerate, or gain speed, very quickly. In just 10 seconds some bikes can accelerate from 0 to nearly 120 miles an hour!

To be safe, bikes must therefore have good brakes to slow them down quickly. Most bikes have two separate braking systems, one on the front wheel, the other on the rear. The rider applies the front brake with a lever on the handlebars, and the rear brake with a foot pedal.

The fastest bikes have three "disk" brakes – two on the front wheel and one on the rear. In a disk brake a pair of tough pads is pressed against a disk rotating with the wheel. This stops the wheel turning. Disk brakes work by hydraulic (liquid) pressure.

Many bikes have a disk brake on the front, but a drum brake on the rear. Slower bikes have drum brakes on both wheels. In a drum brake, a bowl-shaped drum is fixed to the wheel hub. When the brake is applied, a brake shoe is forced against the drum. Drum brakes work by the pulling action of cables.

When a disk brake is applied, liquid (brake fluid) in hoses is forced into the brake caliper unit. This pushes the brake pistons, which press the pads against the disk in a scissor-like grip.

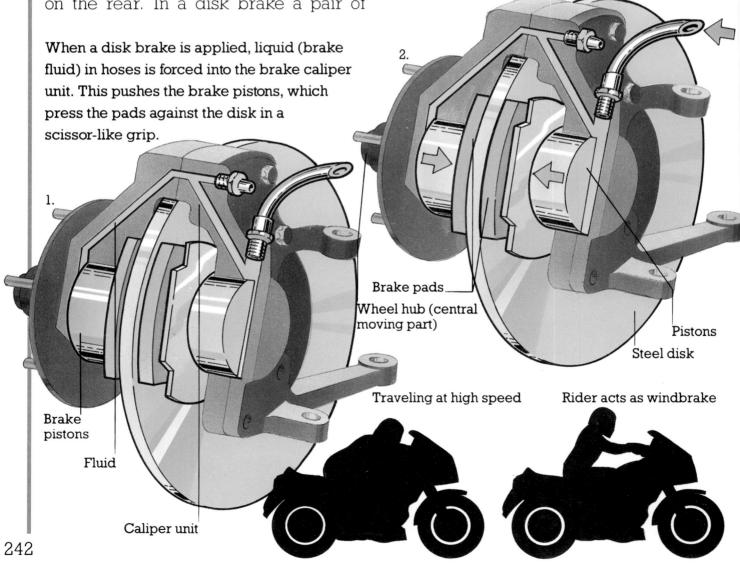

1.

2.

Brake pads

Wheel hub (central moving part)

Pistons

Steel disk

Brake pistons

Fluid

Caliper unit

Traveling at high speed

Rider acts as windbrake

On this bike wheel, the disk brake system is the gold unit and pipes on the the side

These pictures show how a bike behaves when the rider brakes. Using the back brake lowers the back. Using the front brake dips the front. Using both brakes and the gears is critical – it helps keep the bike steadier.

Front brake on   Both brakes on   Slowing down with brakes and gears

As a cross-country bike "takes off," its front telescopic suspension unit fully extends

The suspension helps keep a bike level over a bumpy road. The wheels ride up over bumps and then go down again. The springs act like a cushion to give the rider a comfortable landing, even after a jump in the air!

The air-filled tires of a motorcycle also help to smooth out small bumps in the road. They can be pressed quite flat, and then regain their rounded shape, just as an air mattress does when you lie on it.

SUSPENSION

One of the main jobs of a motorcycle's suspension system is to give the rider a comfortable ride over bumpy roads. The other main job is to stop the bike rocking about too much, which would make it difficult to handle.

A bike has two suspension systems, one at the front, one at the rear. The front suspension is built into the front forks, which hold the wheel. It is telescopic – in each leg of the fork, one part slides up and down inside the other, like a telescope. Each leg contains a spring and a piston inside a fluid (liquid). The spring is squeezed tight when the wheel goes over a bump, then immediately pushes back. Air trapped above the fluid gives the system more bounce. The piston moves back slowly through the fluid to stop the spring pushing back too harshly. It acts as a damper, or shock absorber.

Many bikes have a pair of spring and damper units for the rear suspension. The upper ends are fixed to the bike frame below the saddle, and the lower ends, to the swing arm.

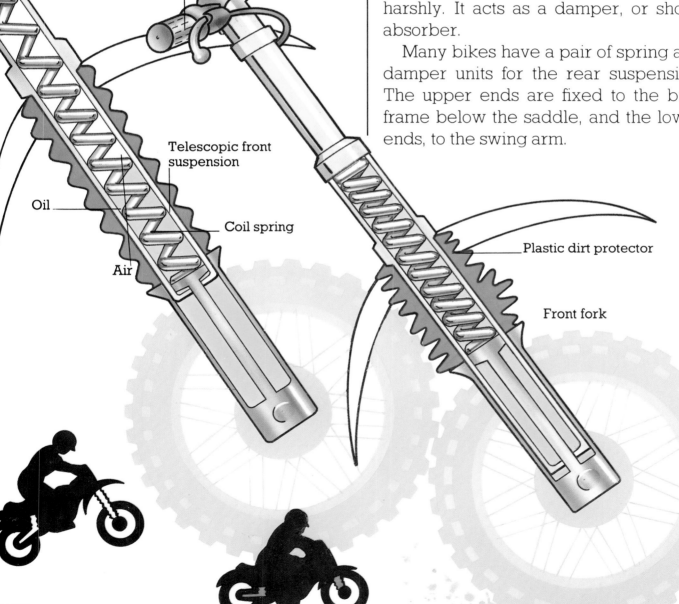

Handlebars

Telescopic front suspension

Oil

Coil spring

Air

Plastic dirt protector

Front fork

SPECIAL BIKES

Apart from the typical everyday motorcycles, many quite different models can be seen on and off the road.

On the road you can sometimes see custom bikes. These are based on ordinary models, but have been "customized," or made individual by, for example, changing the exhaust pipes. "Cruisers" are big bikes with extras such as luggage units. Some superfast bikes race on roads, others around special circuits. They can be recognized by their bubble-shaped windshields and the streamlined shell, or fairing, that covers most of the body.

Another, but quite different, circuit racer is the speedway bike. This has a simple frame and body, and usually only one gear. It has no brakes at all! In some countries speedway riders race on ice, using spiked tires.

For cross-country racing, known as motocross or endures, tough lightweight bikes are used. They have a raised body, knobby tyres and very good suspension. Cross-country riders also race in three-wheelers, called ATVs (All Terrain Vehicles). Originally, they were designed for use by farmers and forestry workers.

A customized bike, with racing car wheels and a luxury passenger cabin

An ATV on a steep slope

A race for bikes with side-cars

Dragsters often look more like rockets on wheels than motorbikes

Dragsters are special bikes that are raced in a straight line over a distance of 1,200ft (400m). The winner is the bike with the quickest time. From a standing start, the bikes can reach a speed of over 180mph (300km/h) after only 7 seconds!

Choppers are bikes with pieces "chopped up," added and changed in other ways. They have a low seat and high handlebars. The front forks are long, so the wheel juts out in front. Many are based on the famous American big bike, the Harley Davidson.

FACTS AND FIGURES

The early days

Two French brothers, Ernest and Pierre Michaux, built a motorized cycle in 1868 – they fitted a steam engine to one of their bicycles. In the United States a year later, Sylvester Roper designed another steam machine. But these powered bikes were not successful.

In 1885 Gottlieb Daimler in Germany fitted a lightweight gasoline engine in a bicycle frame. He later fitted an engine into a carriage to create the first four-wheeled automobile. Soon, European manufacturers were fitting gasoline engines to bicycles and tricycles.

A typical Daimler bike – the Einspor

In 1894, the Germans Heinrich and Wilhelm Hildebrand and Alois Wolf-muller became the first manufacturers to build motorcycles on a large scale. (1,000 built in the first two years.)

In the 1890s motorcycle designers put the engine in different positions in the bicycle frame. In 1901 two French brothers, Michael and Eugene Werner, realized that, for stability, the best place for the engine was low down in the bottom of the frame. And there it has remained to the present day.

1900 – 1950

In the first half of this century bikes were slowly but gradually improved, as a result of road racing.

A 1930 Brough Superior

In 1907 the famous road race, the TT (Tourist Trophy) race, was first run on the Isle of Man off England. The first race was won on a Norton bike.

Norton, and other British makes like Triumph and BSA, came to dominate the motorcycling scene until the 1950s. In the United States, the Harley Davidson and Indian bikes were among the best.

During World War I all the armies used motorcycle messengers. In the 1920s and 1930s motorcycling became a craze throughout Europe, more so than in the United States, where the car was more important.

A TT racing bike of the early 1970s

In the 1920s two of the most famous European bikes appeared for the first time, the Italian Moto Guzzi in 1921 and the German BMW two years later.

By 1939 the world was at war again, and again motorcycles were used on a large scale by messengers. The Germans also used them with sidecars fitted with machine guns as swift road and cross-country attack units.

A Suzuki motorcyle for the 1990s

1950 onwards

After World War II, British bikes such as Triumphs and Nortons led the world for a while. But then they were bettered by the Italian Moto Guzzi, Gileras, and MV Augustas. There was also the "Vespa" scooter.

In the 1950s, Japanese bikes appeared on the scene. First Honda, then Suzuki, Yamaha, and Kawasaki began producing dramatic new bike designs – the bikes were safer, more reliable, more efficient, and cheaper, than their rivals. And these are still the most important names in motorcyling today. Only in the big superbike and touring range can other bikes compete, such as the BMWs, Ducatis and Harley Davidsons.

WORLD-BEATERS

The world record speed for a motorcycle is 318.6 miles an hour, set by Donald A. Vesco in 1978 in a special streamlined body powered by two Kawasaki engines.

Among the fastest road machines is the Honda V65 Magna, which is designed to do up to 173mph (280km/h).

Some racers can travel at speeds of over 180mph (300km/h).

The fastest road race is the 500cc Belgian Grand Prix. In 1977, British rider Barry Sheene averaged a speed of over 135mph (217km/h) for the 88 mile (141 km) race.

The longest racing circuit is the Isle of Man TT "Mountain" circuit, which is over 36 miles (60km) long. Joey Dunlop holds the speed record for the circuit of 118mph (190km/h).

The longest motorcycle was designed and built by Gregg Reid of Atlanta, Georgia. It measures 15ft, 6in long and weighs 520lbs.

Forty members of the Brazilian Army military police rode for just over a mile on a Harley Davidson in 1986.

Yasuyuki Kudo performed the world's longest "wheelie" (riding on the rear wheel only) at the Japan Automobile Research Institute proving ground, Tsukuba, Japan on May 5, 1991.

The highest speed reached on a wheelie is 157.87 mph by Jacky Vranken, of Belgium, on rode a Suzuki GSXR 1100 on November 8, 1992.

Chapter Thirteen
RACING CARS

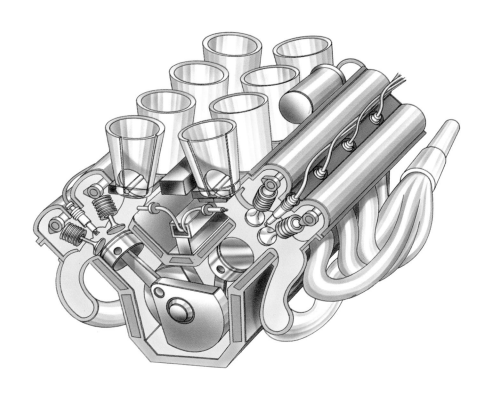

CONTENTS

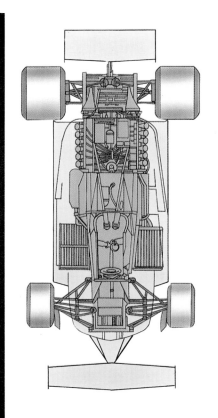

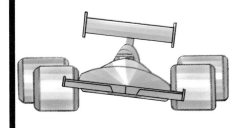

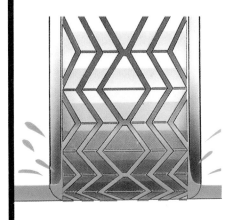

THE WORKING PARTS

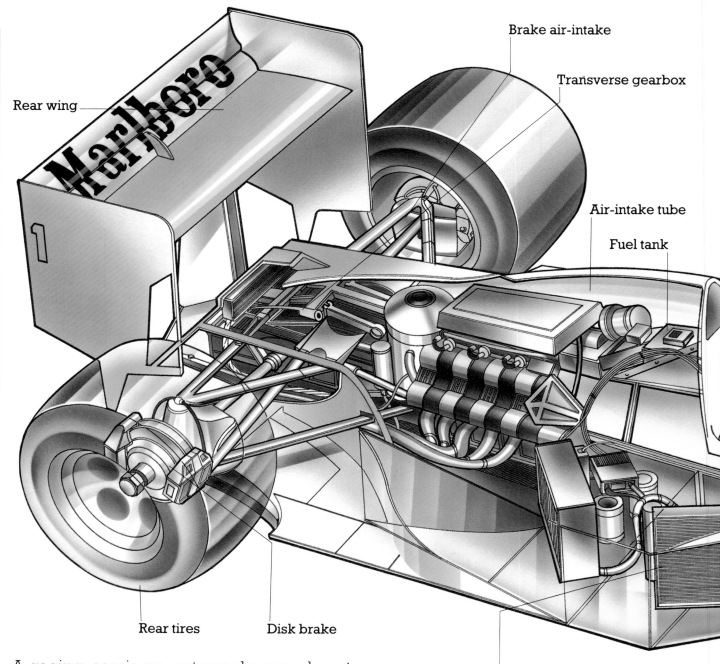

Rear wing

Marlboro

1

Brake air-intake

Transverse gearbox

Air-intake tube

Fuel tank

Rear tires   Disk brake

Water radiators

A racing car is an extremely complex vehicle designed to be driven safely at very high speeds. The "Grand Prix" cars that compete in the famous Formula 1 championship every year can reach speeds of up to 200 mph on specially designed racetracks. Car constructors use all the most modern materials, electronics and body designs to produce very strong and powerful cars that are also lightweight. The car is built around its power unit, the engine. Single-seat racing cars always have the engine have the engine positioned at the rear of the vehicle, turning the rear wheels around. Drivers sit in front of the engine inside a specially strengthened box designed to protect their body against the impact of a crash.

The shape of the car's body is very important. The car is always shaped "aerodynamically," with smooth curving panels to enable it to slip through the air easily. By positioning the wheels out to the side of the vehicle instead of underneath it, the car body can be lowered closer to the ground. This also helps to streamline the car and reduce the air resistance (drag) that acts against it to slow it down.

Small wings, or spoilers, at the front and rear of the car act like upside-down aircraft wings. As the car moves forward and air flows over these, they produce a down-force that pushes the vehicle down onto the track surface. This enables the car to go around corners at higher speeds without skidding.

Although most racing cars look considerably different from normal mass production family cars, a degree of the advanced technology developed for racing cars is later built into the cars that are offered for sale to the public.

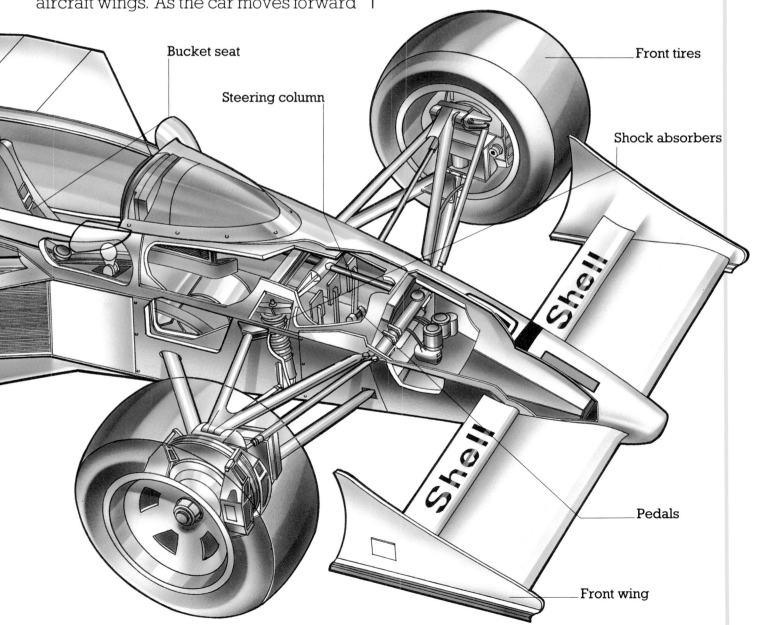

Bucket seat

Steering column

Front tires

Shock absorbers

Shell

Shell

Pedals

Front wing

DIFFERENT TYPES

The earliest motor races involved ordinary road cars, but the cars' owners and makers soon found ways of improving their vehicles' performance for racing. They modified the cars to suit the conditions of the race. Different types of races – over rough countryside, on smooth tracks or on ice – led to different types of racing cars. Modern cars designed for motor sports have become very specialized. Rally cars are designed for speed and endurance over long, winding courses on a variety of roads and loose surfaces. The annual 24-hour race at Le Mans in France involves very powerful sports cars that can travel at over 200 mph.

Single-seat racing cars are divided into several "formulas." Each formula is controlled by strict rules on engine size, car size and weight, and design features. By far the most popular is Formula 1. Others include Formula 2 and Formula 3000. Drag racers are designed to travel as fast as possible over very short, straight courses. Trucks are raced too, and so are some ordinary production cars.

A rally car in action. It is a modified, high-performance production car.

A single-seat racing car.

There are even races for production cars.

Not all races involve specialized "Formula" cars. This is an aerodynamic Le Mans sports car.

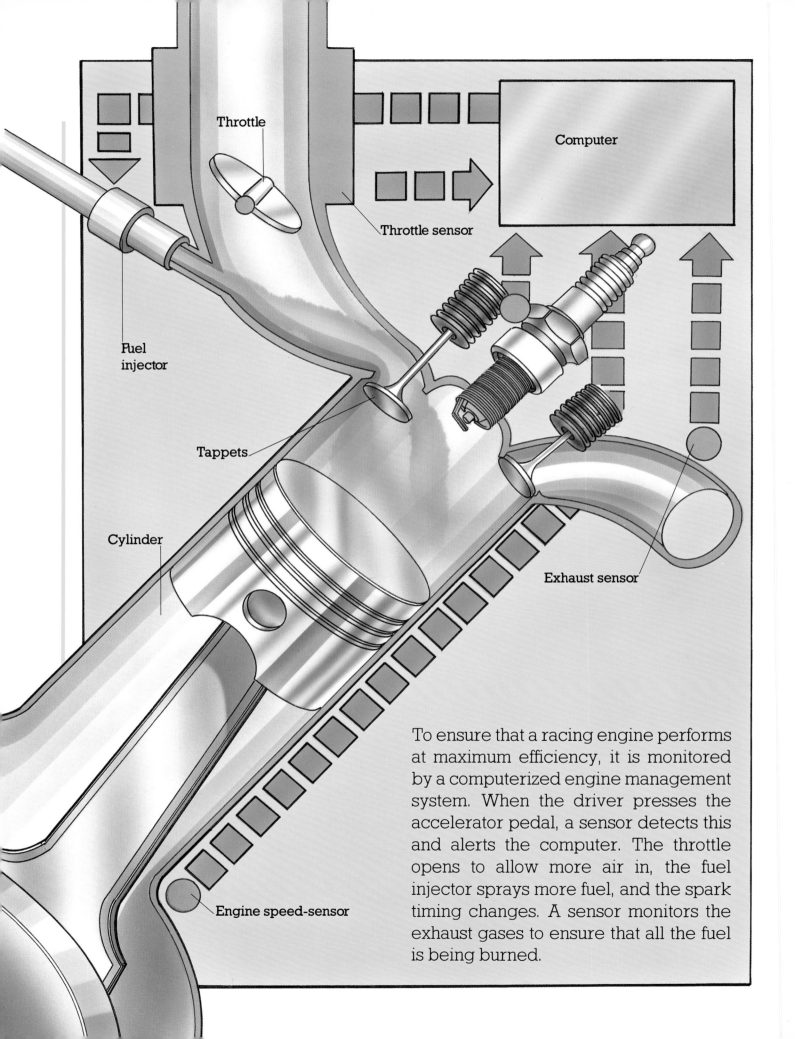

Throttle

Computer

Throttle sensor

Fuel injector

Tappets

Cylinder

Exhaust sensor

Engine speed-sensor

To ensure that a racing engine performs at maximum efficiency, it is monitored by a computerized engine management system. When the driver presses the accelerator pedal, a sensor detects this and alerts the computer. The throttle opens to allow more air in, the fuel injector sprays more fuel, and the spark timing changes. A sensor monitors the exhaust gases to ensure that all the fuel is being burned.

INCREASING THE POWER

Engine power can be increased by boosting the pressure of the fuel-air mixture that is burned inside the engine. This was realized as early as 1923, when the "supercharger" was introduced. The first supercharger was an air pump driven by the engine. It blew air into the engine s cylinders at high pressure. By the end of the 1930s, racing cars fitted with superchargers could travel at well over 186 mph. Superchargers were not readily available throughout World War II (1939-1945). They were not reintroduced to motor racing until 1977, and then under a new name – turbochargers. A turbocharger works using the force of the jet of exhaust gases pumped out by the engine. It increases engine pressure from atmospheric pressure, also called 1 bar, to the pressure allowed by the sport's rules. In 1987, Formula 1 engine pressure was limited to 4 bar (four times atmospheric pressure) and reduced to 2.5 bar in 1988. From 1989, turbocharged engines were banned from Formula 1 racing, but they are still used in numerous other motor sports.

A turbocharger is powered by energy that would otherwise be wasted. A propeller-like turbine in the exhaust pipe is rotated at high speed by hot exhaust gases rushing out of the engine. A shaft connects it to another turbine, called a compressor, positioned in the engine's air-intake. The exhaust turbine forces around the compressor, which increases the pressure of the air entering the engine. This results in greater engine power and also, surprisingly, a saving in fuel.

Drag racers use turbocharged engines for the maximum power and rate of acceleration along a short straight course. They have enormous rear tires to give the maximum grip on the track.

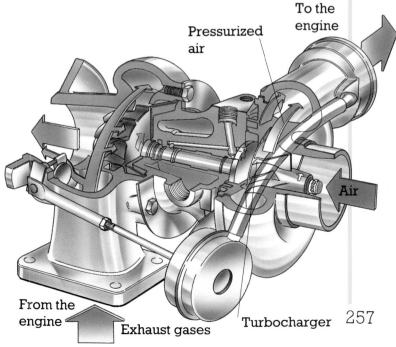

Pressurized air

To the engine

Air

From the engine

Exhaust gases

Turbocharger

POWER TO THE WHEELS

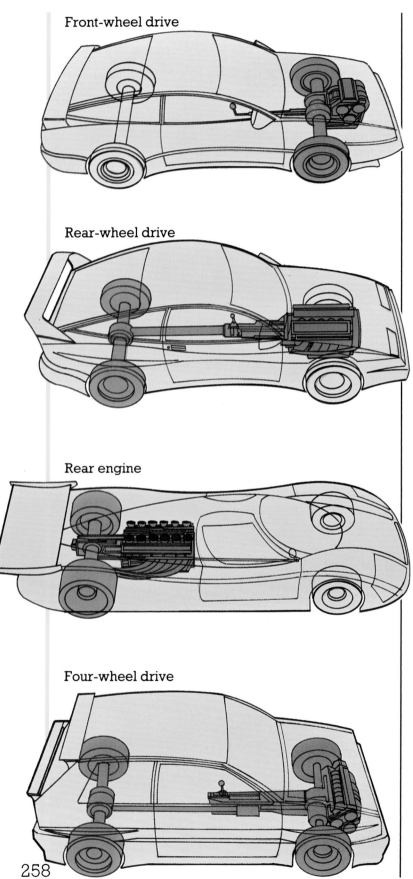

Front-wheel drive

Rear-wheel drive

Rear engine

Four-wheel drive

When a family car's engine is "on" but the accelerator pedal is not pressed, the crankshaft turns at about 750 rpm (revolutions per minute). If the shaft were connected directly to the wheels, this would make the car travel at about 50 mph – it would be impossible to control. In fact, a series of interlinked gear wheels reduces the speed of the crankshaft until the output shaft matches the required speed of the wheels. The gear wheels are contained in the gearbox. The correct gear wheels are linked together by positioning a selector called a gear lever. To change gear, the engine is first disconnected from the gearbox by pressing the "clutch" pedal. The gear lever is moved to the required position and then the clutch pedal is released to reconnect the engine. Some cars have an automatic transmission; they do not have a gear lever or clutch pedal. The gearbox automatically selects the correct gear for the car's speed.

Single-seat racing cars and some specialized sports cars have the engine mounted behind the driver. In this position, the engine's weight is over the wheels it drives, increasing tire grip. It also allows the front of the car to be made lower and thinner to reduce air resistance. Most mass production cars – station wagons, vans, jeeps and popular sports cars – have front engines, driving either the front wheels, the rear wheels or all four for maximum grip. Most front-mounted engines are placed lengthwise in the cars, but some are placed across (transverse engine).

Rally car drivers change gear thousands of times during a rally.

A gearbox contains two sets of gear wheels. The input and output shafts are on top, and the "layshaft" is underneath. When the gear lever is moved, selector rods push certain gear wheels together. If reverse gear is selected, an "idler" wheel slides between the layshaft and output shaft to reverse the direction of spin of the output.

Third-gear mode

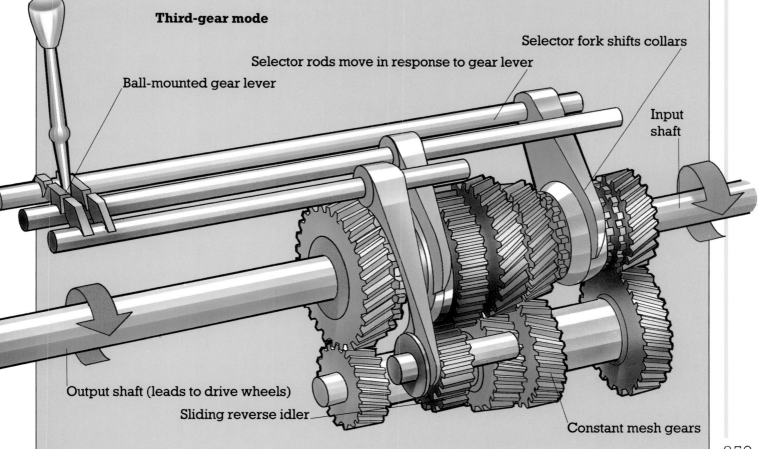

Selector fork shifts collars

Selector rods move in response to gear lever

Ball-mounted gear lever

Input shaft

Output shaft (leads to drive wheels)

Sliding reverse idler

Constant mesh gears

WHEELS

Racing-car wheels developed from the wheels of horsedrawn carriages. The wooden wheels were not strong enough for the powerful racing engines that were developed and they often broke. Solid metal wheels were strong enough, but too heavy. Wheels made from steel rims and hubs, linked by wire spokes (to save weight) were tried, but they were easily damaged. Eventually solid wheels made from lightweight alloys (mixtures of different metals) were developed and they are still used today. The wheels are fitted with tires made from a mixture of different rubbers, called the tire compound. Different compounds behave in different ways. Some compounds give better grip on wet surfaces. Others are more suitable for dry weather.

There are two types of braking systems – disk and drum. Disk brakes were developed for use by aircraft. They were first used in motor racing by Jaguar in the 1953 Le Mans sports car race in France. All racing cars now use disk brakes.

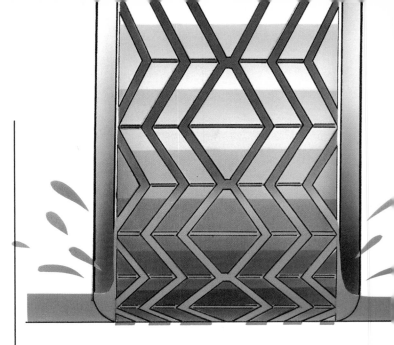

Wets

The tread pattern on rain tires, also called wets, forces water out from beneath the tire and keeps the maximum area of rubber in contact with the track.

In a drum brake, a rough lining material is fixed to the surface of two curved "shoes" inside the drum. Pressing the brake pedal forces the shoes outward and against the spinning drum, slowing it down. In a disk brake, flat friction pads grip a disk which spins with the wheel. The disk can become so hot that it glows red.

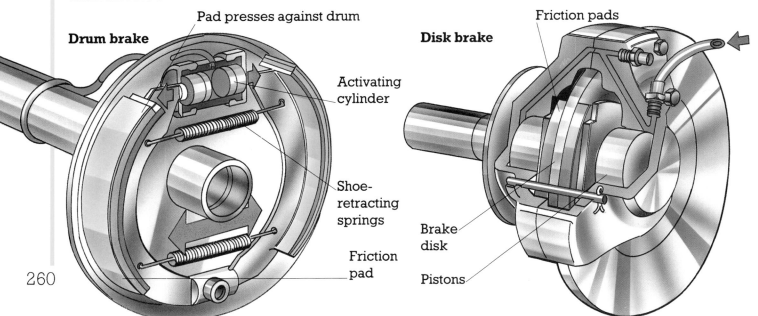

Pad presses against drum

Drum brake

Activating cylinder

Shoe-retracting springs

Friction pad

Friction pads

Disk brake

Brake disk

Pistons

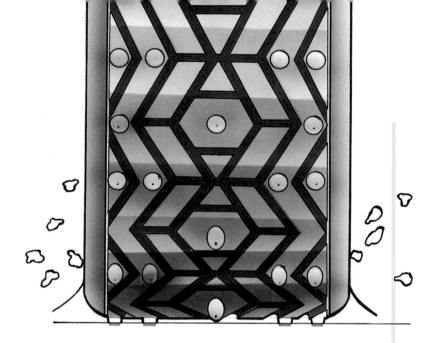

Slicks

In dry weather a tread pattern is not necessary. Dry-weather tires, called slicks, are smooth and made from a soft rubber that is sticky when warm, to give maximum grip.

Snow tires

Rally cars often have to be driven over snow or ice-covered roads and tracks. To give them some grip on these slippery surfaces, they may use tires with metal studs.

Rain tires gripping a wet track in spectacular fashion.

SUSPENSION

If a car were connected to its wheels by rigid shafts and struts, it would be uncontrollable at high speed. The whole car would vibrate and jump as the wheels bounced over every little bump in the road surface. Every racing car is therefore linked to its wheels through a system of levers, springs and pistons called its suspension system. This allows the wheels to bounce over bumps without the rest of the car doing the same. The suspension system is said to absorb or damp unwanted movements.

In the 1970s the Lotus Formula 1 racing team began to develop a completely new type of suspension system. A car's aerodynamics works at its best if the car body can be kept at a constant height from the track surface. Normal suspension systems cannot achieve this. If the driver brakes hard, the car's nose dips down. When the car goes around a corner, it rolls toward the outside of the corner. And when it accelerates, the nose comes up and the rear of the car dips down. All these changes in position upset the car's aerodynamics. The active suspension system developed by Lotus used fast-acting jacks controlled by a computer to raise or lower each corner of the car when necessary, so that the body remained level at all times.

The size of the wheels is important, too, for smooth traveling. Racing cars have larger wheels than production cars.

In some motor sports on rough ground, suspension systems must be very strong indeed!

A shock absorber consists of a piston with a spring coiled around it. When a wheel goes over a bump, the pushrod is forced upward. The spring is compressed and then released. The oil-filled piston prevents the spring from bouncing up and down. It "damps" the spring.

An active suspension system keeps a car level, at a constant "ride height," by replacing the normal coil springs and dampers with computer controlled jacks. If the car's nose tries to dip, sensors detect the movement and alert the computer. In a fraction of a second, the computer calculates the action necessary to counteract this unwanted movement and instructs the front jacks to raise the nose.

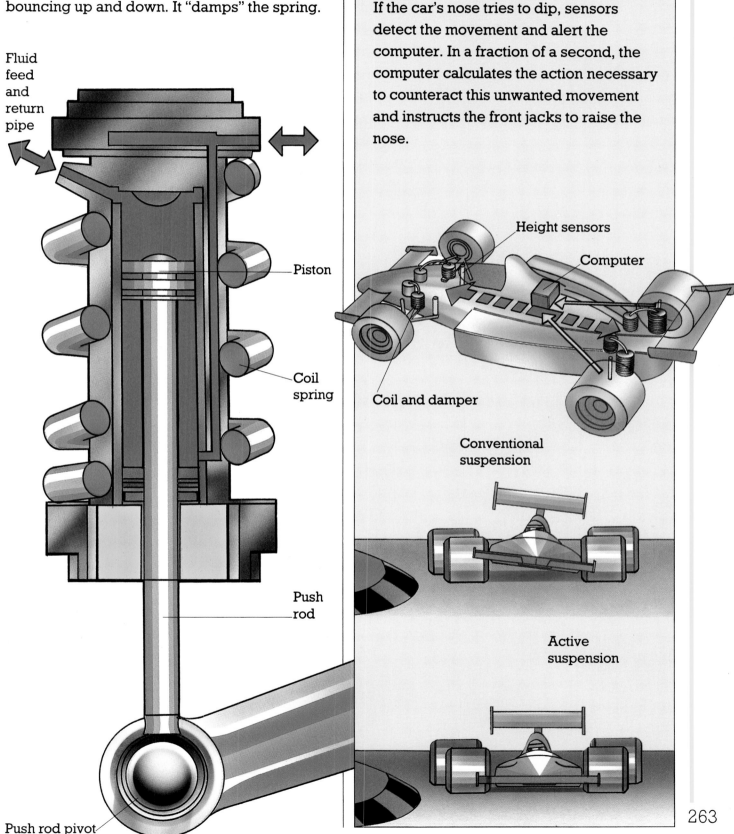

Fluid feed and return pipe

Piston

Coil spring

Push rod

Push rod pivot

Height sensors

Computer

Coil and damper

Conventional suspension

Active suspension

263

AERODYNAMICS

The way that air flows around a car creates forces which affect the car's speed and performance. The study of airflow around objects is called aerodynamics. Racing car designers make their cars low and slim with a smooth curving shape to keep air resistance to a minimum. In the late 1960s, designers all began to use aerodynamics to improve racing car performance. The first development was the nose winglet. A pair of wings, or spoilers, were fixed to the car's nose. They behaved like upside-down wings and helped to force the front of the car down onto the track. A rear wing, running the full width of the car, was added to hold the rear of the car down at high speed.

Designers then examined how to use the shape of the car itself to improve its performance. By using "side skirts" extending down to the ground and by shaping the bottom of the car, the air pressure underneath the whole car could be reduced to create more down-force. A good number of these developments, including moving wings and underbody shaping, were banned within a year or two when the rules governing Formula 1 car design were changed by the sport's authorities.

To develop a new racing car shape, designers make scale models of the car and test them in "wind tunnels." Here they study the flow of air over the bodywork using cameras and computers.

Grand Prix racing cars and some sports cars use wings to produce a down-force which improves road holding and allows faster cornering. Air flowing under the curved front and rear wings travels further than the air flowing over the flatter top surface. This creates a difference in air pressure above and below the wings and causes the down-force.

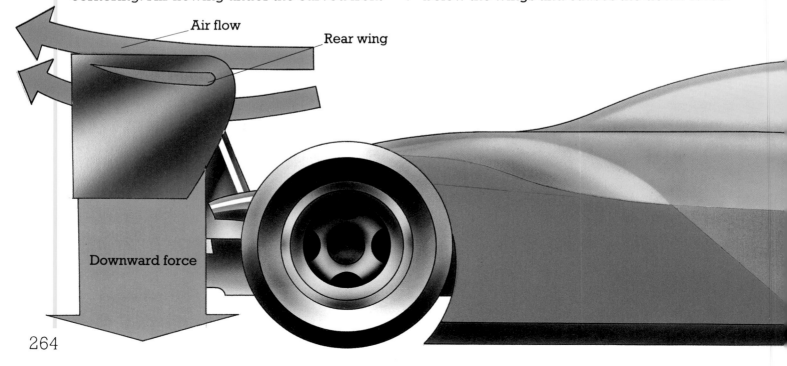

Air flow

Rear wing

Downward force

264

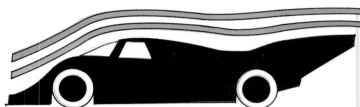

The angular shape of most family cars causes turbulence in the air flowing over the car, particularly at the rear end.

Racing cars are shaped to allow air to flow over them smoothly without causing any turbulence.

Turbulent "vortexes" of air spiral away from the rear wing of a Formula 1 car.

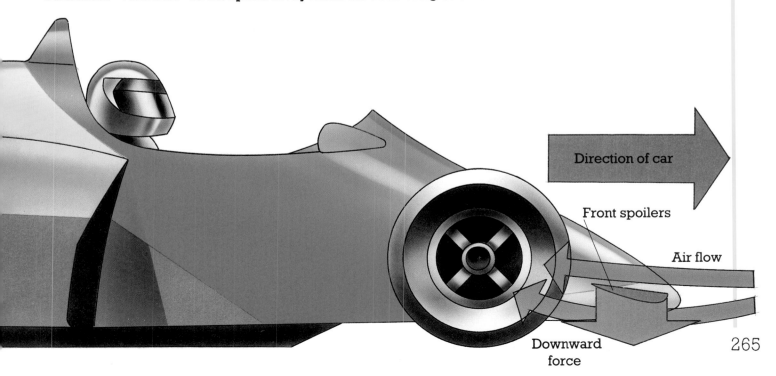

Direction of car

Front spoilers

Air flow

Downward force

BEHIND THE WHEEL

Driving a racing car is very difficult and tiring. Cornering at high speed creates forces on the driver which can double or triple his weight. A driver's head and helmet normally weigh about 15lbs, but during a race his neck muscles may have to cope with more than double that as the car weaves in and out of corners.

Rapid acceleration and braking also throw the driver's head backward and forward. Racing car drivers must be very fit to withstand these forces.

To keep the car as low on the road as possible, the driver lies on his back in a seat specially shaped to fit the shape of the driver's body. The seat's close fit

The view inside driver Nigel Mansell's Formula 1 Ferrari racing car.

helps to spread the effects of cornering and great accelerating forces more comfortably over the whole body.

There are few instruments on the dashboard in front of the driver, because there is little time to look down at them during a race. The most important controls – steering wheel, gear lever and foot pedals – are similar to those in a normal production car. The instruments show fuel and oil pressure, oil temperature and water temperature. The largest instrument is usually the rev counter which shows engine speed. The driver uses this and engine noise to decide when to change gear.

The dashboard of a modern racing car.

A racing car's steering wheel (1) is smaller than in a normal car. Dials and indicators on the dashboard (2) give important information about the engine. The driver's feet operate three pedals. The clutch (3) disconnects the engine from the wheels during gear changes. The brakes (4) slow the car down when necessary. The accelerator or throttle pedal (5) is pressed to make the car go faster. To the driver's right, a short gear lever (6) is used to select the correct gear to match the engine's speed with the car's speed. The specially shaped seat (7) holds the driver firmly in the right position. In Formula 1 racing cars especially, the driver lies, rather than sits, in position, with arms and legs outstretched. A harness holds him in securely.

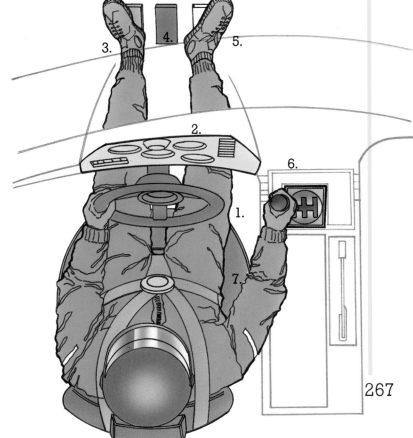

RACE TACTICS

Before a race, teams plan what they are going to do during the event – their race tactics. If the track is wet, some may start with wet-weather tires on the car and change to dry-weather "slick" tires later on. Pit teams practice until they can change all four wheels in about eight seconds! Other teams may start on slicks and hope that the track dries out so that a pit stop is not needed.

The start of a race is a dangerous time. Any driver who is unable to start must raise his hand to warn other drivers. When the starter decides that the time is right, he switches lights that all the drivers can see from red to green. All the cars accelerate rapidly and try to slip past slower cars in front.

Unless a driver can lead a race from start to finish, which is rare, he must pass all the cars in front of his to win. As one car nears the rear of another, the aerodynamics of the leading car causes a suction effect called a "slipstream" that pulls the chasing car along behind. At the right moment, perhaps as they approach a bend, the chasing driver steers his car out from behind the leader and tries to delay his braking to reach the corner first.

Every driver is eager to get a fast start at this Formula 1 race line up.

Drivers must choose the right moment carefully to overtake cars in front.

Pit mechanics practice their work to make pit stops as short as possible.

Colored flags are used to send messages to drivers. If the race has to be stopped, a red flag is waved. A yellow flag warns drivers not to overtake cars in front. A blue flag shows a driver that a car is closing fast from behind. The checkered flag marks the end of the race. With many cars on the track, lights, not a person with a flag, start a race.

Stop the race

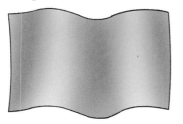

No overtaking

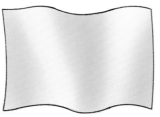

Car behind

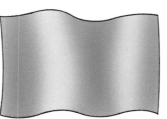

End of race

HISTORY OF THE RACING CAR

The first motor races were held in France in the 1890s. Only the car makers and a few wealthy car owners had enough time and money to take part. Each car carried a driver and a mechanic. The cars were so unreliable that the mechanics often had to repair their cars during a race. Neither the driver nor the mechanic wore a crash helmet or a seat belt.

One of the first motor races in 1905.

In 1906, rules were drawn up by the sport's authorities to control the design of cars that could enter races and to control the races themselves. This special "formula" later became known as Formula 1. The cars were huge and very powerful. They could weigh up to one ton and be powered by engines of 10 liters or more at over 90 mph. One of their cylinders was as big as the whole engine of a modern production car. Their tires, steering and brakes were not good enough to cope with these speeds and engine power and so there were many accidents.

D-type Jaguar in the 1950's

Bigger and more powerful racing cars were continually developed. The introduction of the supercharger in 1923 boosted engine power even more. The sport's authorities agreed that the rapid increase in engine power had reached dangerous levels. In 1934, they made new rules limiting the weight of a racing car to 1,650lbs in an attempt to prevent top speeds from rising any further. Manufacturers overcame these rules by building cars from very light materials and using new mixtures of fuels to create more power. The most powerful car of the time was the Mercedes W125. In 1937, this managed to reach almost 200mph.

The Lotus 25 introduced the monocoque.

In the 1930s Auto Union turned a car back to front and put the engine behind the driver. They were the first to win races with a rear engined car, including the Grand Prix. Other manufacturers preceeded to copy them. Then in 1962, Colin Chapman's Lotus team introduced the monocoque, meaning single shell, which replaced the car's basic frame-work or "chassis" with a single strong yet lightweight structure. Everyone copied this.

Formula 1 racing car.

Car aerodynamics developed rapidly during the 1970s. In 1977, Lotus introduced the ground effect car, which used the car's shape to create a down-force. Also in 1977, Renault introduced a new engine to challenge the 3-liter Ford-Cosworth engine. It was half the size of the Cosworth, but turbocharged. At first it was not reliable, but quickly improved. More teams began to use them. By the late 1980s, the sport's authorities felt that the engines were too powerful and costly. From the 1989 racing season, turbochargers were banned.

FACTS AND FIGURES

The first motor race was held on June 11-13, 1887 in France, from Paris to Bordeaux and back, a distance of 730 miles. The winner, Emile Levassor, traveled at an average speed of 15 mph.

The world's largest sporting event is Indianapolis 500 motor race, with a race-day crowd of over 300,000 people.

The Monaco Grand Prix, driven on the roads of Monte Carlo, is thought to be the toughest Grand Prix circuit. During the 160 mile race, drivers have to change gear about 1,600 times.

The first motor race on a circuit was held on the Circuit du Sud-Ouest at Pau, France, in 1900.

A car driven by Bobby Unser was refueled in only four seconds during the 1976 Indianapolis 500 race – the fastest pit stop on record.

Over 2.5 million people attend the 16 Formula races held around the world, an average of over 150,000 spectators per race.

Between February 1961 and June 1964, Stan Mott of New York, drove his go-kart around the world, a distance of 23,000 miles on land through 28 countries.

Chapter Fourteen
NUCLEAR POWER STATIONS

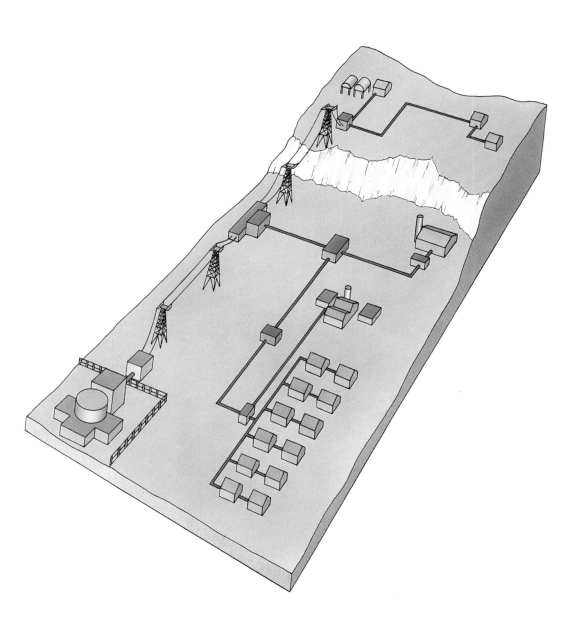

CONTENTS

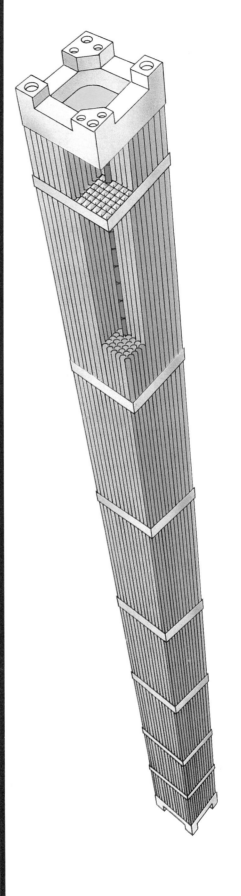

THE WORKING PARTS

Power stations are factories that produce energy. Most of them use the heat from burning coal or gas to make steam. The steam is then used to drive machines called turbines which make electricity. The electricity is supplied through cables to our homes where we use its energy in a variety of ways.

In a nuclear power station the heat for making steam comes from a material called uranium. This is not burned

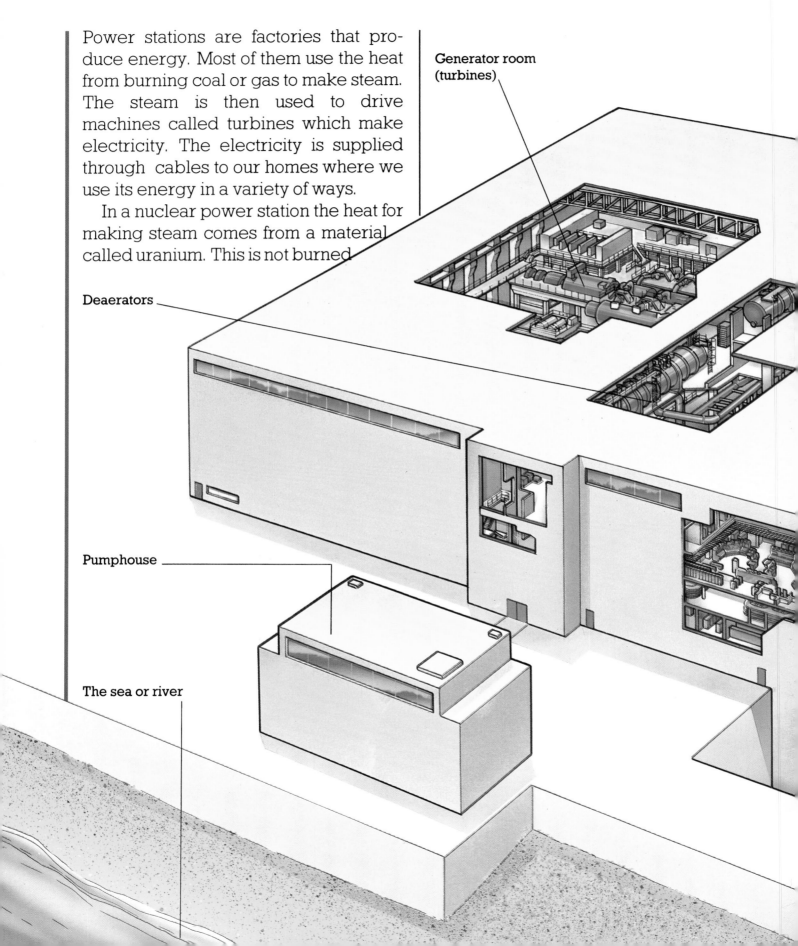

Generator room (turbines)

Deaerators

Pumphouse

The sea or river

like coal or oil – the atoms of the uranium are split in a process called nuclear fission, which creates a very intense heat. This process takes place in the reactor – the nuclear power station's equivalent to a coal or oil furnace.

In the reactor's core, a strong container called a pressure vessel holds rods of uranium fuel, together with systems to control the amount of heat produced. A coolant flows through the reactor, absorbs the heat and carries it off to make steam.

The reactor is housed in a structure called a containment building. This is made of very thick concrete and steel to stop any radioactive particles escaping.

Since even small amounts of radiation can be harmful to people, other parts of the nuclear power station must also be made strong and safe. This means that nuclear power stations are much more costly to build than conventional coal or oil ones. Moreover, disposing of the nuclear waste material presents enormous, and expensive, problems.

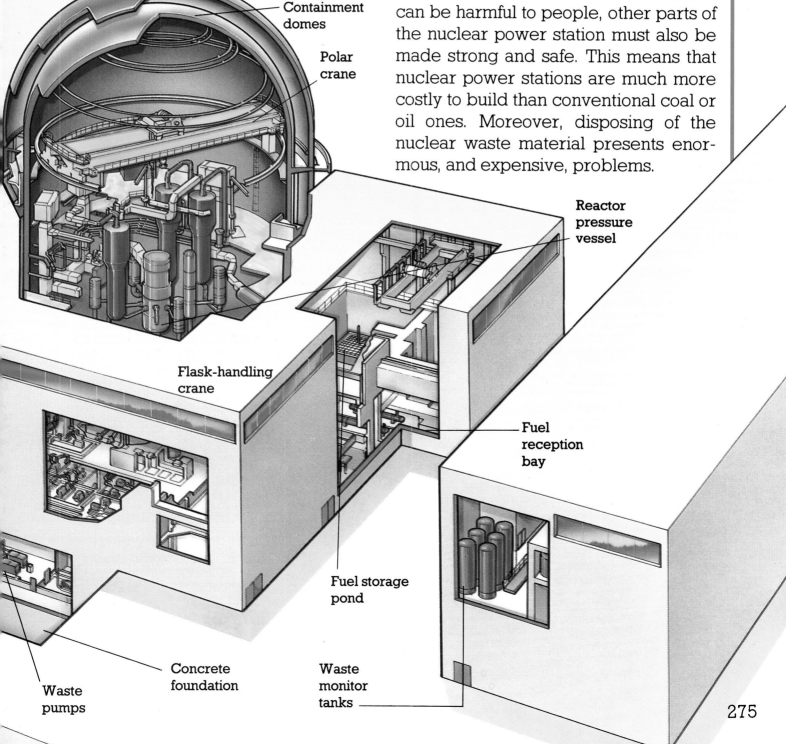

Containment domes

Polar crane

Reactor pressure vessel

Flask-handling crane

Fuel reception bay

Fuel storage pond

Concrete foundation

Waste monitor tanks

Waste pumps

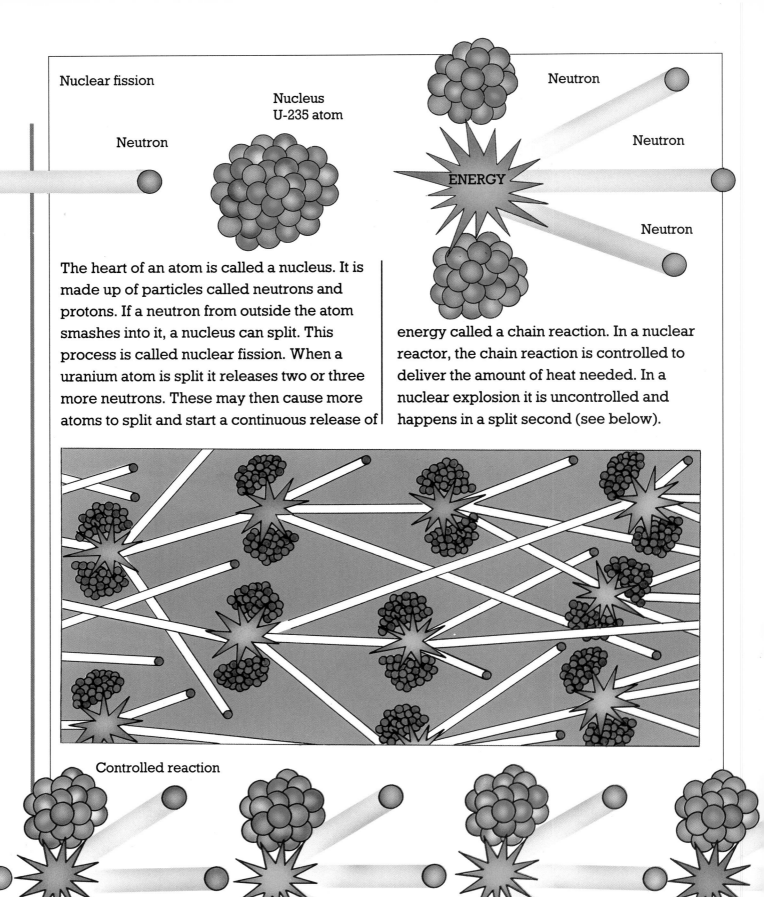

Nuclear fission

Neutron

Nucleus
U-235 atom

Neutron

ENERGY

Neutron

Neutron

The heart of an atom is called a nucleus. It is made up of particles called neutrons and protons. If a neutron from outside the atom smashes into it, a nucleus can split. This process is called nuclear fission. When a uranium atom is split it releases two or three more neutrons. These may then cause more atoms to split and start a continuous release of energy called a chain reaction. In a nuclear reactor, the chain reaction is controlled to deliver the amount of heat needed. In a nuclear explosion it is uncontrolled and happens in a split second (see below).

Controlled reaction

NUCLEAR FISSION

The process of nuclear fission, illustrated and described on the opposite page, only occurs easily with a natural element called uranium which is both plentiful and inexpensive. It is also said to produce much cheaper energy than other fuels. The cost of fuel in a nuclear power station is about ten percent of the the total cost of electricity produced. In coal or oil power stations it can be as high as 65 percent.

Uranium found in nature is not all one kind. It is necessary to enrich nuclear fuel by increasing the "cream," uranium-235, relative to the "milk," uranium-238. Once it has been mined and purified, uranium oxide is made into small pellets and packed into metal rods. But uranium becomes radioactive in a reactor, and precautions have to be taken to safeguard against the dangers of radiation throughout the process of generating power and afterward.

Special machines such as Geiger counters are used to detect radioactivity and check that an area is safe for materials or people. There are three main types of radioactive rays: alpha particles which can be stopped by an object as thin as a sheet of paper; beta particles which can be stopped by a thin sheet of metal like aluminum; gamma rays which can only be stopped by thick layers of very dense materials like lead.

RADIATION AND HALF LIVES

The atoms of materials like uranium or radium are unstable and break up naturally, forming other materials and giving off radiation. This is called radioactive decay. The intensity of radiation slackens with time. The time a material's radioactivity takes to reach half its original intensity is known as its half-life. Depending on the material, this varies from less than a second to billions of years.

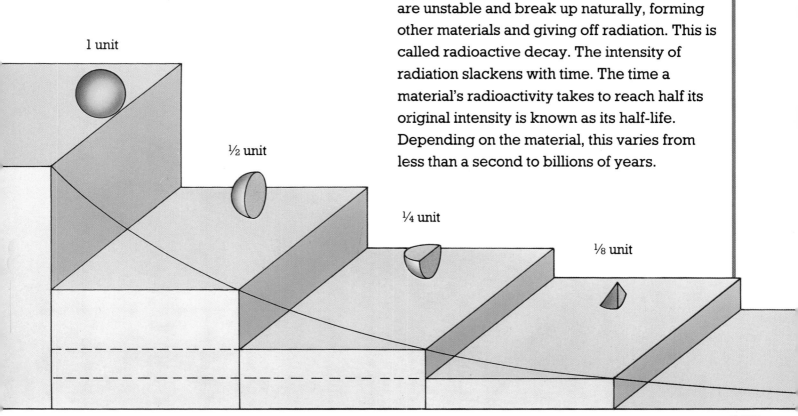

1 unit

½ unit

¼ unit

⅛ unit

Half-life

THE REACTOR

The core of a reactor is mounted in a very strong container called a pressure vessel made of steel up to 10 ins thick. This is able to withstand very high temperatures and pressures, but is shielded further as an extra precaution. Inside the pressure vessel, nuclear fuel is held in rods running vertically. Parallel with these run control rods which will absorb neutrons. The control rods govern the amount of neutrons available to cause fission. If more power is required they are pulled up out of the center of the core. If they are pushed fully down into the core, the fission reaction will stop and the reactor will shut down.

Fuel and control rods are held in the moderator – this is a material, like water or graphite, which makes a chain reaction possible by slowing down neutrons. It must do this because U235 undergoes fission easier with slower neutrons.

The coolant also runs through the core. It can be water, liquid metal or gas, depending on reactor type. Without a steady flow of coolant, the fuel would soon overheat and melt.

While there are different types of reactors, their cores are generally similar. The exception to this rule is the fast breeder reactor (FBR), which is still largely experimental. The plutonium which an FBR uses as fuel will sustain a chain reaction with fast neutrons. Therefore FBR core is, for example, only one third the size of the AGR illustrated opposite.

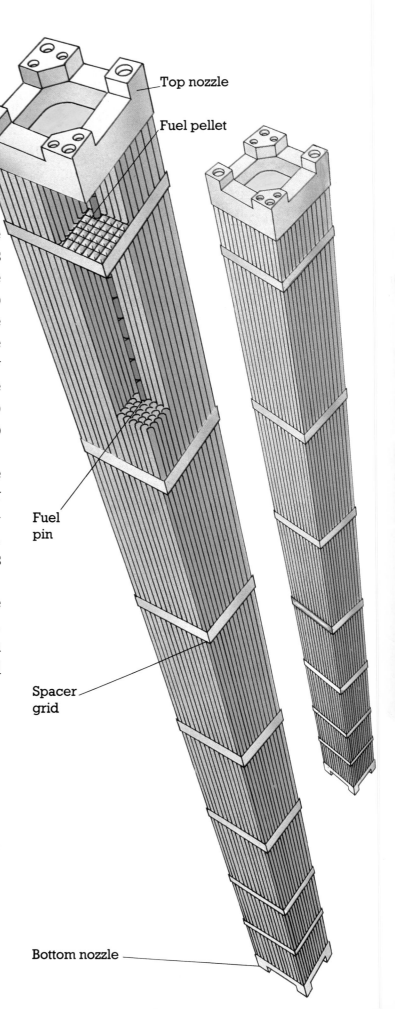

Top nozzle

Fuel pellet

Fuel pin

Spacer grid

Bottom nozzle

The reactor.

Illustrated below is a high temperature gas cooled reactor (AGR). Carbon dioxide gas passes over the hot fuel rods in the reactor core. It then transfers its heat to water in the heat exchangers. This is turned into steam to drive the turbines. Temperatures, pressures and radiation are closely monitored and adjusted from a control room which is usually sited in another part of the power station.

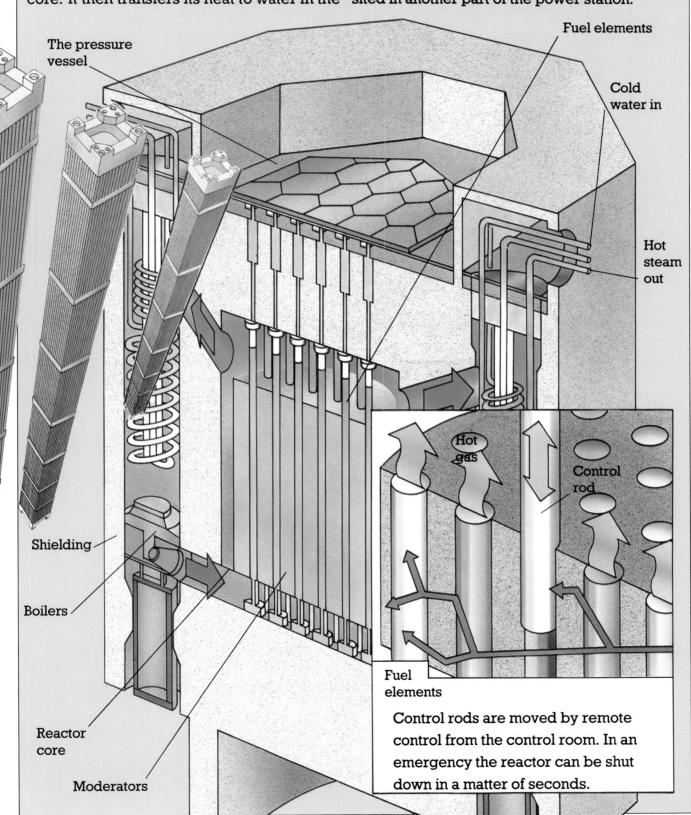

The pressure vessel

Fuel elements

Cold water in

Hot steam out

Shielding

Boilers

Reactor core

Moderators

Hot gas

Control rod

Fuel elements

Control rods are moved by remote control from the control room. In an emergency the reactor can be shut down in a matter of seconds.

GENERATING THE POWER

In very simple terms, a power station is similar to a huge boiling kettle with its steam turning a propeller in front of the spout. The force of the revolving propeller is used to generate electricity. In a nuclear power station the reactor is the heating element. Because of the dangers of radioactivity it does not make steam directly but transfers its heat to a coolant which is pumped into a heat exchanger where the steam is then produced. This travels through pipes to turbines where it forces the propeller blades inside to revolve very fast. The turbines are linked by a shaft to an electrical generator which converts all this movement into electricty.

Big power station cooling towers are there to cool the condenser water: exhausted steam is piped through a mass of cold water in the condenser. The condenser water heats up in the process and is itself cooled by being passed through coils in the towers where it transfers its heat to air.

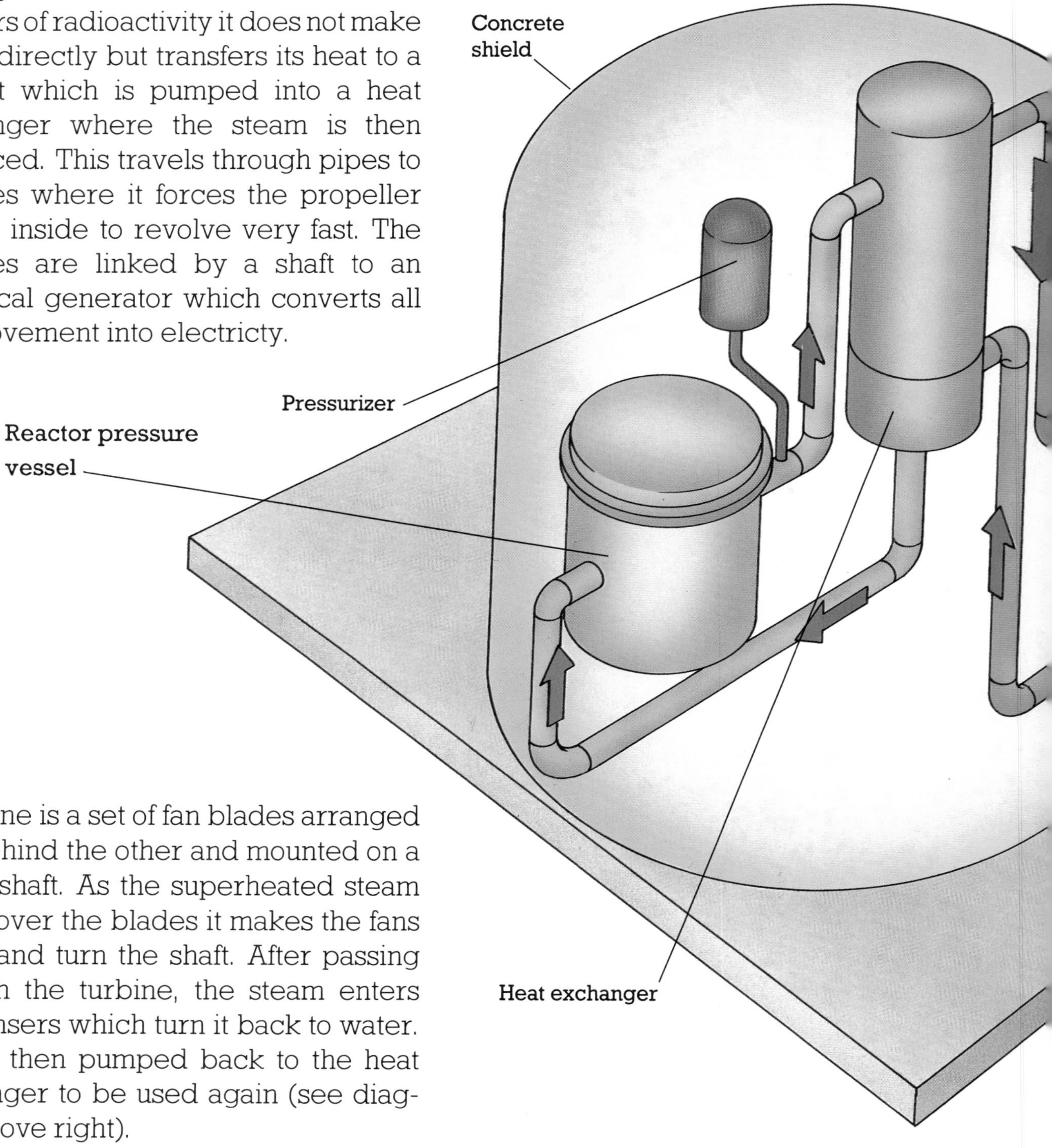

Concrete shield

Pressurizer

Reactor pressure vessel

Heat exchanger

A turbine is a set of fan blades arranged one behind the other and mounted on a single shaft. As the superheated steam blows over the blades it makes the fans rotate and turn the shaft. After passing through the turbine, the steam enters condensers which turn it back to water. This is then pumped back to the heat exchanger to be used again (see diagram above right).

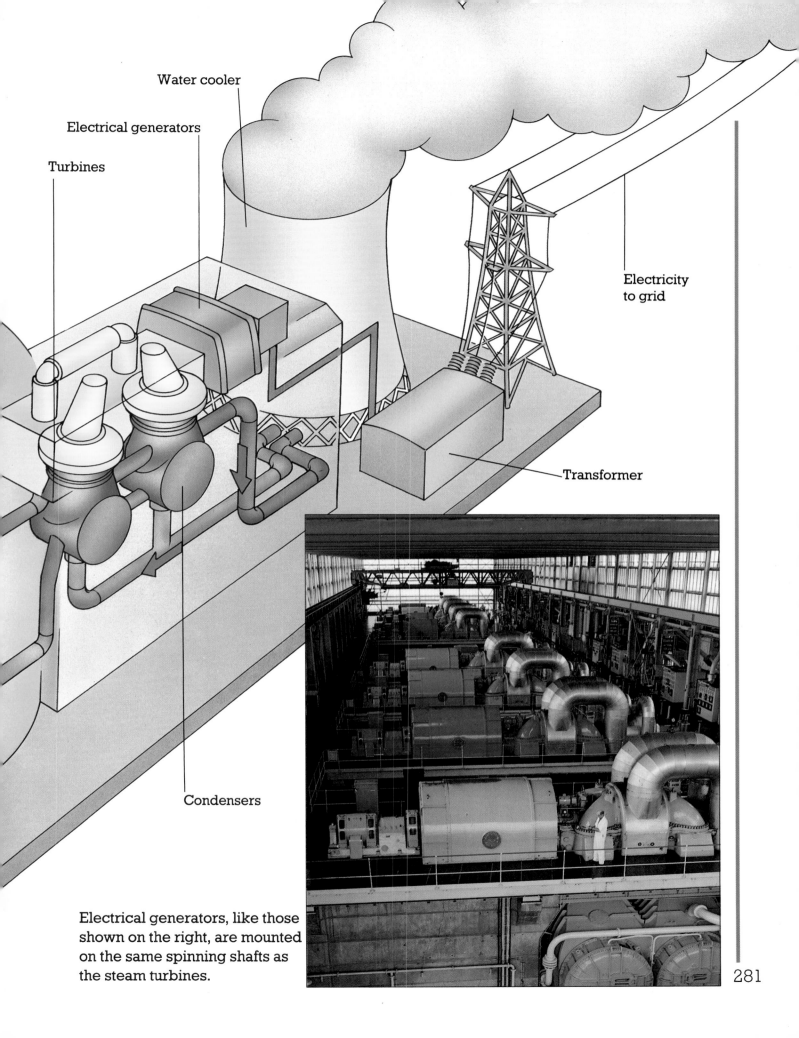

Turbines

Electrical generators

Water cooler

Electricity
to grid

Transformer

Condensers

Electrical generators, like those
shown on the right, are mounted
on the same spinning shafts as
the steam turbines.

281

POWER TO THE GRID

Electricity is made in the power station as the turbine shaft turns the coil inside the magnetic field of a generator. The electricity leaves the generator via a tranformer which increases its voltage to the high values needed to send it long distances to our homes. It normally leaves the power station at 275,000 or 400,000 volts in overhead lines (see photo right). Along the way a network of transformers and substations reduce the voltage to the 220 and 110 volts used at home or the higher voltage used in factories. Nuclear power stations, because they are cheap to run, are used to generate base load - they deliver bulk power to the grid 24 hours a day. Peak loads, when extra demand is required, such as when most people come home, are handled by quick reacting stations, burning gas.

High voltage cables carried on pylons.

Transformers (see photo below) form key stages in the national grid.

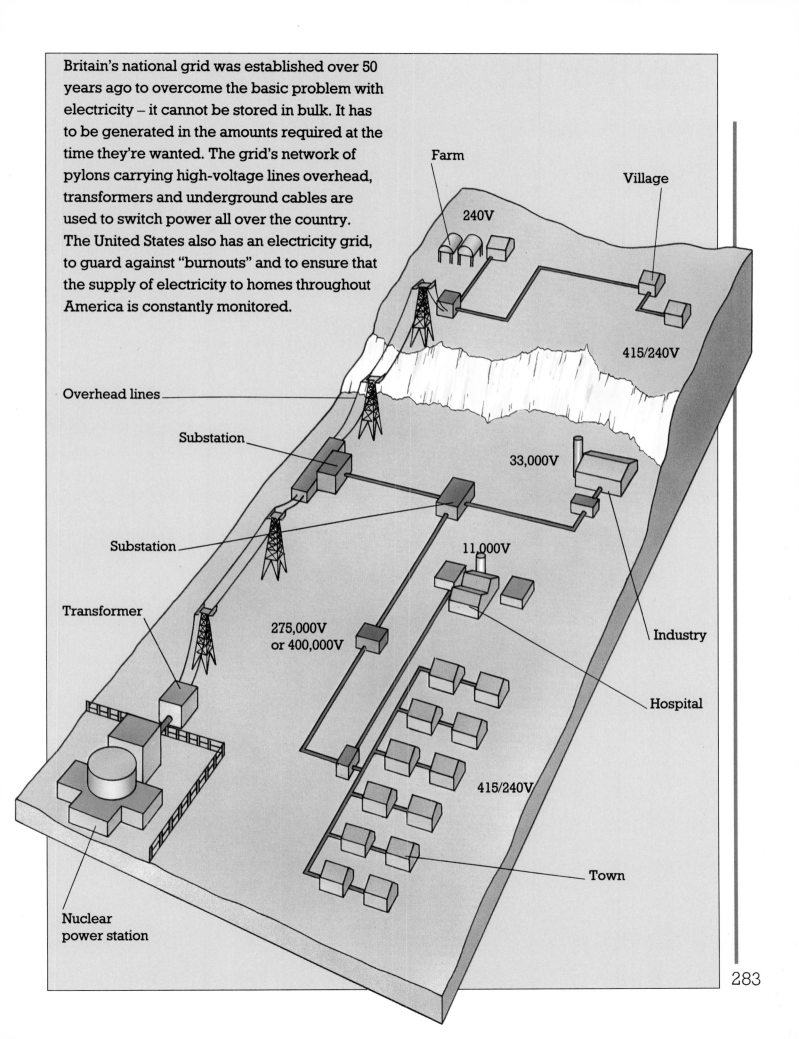

Britain's national grid was established over 50 years ago to overcome the basic problem with electricity – it cannot be stored in bulk. It has to be generated in the amounts required at the time they're wanted. The grid's network of pylons carrying high-voltage lines overhead, transformers and underground cables are used to switch power all over the country. The United States also has an electricity grid, to guard against "burnouts" and to ensure that the supply of electricity to homes throughout America is constantly monitored.

Farm

240V

Village

415/240V

Overhead lines

Substation

33,000V

Substation

11,000V

Transformer

275,000V or 400,000V

Industry

Hospital

415/240V

Nuclear power station

Town

REPROCESSING FUEL

Uranium fuel from reactors does not burn away like coal or oil. It does, however gradually get less efficient and eventually must be replaced with fresh material. What to do with the used uranium - known as spent fuel - is one of the nuclear industry's most pressing problems.

To throw away this waste is impossible since spent fuel is dangerously radioactive. Moreover, about 95 percent of it can be cleaned up for reuse.

◄▼ To make spent fuel elements easier and safer to handle they are allowed to cool for several months in special cooling ponds (see photos left and below). During this time some radioactivity will die away.

Cooling is the first stage in reprocessing. Spent fuel still gives off a lot of radiation and heat so it is first stored in specially constructed ponds of water. The fuel is then taken to the reprocessing plant. This is where the rods are dissolved in acid and the unused uranium is extracted along with radioactive plutonium, a by product of nuclear fission. All this is done by remote control with all operators shielded behind thick layers of concrete.

The recovered uranium is used to make new fuel rods. The plutonium can be used to enrich fuel for fast-breeder reactors or in nuclear weapons. What is left, usually around three percent of the original material, is dangerous and unusable waste, which must be stored in complete security. This high-level waste, which will remain radioactive for thousands of years, is sealed in thick containers and stored to await disposal. Although burial deep underground or under the sea has been suggested, no one has yet found a satisfactory way of disposing of it. Some countries have found this side of the nuclear power industry so troublesome that they have given up reprocessing altogether.

Another major problem is that in the past reprocessing plants have released large amounts of radioactivity into the air and sea nearby. One such plant in Britain, Sellafield, has a long and sorry history of leaks.

Plutonium is used to make nuclear weapons. The photo below shows the test firing of a missile with a nuclear warhead. Besides its uses in nuclear power stations and weapons, there are no other uses for plutonium.

GETTING RID OF THE WASTE

Nuclear waste is classified into three levels, low, intermediate and high. It can range from things like clothing or packaging which have been made mildly radioactive in the power station (low level) to spent fuel rods (high level).

Low- and intermediate-level wastes used to be sealed in containers and dumped at sea or in shallow land sites. But public pressure led to a ban on sea dumping and only the lowest level wastes are buried in shallow sites.

Some more hazardous intermediate-level wastes are sealed into thick containers and buried in deeper sites like disused mines. Acid from reprocessing plants, with radioactive waste still dissolved in it, can be stored in tanks or evaporated and turned into a type of glass in a process called "vitrification."

High-level wastes pose the most difficult problem. Suggested solutions have included dumping in deep-sea trenches, launching into outer space or burial under polar ice. All of these are dangerous and the favored method at present is burial in specially constructed underground chambers.

Nuclear waste has a lifetime of hundreds of thousands of years. Even if current storage methods are "fail-safe" (totally secure), there can be no guarantee of this far into the future.

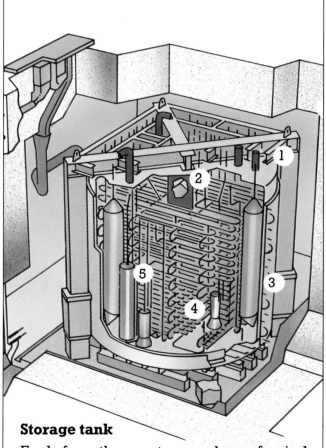

Storage tank

Fuels from the reactor ponds are ferried to a reprocessing plant where they are stored underwater for 140 days before reprocessing. Next, the spent fuel rods are chopped up and dissolved in nitric acid. Uranium plutonium and waste are separated, and the liquid waste stored in the stainless steel tank pictured above. These tanks are specially designed with five seals so that no radioactivity can escape.

Low level waste disposal

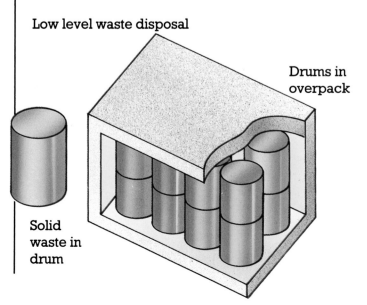

Drums in overpack

Solid waste in drum

Great Britain plans to house its low and intermediate nuclear waste in a specially constructed underground vault called a repository, illustrated on the right. It will be 2,300 feet deep, cost $5 billion to build and should start operating early next century. The first chosen site is at Sellafield, and planners have had to predict all the risks that might threaten the repository over the next 25,000 years – including ice ages.

Low level waste is dumped in the Irish Sea.

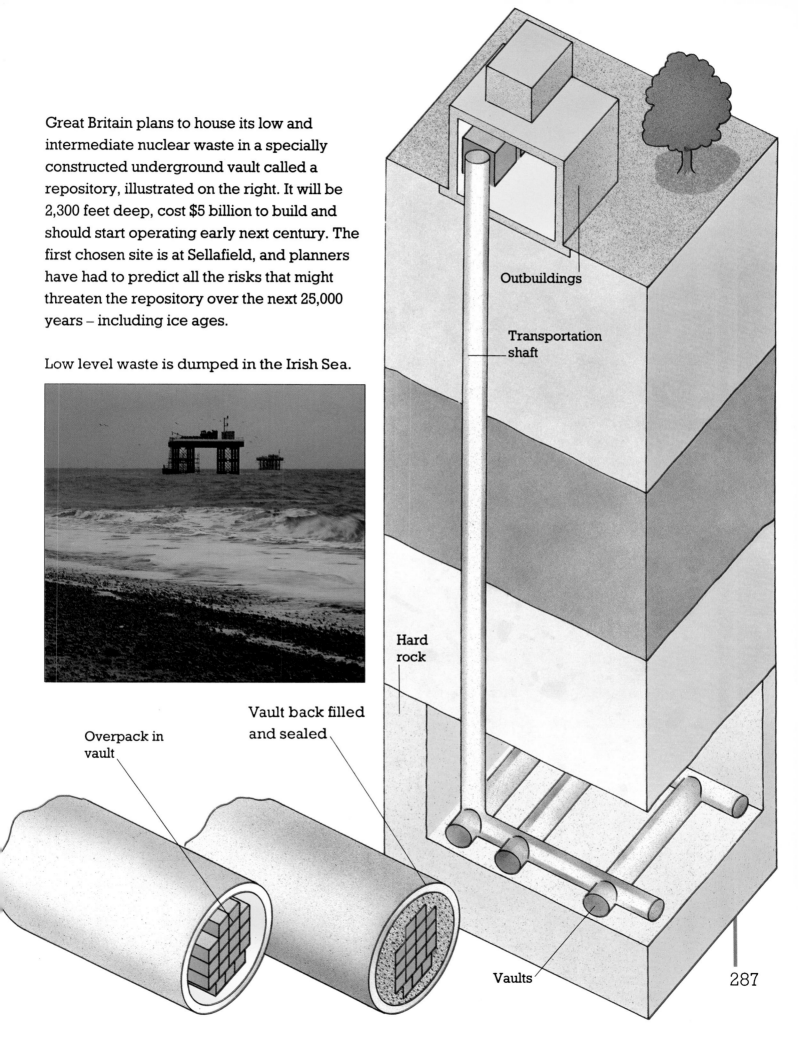

Outbuildings

Transportation shaft

Hard rock

Vault back filled and sealed

Overpack in vault

Vaults

HOW SAFE IS SAFE?

The accidents at Sellafield and Three Mile Island, both close to big cities, could have claimed thousands of lives. If Chernobyl had been close to a city, it would have done so. Safety inside nuclear plants depends on a number of factors: the machinery must be designed to be as reliable as possible, expert staff are needed to check radiation levels. If systems fail, they must do so safely. Such safety procedures need money to put into practice. In the end, it depends on how much governments or private companies are prepared to spend to ensure the safe operation of their nuclear power stations.

Until the Chernobyl accident, supporters of nuclear industry could point to the safety record of other types of power generation and say how safe atomic power has been. Accidents on oil rigs and coal mines have cost many thousands of lives – the worst coal mine disaster claimed 1,572 lives in China in 1942. There are environmental costs too: coal/oil-fired power stations produce greenhouse gases and pollution which could lead to global warming and acid rain; oil spills from tankers can cause environmental disasters.

After Chernobyl, the International Atomic Energy Agency set out to establish a worldwide safety code. The plan includes rules for notifying other countries when accidents occur and assistance afterward. But while international cooperation is an essential factor, special attention to power station design, construction, and safety procedures is even more important.

Making and testing systems and machines to handle nuclear materials is one of the industry's biggest costs. Spent fuel rods are moved around in containers called flasks. Each 48 metric ton flask carries only two metric tons of fuel. The photo above shows the most spectacular test of a flask ever made. A remotely controlled British Rail train was crashed into an experimental flask at high speed. The flask was recovered intact and undamaged while the train itself was demolished. The photo on the right shows the remote control equipment which operators use to handle high-level radioactive materials and, on the far right, are the thick concrete containment buildings.

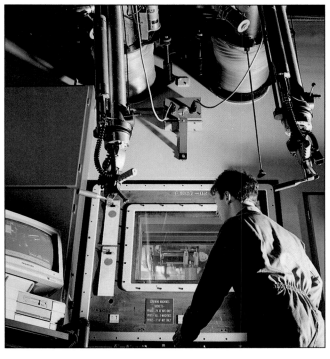

Energy can also be created when atomic nuclei are joined together. In a nuclear fusion reactor atoms of deuterium and tritium would be held in place as a plasma in a torus – or doughnut-shaped – vacuum vessel. Very powerful magnetic coils (toroidal coils) could do this. This plasma would then be heated using lasers, radio waves, and electric fields, bombardment with neutral particles or by some combination of these methods.

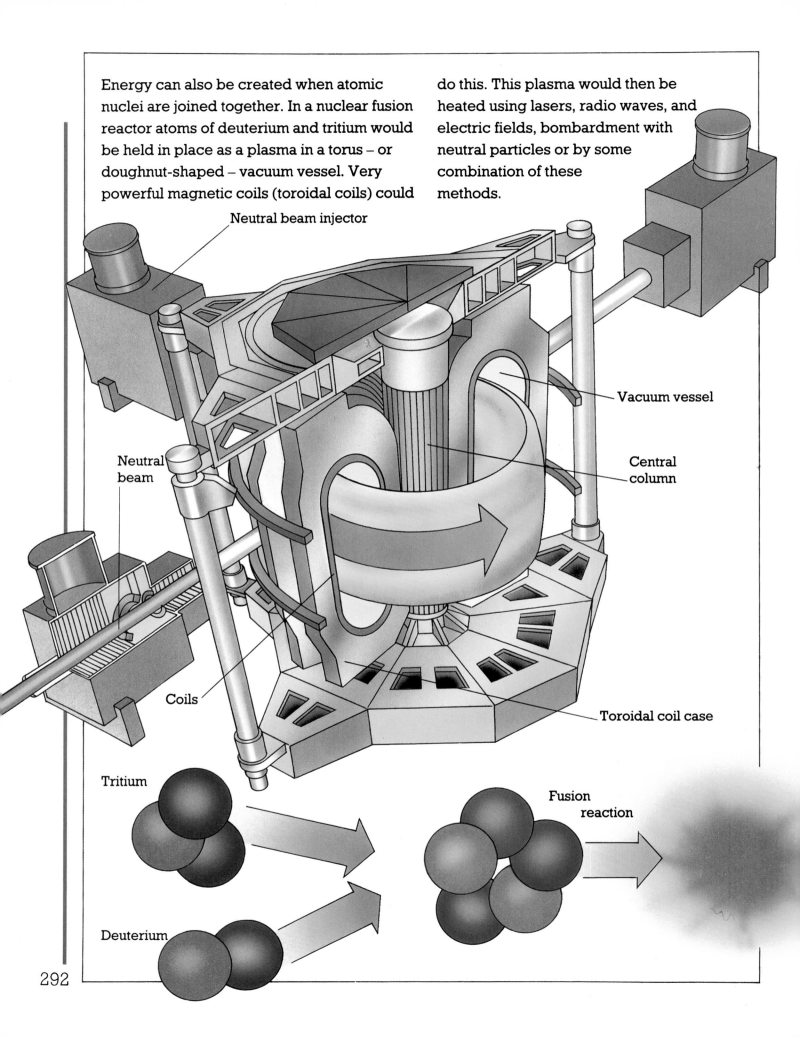

Neutral beam injector

Vacuum vessel

Central column

Neutral beam

Coils

Toroidal coil case

Tritium

Deuterium

Fusion reaction

THE FUTURE

Nuclear power used to be thought of as the answer to all our energy worries. But now, some 35 years after it was first used, difficult waste products and decommissioning have pushed the real cost higher and higher. And with a number of worrying accidents, particularly Chernobyl, nations are now questioning its future.

Many countries have canceled planned power stations. Sweden, for example, has decided to cease using nuclear power altogether by the year 2010. And this comes at a time when our coal and oil reserves are running out. So a usable and plentiful form of power will be needed by the middle of the next century.

Nuclear fusion, described on these pages, may be one answer. If we can master fusion it will deliver limitless and safe energy, with little pollution and dangerous waste. (It makes no long-term waste like spent fuel, and what radioactive materials it does make are safe for recycling in 100 years.) But it is still in a very early stage – no fusion reactor has achieved a sustained chain reaction yet. A practical version is at least 50 years in the future.

Alternative energy sources such as wind, tidal power, and solar energy also offer some hope. But even these clean sources are not without their problems – tidal generators can, for example, disrupt coastal wildlife.

The way ahead calls for money to be invested in all new forms of energy production – not just fusion – and a real effort to clean up and keep safe our present sources. To preserve resources for future generations, contemporary societies have an obligation to use fuels in moderation.

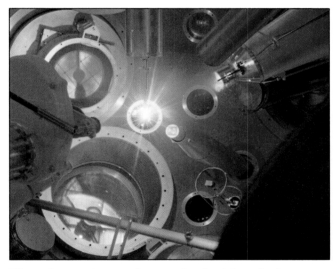

The photo above shows the inside of a laser fusion chamber.

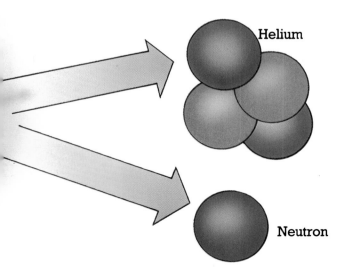

Helium

Neutron

Nuclear fusion is the process taking place in the sun and other stars. It involves making two atoms join together, or fuse, rather than splitting one apart as in nuclear fission. The atoms must be heated to more than 180 million degrees F and held at that temperature for over 1.5 seconds. The process should then become a self-sustaining chain reaction releasing great amounts of heat.

HISTORY OF NUCLEAR POWER

1841: Péligot isolates uranium.

1896: The French chemist Henri Becquerel discovers radioactivity. The amount of energy observed being released is thought too small to be usable in any existing device.

1905: Scientist, Albert Einstein, publishes his theory of relativity. He proved that mass and energy are essentially the same thing, and his equation showed how much energy could in principle be obtained from a given mass.

A nuclear bomb exploding

1919: New Zealand physicist, Ernest Rutherford, succeeds in splitting the atom after many attempts.

1938: In Berlin, German and Austrian scientists discover that self-sustaining fission is possible in uranium.

1939: Einstein writes to President Roosevelt urging the production of an atomic bomb.

1940: The discovery of plutonium by Glenn Seaborg.

1942: Italian physicist Enrico Fermi starts Chicago Pile Number One, the first atomic reactor in a disused squash

Calder Hall, an early nuclear power station

court at the University of Chicago. The reactor was started on December 2, 1942 and this date is now regarded as the dawn of the nuclear age.

1944: The world's first industrial scale nuclear reactor starts at the Hanford works alongside the Columbia River in the U.S..

1945: The Japanese cities of Hiroshima and Nagasaki are destroyed by atomic bombs dropped from U.S. aircraft.

1946: Soviet Union starts a research reactor.

1947: The first British research reactor starts at Harwell.

1949: First Soviet A-bomb test.

1949: Britain decides to use nuclear

An American research reactor in the 1950s

energy to generate electricity for the national grid.

1950: First Windscale plutonium-producing reactor comes into operation.

1951: First electricity is generated by U.S. experimental reactor.

1952: First British A-bomb test.

1955: USS Nautilus starts sea trials powered by a small, pressurized water reactor.

1956: British Calder Hall power station starts up, producing electricity as a byproduct of plutonium manufacture.

1957: Fire and leak at Windscale. The

Interior of a modern nuclear power station

first of the large nuclear accidents.

1958: First French commercial reactor starts at Marcoule.

1978: Europeans decide to start the Joint European Torus (JET) project to test nuclear fusion as a source of power.

1979: Accident at Three Mile Island.

1983: JET starts experiments at Culham in Oxfordshire.

1986: The world's worst nuclear accident, a meltdown, occurs at Chernobyl in the former Soviet Union.

FACTS AND FIGURES

Nuclear power is used to generate around 17 percent of the world's total of electricity.

A total of 429 nuclear reactors have been built worldwide. Another 156 are under construction and a further 105 are planned.

Belgium and France are the world's largest users of nuclear power – both countries produce around 70 percent of their electricity using it.

Over 350 nuclear powered vessels have been built.

In Great Britain the average person's annual dose of radioactivity from nuclear power is 0.4 percent of the total radiation. Cosmic rays account for 13 percent, natural radiation from rocks 16 percent and medical radiation such as X rays 20 percent.

One kilogram of uranium 235 – a lump the size of a tennis ball – contains enough energy to power one million one-bar electric fires continuously for 2,500 years.

To provide an average year's energy consumption for the whole world takes 1,700 metric tons of coal or 85,000 metric tons of uranium in conventional reactors or 1,000 metric tons of uranium in fast breeder reactors.

The Chernobyl accident releases radioactivity equivalent to 90 Hiroshima bombs. An area of 3,900 square miles was evacuated of some 272,000 people.

GLOSSARY

active suspension
A computer controlled system that keeps a car at a fixed height above the ground.

airfoil
A surface such as an aircraft wing that is shaped to produce lift.

aileron
A movable flap on a wing's trailing edge, used to make an aircraft roll to one side.

altimeter
An instrument for measuring and displaying the height of an aircraft.

aperture
The hole in the front of a camera or lens that light passes through to reach the film. The size of the aperture is adjusting on most cameras.

atoms
The tiny particles that make up all matter - there are billions of them in the period at the end of this sentence. Atoms themselves are made of even smaller particles called protons, neutrons and electrons.

autogyro
An aircraft that uses a freewheeling overhead rotor to generate lift when the craft is driven forward by a powered rotor.

ballistic
A missle that follows a high, curving flight path under gravitational forces alone, then plunges down on to its target.

blitzkrieg
From the German words meaning a lightning war. A powerful, swift attack intended to defeat the enemy quickly.

carburettor
In the carburettor, gasoline and air mix to form an explosive mixture.

chassis
A vehicles basic frame, to which the engine, wheel and body are attached.

chicane
A corner or a series of barriers added to an existing racetrack to reduce the car's speed.

chip
A single piece of silicon containing a complete electronic circuit. Also called an integrated circuit, or IC.

clutch
This part disconnects the engine from the gearbox during gear changing. It can work manually or automatically.

cockpit
The part of an aircraft where the pilot sits and controls the aircraft.

compressor
A turbine used to squeeze a gas (usually air) into a smaller space,

and, therefore, increases its pressure.

constellation
A group of stars. In the past, constellations were named after animals or figures from legend that their patterns appeared to resemble, for example The Great Bear, The plough, Taurus the Bull, Cancer the Crab. In reality, the stars were not close to each other at all. The whole sky is now divided into 88 areas named after the old constellations.

crankshaft
The main shaft in the engine, which changes the up-and-down movement of the pistons into a turning movement.

cruise missile
A winged missile that is usually powered by a rocket and fitted with an electronic guidance system. Cruise missiles fly low over water and land to avoid detection by radar.

CPU
Central Processing Unit. The part of a computer that performs most if not all the calculations and also controls the rest of the computer if there are not coprocessors or chips to do so. The CPU may be contained in a single chip called a microprocessor.

dead reckoning
A method of navigation in which a vessal's current position is calculated from its last known position, speed course and tides.

decommissioning
The process of shutting down and dismantling and/or making safe a disused nuclear power station.

diaphragm shutter
A camera shutter made from overlapping metal leaves which swivel open to expose the film when the shutter release button is pressed.

drag
A force that resists the movement of an object such as a car or aircraft through air and tries to slow it down.

electromagnetic spectrum
The range of frequencies and wavelenghs of electromagnetic energy. The lowest frequencies (longest wavelengths) correspond to radio waves, the highest frequencies (shortest wavelenghs) to gamma rays.

fiber optics
Long, fine strands of glass used to transmit information in the form of an intense beam of light produced by a laser. The strands are bundled together to form fiber optic cables. Most cable television stations now use fiber optic cables instead of metal cables to feed television channels into people's homes.

field
A television picture composed of

half the normal number of scanning lines. Two fields form one complete picture.

filmless camera
A camera that uses a medium other than film for recording images, such as magnetic tape.

fission
The breakup of an atom by splitting its nucleus apart: the process leads to creation of new elements and the release of neutrons and energy.

flight envelope
The limits of speed and altitude that an aircraft must stay within.

floppy disc
A thin plastic disc with a magnetic coating, used to store computer programs and data. The disc is protected from damage by a card or plastic sleeve. Discs come in standard sizes. The most common are 3.5 inches and 5.25 inches in diameter.

four-stroke engine
One in which the piston makes four movements, or strokes, to produce power.

frame
A single complete television picture. 25 PAL frames and 30 NTSC frames are transmitted every second, a speed so fast that our eyes see them as a moving picture.

frequency
The number of cycles or vibrations of a wave that pass a point every second. Frequency is measured in hertz (1 vibration per second = 1 hertz). Light waves to which our eyes are sensitive range in frequency between 400 million million and 750 million million hertz.

fusion
The joining together of atoms by fusing their nuclei to form heavier elements. Fusion is the process that powers the sun and other stars.

gamma rays
Electromagnetic radiation with wavelengths shorter than X-rays.

geostationary/geosynchronous
An orbit 21,600 miles above the Earth's equator. A satellite in this orbit keeps pace with the Earth as it spins around, and appears to hang over the same spot on the Earth, all the time.

gearbox
A collection of toothedged wheels that can be linked together in different ways. These gearwheels change the speed of the engine into a faster or slower drive at the rear wheel.

gravity
The force of attraction between two large objects. The "pull" of the Earth's force of gravity must be overcome to launch a shuttle into space.

half-life
The length of time taken for a radioactive substance to decay to half its original intensity.

hard disc
A rigid disc used to store tens of megabytes of computer data. Also often called a fixed disc, because the disc or discs cannot be removed from the sealed drive unit inside the computer. Mainframe computers are an exception to this since they can use hard disc units which are interchangeable.

horsepower (HP)
A unit of power used to measure the power output of an engine, based on the power of a horse. One horsepower is equivalent to about 746 watts of electrical power.

internal combustion engine
Any engine in which the combustion (burning) occurs inside the engine - for example, a truck's diesel engine.

k
A unit of measurement of the size of a computer's memory. K or kilo, normally indicates 1,000, but in relation to computers, 1k means 1,024 bytes.

latent image
The invisible image on an exposed film that is revealed by developing the film.

lidar
Light Detection And Ranging. A system for detecting objects and measuring how far away they are by bouncing a laser beam off them.

lift
A force that tries to raise an aircraft as it moves through the air. The amount of lift produced by an aircraft depends on its speed, weight, wing area and wing shape.

light
Electromagnetic radiation with wavelengths from 0.4 to 0.77 millionths of a meter. The human eye is sensitive to this narrow band of radiation only.

Mach
A number named after the Austrian physicist, Ernst Mach, relating an aircraft's speed to the speed of sound. Mach 2 = twice the speed of sound, which equals 1,410 mph at an altitude of 9,600 yards.

machine code
A language used by computers consisting of zeros and ones only.

microprocessor
The chip or chips that contain a computer's master control circuit, the Central Processing Unit (CPU).

orbit
The flight path of a spacecraft or satellite as it circles the Earth.

parabola
The shape of an optical telescope main mirror and radio telescope dish. It focuses radiation from space on a point in front of the mirror or dish.

payload
The cargo, passengers, weapons or any other extra weight carried by an aircraft.

piston
A part that moves up and down in an engine cylinder. It produces power when it is forced down by exploding fuel.

pitch
A front-up/ front-down motion of an aircraft.

pixel
A shortened form of the words "picture element." The smallest point on a computer screen that can be controlled individually.

production cars
Ordinary road cars produced in great numbers for sale to the general public, for example station wagons.

projectile
An object fired from a gun, such as a bullet, shell, shot or missle.

RADAR
RAdio Detection And Ranging. A system invented in the 1940s for locating objects by bouncing radio waves off them and analyzing the echoes.

radioactivity
The result of unstable elements breaking down or decaying into other elements. It results in the production of tiny particles and radiation and can be very dangerous to living things.

reprocessing
Taking spent nuclear fuel and extracting from it the unused uranium and the plutonium byproducts. Both of these can be used again.

reversal film
Film designed to produce a positive image after exposure and development, without the need to make a print from the film. Slide, or transparency, film is a reversal film and can be projected.

safestore
The planned "concrete coffin" that would be built around the cores of decommissioned nuclear power stations to seal in radioactivity.

shock absorber
A device used to prevent a vehicle from bouncing up and down on its suspension on a bumpy road.

solid state
Any device in which the active parts are solids. A solid state laser usually has a rod of crystals as the light pro-

ducing material.

sonar
SOund NAvigation Ranging. The use of sound waves to detect objects near a submarine.

streamlining
Smoothing the shape of an object like a car, so that air flows over it with little or no turbulence.

throttle
A control used to vary the amount of fuel fed to an engine. Opening the throttle increases the engine speed.

thrust
The pushing force of an engine or the propeller or rotor that it drives.

transmission
The system that carries engine power to the rear wheel. It includes the clutch, gearbox and final drive.

turbine
A motor made up of a series of fan blades. The blades are made to turn by high pressure steam or gas. In power stations, massive turbines are connected to electrical generators.

two-stroke engine
One in which power is produced every two strokes of the piston.

variable geometry
Also known as swing-wing. An aircraft with movable wings that can be swept backwards for supersonic flight or swung forward for better performance at lower air speeds.

wavelength
The distance between the peaks of a wave motion. The wavelength of visible light is 0.4 to 0.7 millionths of a meter.

x-ray
Electromagnetic radiation with shorter wavelengths than ultraviolet radiation, ranging from a thousand millionth of a meter down to a billionth of a meter.

yaw
A turning motion to the left or right, like a car turning around a corner.

INDEX

Photographic credits
Thanks to: Science Photo Library, Dounreay AA Technology; British Nuclear Fuels; AEA Technology; Atomic Energy; Nuclear Electric Nombel; Taillade, De Vries, Jumbo, Sellinger, Tavernier, Klein, Maindru, and Prior Colorsport; Allen Cash Photo Library; Motor Group Archives; Haymarket Publishing; Kel Edge; Yamaha; Honda; BMW; Aladdin Books; Frank Spooner Agency; NASA via Astro Information Service; Associated Press; Aerospatiale; British Aerospace; Rockwell Int.; Salamander Books; Aviation Picture Library; Quadrant Picture Library; Rex Features; Planet Earth Pictures; MoD RN PR; MARS/ General Dynamics; Popperfoto; William Fowler; Military Archive Research Services; Swedish Defence Force; Topham Picture Library; Spectrum; Ford Motor Company; Robert Harding Library; Zefa; Eye Ubiquitous; Roger Vlitos; QA Photos; STL Designs; Mercury Communications Ltd.; Angela Graham; Olivetti; Hewlett Packard; Amsted UK Ltd.; BT; Mitubishi; Bull HN Information Systems Ltd.; Mary Evans Picture Library; IBM; University of Pennsylvania; JVC Ltd.; Sanyo; ITN Ltd. GEC Sensors; Sony UK; Lionheart Books; Autocue Ltd.; The Studio Workshop; British Film Institute; National Museum of Film; The Howarth- Loomes Collection.